PRIMITIVE MAN AND HIS WAYS

PRIMITIVE MAN AND HIS WAYS

PATTERNS OF LIFE
IN SOME NATIVE SOCIETIES

KAJ BIRKET-SMITH

Translated from the Danish by

ROY DUFFELL

THE WORLD PUBLISHING COMPANY

CLEVELAND AND NEW YORK

Published by The World Publishing Company
2231 West 110th Street, Cleveland 2, Ohio

Library of Congress Catalog Card Number: 61-9764

FIRST EDITION

GBWP

CONTENTS

ILLUSTRATIONS

FOREWORD

THE SCIENCE of Man has many aspects. We can study humanity as a zoological species, we can investigate the manifestations of the mind, try to penetrate the mysteries of language, or delve into the problems connected with man's life as a more or less civilized being. As far as the so-called primitive or backward peoples are concerned (deplorable terms suggesting a quite unjustifiable evaluation), the latter part of the science is called variously ethnography, ethnology, and cultural anthropology, but the subject is properly speaking the same. Nevertheless, two different trends of approach are clearly in evidence. One aims at describing each culture as a functional whole and thus has a strong touch of sociology. In Great Britain, where this view is nowadays very conspicuous, the term cultural anthropology is sometimes even replaced by social anthropology. In many other countries, including Denmark, the prevalent method is more historical, on the assumption that present conditions are only understood on the background of the past. In accordance with this view I have here attempted to give an outline of six characteristic cultures from widely different parts of the world as they have developed, adapted to their environment.

It is a pleasant duty to express my sincere thanks to Dr. Ernst Manker, Stockholm; Dr. Johs. Falkenberg, Oslo; Mr. Jens Bjerre, Copenhagen; and Michael Joseph Ltd., London, for photographs placed at my disposal. For the same reason my thanks are due to Mr. Johs. Nicolaisen, Fellow of the University of Copenhagen, who in addition has supplied much information based upon his profound knowledge of the Tuareg. And finally I feel deeply obliged to my friends and colleagues in the Danish National Museum for untiring help and encouragement.

KAJ BIRKET-SMITH

Copenhagen, *June, 1959*

ENVIRONMENT AND CULTURE

Accessibility and Adaptation

FEW PLACES on earth give such an impression of hostility to life as the south coast of Arabia. The dark, jagged cliffs, and a blistering sun, which seems to have scorched away all traces of plant life, conjure up an inhospitable picture of endless desert. A fierce heat quivers over the streets of Aden. Small goats trip between the legs of turbaned Arabs and Indians, between black Somalis, with their thick crop of fuzzy hair, and an occasional woman, heavily veiled. At street corners the water sellers squat beside their skin bags, while on the steps inside the cool shade of the doorways beggars and cripples lie sleeping. A camel draws a two-wheeled cart sedately by. . . . For years not a drop of rain has fallen, yet here in the midst of the desert is this patch of life created by man: a small cosmopolitan centre, its existence due to the harbour hard by one of the world's oldest waterways, the link between the Mediterranean and India.

The importance of Aden goes right back to ancient times. Outside the city, surrounded by dusty bushes which seem to grow out of the bare sand, the impressive remains of enormous cisterns for collecting each precious drop of life-giving water lie one below the other. How old are they? No one can say with certainty; their origin is lost in the mists of antiquity. But even then men had overcome the inhospitality of nature.

Another picture involuntarily comes to mind—this time of the Arctic wastes, where in my youth I struggled step by step with a heavily-laden dog sledge through the snowdrifts. Days, even weeks, passed before a small settlement of snow huts broke the deadly monotony, and fur-clad Eskimos emerged from their entrance passages to bid the strangers welcome. Today with wondering eyes they watch luxurious airliners cross the very same territory on their way from Scandinavia to the Pacific coast of America. Here too mankind has bent nature to his will. In very truth man would seem to have obeyed the old commandment to replenish the earth and subdue it and have dominion over the fish of the sea and over the fowl of the air and over every living thing that moveth upon the earth.

Cultural development has been going on for a long time. It must be several hundred thousand years since our earliest ancestors formed the first piece of flint into a handy tool. Since then progress has been mainly forward, and the nuclear age offers a dazzling future. Is there then no limit to what man can achieve? Materially, he has achieved a great deal and a great deal more is within his grasp. Spiritually, progress has been much slower. One sincerely hopes that the time will come when progress will not be exclusively measured by the incidence of cars and television sets. But one thing must never be forgotten: we are ourselves part of nature and must always be so. The resources of nature are limited, even as our own spiritual resources are limited. We can exploit nature's resources to the limit of our abilities; we can never exceed them.

* * *

There are two ways in which nature influences cultural development. The situation of a culture in relation to other cultures conditions the extent to which fertile new ideas can find their way in. Not for nothing are the lowest forms of culture to be found on the fringes of the habitable world—in the "marginal peoples", as the founder of human geography, F. Ratzel, called them—and in such inaccessible places as the depths of the tropical rain forest. The other kind of influence exercised by nature is more immediate—through adaptation to local conditions.

Each form of culture makes its own special demands on its surroundings, just as the surroundings define the limitations of each individual culture. A culture will always be the joint product of the human spirit and the environment. There is a constant interaction, differing from place to place and from age to age. But one thing all cultures have in common: they have to adapt themselves to the conditions under which they live.

Not all cultures, however, exhibit the same degree of adaptation. The lower in the scale and the less specialized they are, the better they will be able to survive under changing conditions. On the other hand, some regions presuppose a high degree of adaptation if human life is to exist at all. But like all specialization, adaptation is a two-edged sword. The more one-sided a culture is, the more limited are its possibilities. The further it has gone in adapting itself, the greater the danger that development will come to a halt. Complete equilibrium with the surroundings is the death of a culture.

How then do we define adaptation? It has both positive and negative sides. On the positive side it can either be creative or selective, selecting from outside only such elements as will fit into the particular pattern of its culture. The line between these two possibilities is not always sharply drawn since cultural loans are often coupled with certain changes resulting from the new conditions. Negative adaptation is to be found when the natural conditions entirely preclude or at least check the development of certain characteristics. It can, however, also result in a culture being forced to abandon elements which once belonged to it but which, because of the changed conditions, no longer fit into the pattern. There will be an opportunity later on for elaborating all this.

No part of a culture is beyond the range of influence of its surroundings; but not all parts are equally exposed to their action. It is this factor which has produced the branch of geography known as cultural geography or human geography in a more restricted sense. Its purpose is to examine those aspects of the culture which are mainly dependent on the nature of the country, i.e. the distribution of the population, their occupations, dwellings, communications and polity. Such an investigation will, however, fail to have any realistic basis if it is not founded on history. No one has put this more clearly than Gudmund Hatt:

"The various natural conditions tell us of the cultural possibilities of the different countries and this enables us to draw conclusions regarding the routes taken by migrant peoples and the directions in which currents of civilization have flowed. How the cultural possibilities of a country are, or have been, in fact exploited, and which particular routes peoples and culture waves have taken in preference to other possible routes—of all this we can only have positive knowledge by studying the cultures and the peoples themselves or the possessions they have left behind them. When human geography forgets this limitation to which it is subject, it comes to fanciful and uncertain conclusions."

The object of this book is to give a picture of a number of cultures under differing climes and to show how in the process of their development they have adapted themselves to the conditions under which they exist. The description starts with the basic types of occupation, for natural conditions are most clearly reflected in economy. To this extent the geographical point of view prevails; but this is not in fact a geographical work. Any culture constitutes a working organism, in which each active part works in close interaction with the whole. For this reason I have felt that the description must cover each culture in its entirety. This may well result in their background being geographical, but the actual description will be ethnographical.

BIBLIOGRAPHY

On cultures and their development in general, see KAJ BIRKET-SMITH: *Geschichte der Kultur*, 3rd ed., Zurich, 1956.

The pioneer work on human geography is FRIEDRICH RATZEL: *Anthropogeographie*, i-ii, 2nd and 3rd ed., Stuttgart, 1909-12. The study has been particularly developed by French scientists, cf. e.g. JEAN BRUNHES: *La géographie humaine*, i-iii, 3rd ed., Paris, 1925. DANIEL FAUCHER: *Géographie des cultures*, Paris, 1949. ALBERT DEMANGEON: *Problèmes de géographie humaine*, Paris, 1942. MAX SORRE: *Les fondements de la géographie humaine*, i-iii, Paris, 1943-52. P. VIDAL DE LA BLACHE: *Principes de géographie humaine*, Paris, 1922.

Cf. also C. DARYLL FORDE: *Habitat, Economy and Society*, London, 1953.

AUSTRALIAN ABORIGINES

Food Gatherers and Primitive Hunters

Isolation and Uniformity

AUSTRALIA is not only the smallest continent—smaller than Europe, smaller even than the United States excluding Alaska—it is also the most inaccessible. Vast stretches of water separate it from countries to the west, south and east, disregarding Tasmania, of course, which in every respect constitutes a detached part of the Australian mainland, to which as late as the Ice Age it was joined by a land bridge. Only from the north is Australia accessible, and even here the Timor Sea and to a still greater extent the Coral Sea form a considerable barrier to passage from Indonesia and Melanesia. Access is easy only across the narrow, reefy Torres Strait from New Guinea. And so it was not before the first half of the seventeenth century that Dutch seafarers discovered the north and west coasts of Australia; and over a hundred years later before European colonization began.

This isolation has left its mark on the flora, fauna and human life of Australia and set them apart. No less than seven-eighths of its flora are peculiar to the continent—are endemic. In appearance they are often equally remarkable; this is as true of the countless eucalypti, which occur in all guises from giant trees with straight trunks and lopsided leaves to dry, twisted bushes, as of the casuarinas with their dark and mournfully drooping branches, the leafless thorny acacias, the grass trees crowned with a bristly tuft of leaves and the curious swollen bottle trees, whose water has saved more than one traveller from dying of thirst. But common to all plants is the fact that though many of them are suitable for food, none is suited to cultivation. The whole continent has not yielded a single cultivated plant.

Strange and primitive forms of animal life have also found sanctuary in Australia: the lung fish in the rivers of Queensland, the egg-laying duck-billed platypus and spiny anteater—lower in the scale than all other mammals. Above them all the marsupials have taken over the rôle of the remaining mammal orders, from the giant kangaroos to the tree-kangaroos, the vulpine opossums, the cuscus and the koala bears—which in spite of their name are harmless vegetarians leading a sleepy existence in the crowns of the eucalyptus trees. Finally there are the predatory dasyures and the bloodthirsty Tasmanian wolf. The only higher mammals are the bats, rats and the semi-wild—often completely wild—dog, the dingo, rats involuntarily and dingoes voluntarily introduced by man. It is significant that here again not one of the continent's original mammals can be tamed. No less strange is the bird life: the Australian ostrich, the emu, the parrots, of which there are more than fifty species, the black swans and the brilliantly coloured doves. Of the snakes no less than two-thirds are poisonous.

Isolation is one of the characteristics of nature in Australia; another is uniformity. A single wide gulf, the Gulf of Carpentaria, bites deep into the north coast of the continent, with the Cape York Peninsula on its eastern flank. Otherwise the continent forms a compact land mass with no extensive lowlands and no great peaks; the highest point would not reach half-way up Mont Blanc. For millions of years the country has lain exposed to the destructive forces of the climate. The whole of the western half, and more besides, consists of an almost flat plateau where only isolated hills of exceptionally resistant rock or ridges raised along fault lines rise above the ancient peneplain. To the east the plateau drops to the low-lying plains in the region of Lake Eyre and the Murray and Darling river system; but from there the terrain rises again to the eastern mountains, which drop more or less sheer towards the Pacific coast, and are, in fact, nothing but a number of plateaux separated by faults in the earth's crust and deeply furrowed.

Aided by reputedly magical drawings upon the rocks, a clan chieftain of the Wailbri tribe recites the myth of the sacred snake.

Left: A craftsman of the Wailbri tribe chipping stone knives.

Below: A hunter of the Murimbata tribe using a spear-thrower. With this implement the spear normally can be cast accurately to a distance of sixty yards and casts of up to 100 yards have been achieved.

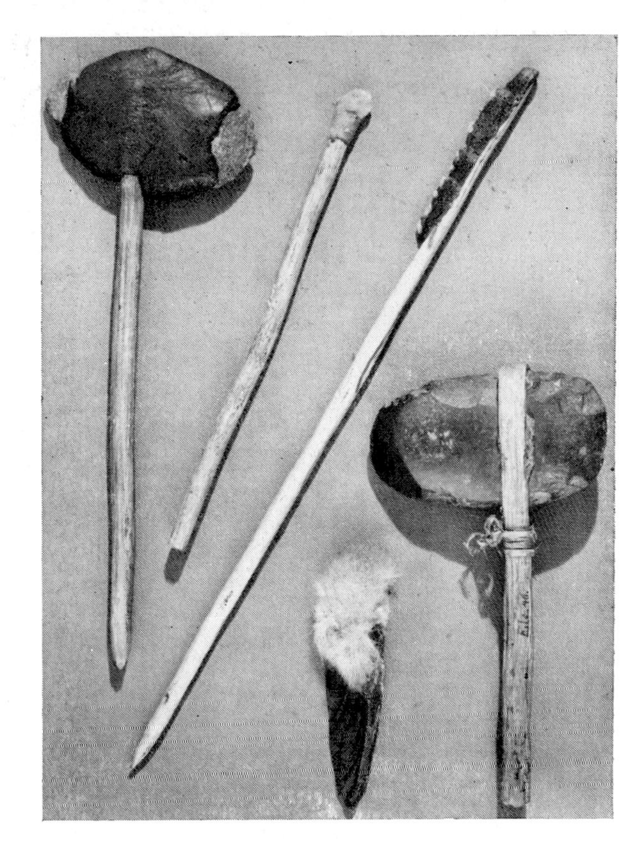

Right: Among these implements, which come from south-western and north - eastern Australia, and now are in the National Museum at Copenhagen, can be seen stone axes and a knife.

Below: Ceremonial objects used by the Aranta tribe: the two lower ones are of elaborately carved stone; the painting above is on bark, comes from Arnhem Land and depicts a stone axe and two jungle fowl in a camp area. The decoration on the borders represents grass. All are in the National Museum at Copenhagen.

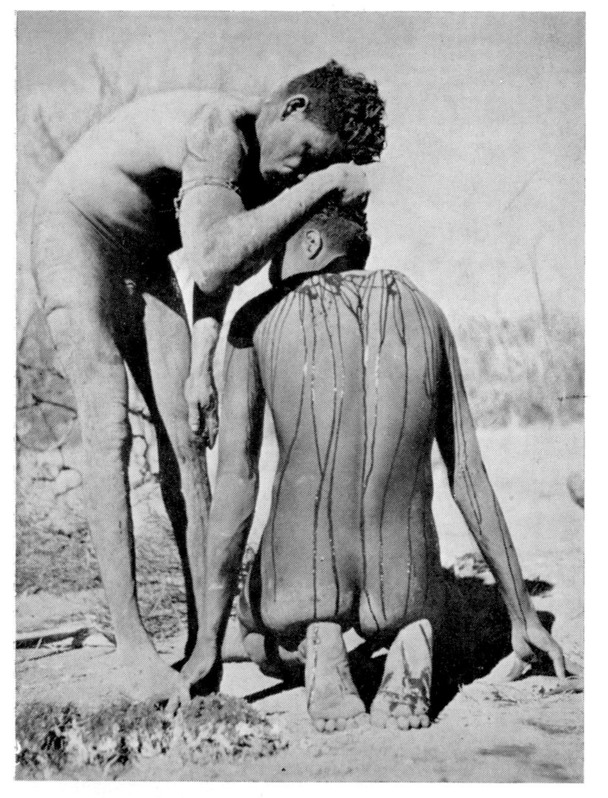

Above: Aborigines at their huts in Queensland.

Left: Among aborigines there is strong belief that blood possesses magical power; in this ceremony a transfer of that power is seen taking place between men of the Wailbri tribe.

A similar uniformity is found to a certain extent, though only to a certain extent, in the climate and flora. Australia is situated on both sides of the Tropic of Capricorn, which means that the greater part is in the sub-tropical zone. Only a small section to the north extends into the tropics. Here the summer, which of course falls in our winter months, is also the rainy season, when the monsoon from the sea heads for the shore, and the vegetation consists of grass, with scattered trees and small forests. But only on those mountain slopes facing eastward is the rainfall large enough for the tropical rain forest to develop in all its luxuriance.

The sub-tropical zone is quite different. The coastal mountains get plenty of rain and in many places they are covered with forests; if these cannot match the splendour of the tropical forest, their palms, lianas and tree ferns provide something of its luxuriance. But the very fact that the moist sea winds get rid of most of their moisture near the coast has dire consequences for the climate farther inland. From a distance the countryside would seem to be well covered with forest; in reality the trees are widely separated, with open stretches of grass between them. This curious shadeless vegetation of high-stemmed eucalypti is characteristic of many districts of eastern Australia.

But the shortage of water has far direr consequences in the interior of the continent. Both here and in the extreme south, night frosts are by no means rare; but while the variations in temperature are comparatively moderate at the coast, they are quite violent in the interior, where the average shade temperature during the summer is 86°F. Dry southerly winds blow throughout the year and over vast areas the rainfall is insignificant. The rivers, incapable of reaching the coast, disappear into salt lakes and marshes, so that nearly two-thirds of the continent has no outlet to the sea. Only the Murray River with its source in the eastern mountains still carries a considerable volume of water, while in the dry season its even longer tributary, the Darling, is scarcely able to link up with the main stream.

It is hardly surprising then that as soon as we reach the central area the vegetation becomes poorer and poorer. Patches of bush steppe start to appear and finally dominate the scene. As far as the eye can reach all that can be seen is dry scrub punctuated by patches of bare earth covered after a shower of rain with a profusion of annuals, or by salt-encrusted clay marshes where nothing but thick-leaved glassworts will thrive. Large tracts of West Australia are complete desert. On enormous sand dunes three-foot-high tufts of porcupine grass eke out a miserable existence.*

Penetrating into the south-westerly corner of Australia and to that part of the south coast facing west, we find districts resembling the Mediterranean where the winter is the rainy season, and miles of evergreen scrub alternate with grassland and monotonous eucalyptus forests. Thus it is mainly climate and vegetation which account for the differences in the Australian landscape.

Isolation, which has been of such significance to the continent, has also left its mark on the original inhabitants. Both in physical characteristics and way of life they seem curiously primitive. Racially they are in many respects similar to the most ancient forms of modern peoples as we know them in Europe, Asia and America. They are closest to certain small primitive tribes in southern Asia, though physically they appear to combine several of the characteristics which later became more pronounced in more highly developed races. The wavy hair, entirely different from the woolly hair of the Negro, is reminiscent of the European; so is the plentiful growth of hair on the face and body, and to some extent the coarse features. The dark, chocolate-brown colour of the skin, the broad nose and long arms and legs call to mind Negroes, though the type towards the north is somewhat slighter built, more dark skinned and less hairy than those farther south. Then there are other features which at once betray the low stage of development of the race: the receding forehead, the heavy eyebrow ridges, the prognathic mouth region and the low, narrow skull with its incredibly thick brain case.

Broadly speaking, the Australians are similar in appearance throughout the continent. There is only an occasional suggestion of

* This grass, which is of some significance to the natives, is called *Spinifex* by the white population of Australia. Actually, however, it belongs not to the botanical genus of this name but to the *Triodia* genus.

a possible foreign strain in the form of an element corresponding to the now extinct Negroid aborigines of Tasmania. There is thought to be evidence of this in the west and in northern Queensland, where a woolly-haired pygmy type is described. This, however, seems to be insufficiently investigated as yet. In the matter of language, too, isolation and uniformity are again characteristic: all Australian languages appear to be interrelated, though without demonstrable connexion with others.

The primitive racial characteristics of the Australians are consistent with the theory that their forefathers immigrated as far back as the close of the Ice Age. Skulls found at Talgai in the south of Queensland and at Keilor not far from Melbourne undoubtedly date from that time. By means of radioactive carbon the date of the archæological strata from Pejark Marsh has been put at about 11,500 B.C. Unfortunately, Australian archæology is still in its infancy; but the little that is known confirms the age of the skulls. The oldest known tools have come from excavations near the mouth of the Murray River and on Kangaroo Island off the south coast. These implements are pebbles roughly shaped on one side, and simple stone chippings somewhat like a horse's hoof—obvious forerunners of better fashioned scrapers used right down to the present day.

At Tartanga on the lower reaches of the Murray River and on Devon Downs it has fortunately been possible to work out a chronological sequence of the various cultures. Here too development starts with quite primitive tools and ends with ground-edged axes and other well-made implements. Most excavations have been carried out in the south-eastern corner of the continent; but archæological investigations have also been made in Arnhem Land in the north. All in all, twelve different prehistoric cultures can be traced in Australia; so far, unfortunately, the finds have been too few and too scattered for their interconnexion to be established.

So much is certain, however: the oldest forms show an unmistakable relationship with similar finds in Indonesia, Malaya and Tonkin. It is in south-east Asia that the foundations of Australian culture must be sought, and it is in the last resort from there too, with New Guinea as the connecting link, that with one or two exceptions later currents of civilization have flowed. An evident predilection for microliths—small flint flakes used as side blades in spears—suggests the transition period between the Old and New Stone Ages. From a still later period, the fully developed New Stone Age, there are axes made by pecking and axes polished in varying degrees. Agriculture, on which the whole of New Guinea's Stone Age culture is based, has never secured a foothold in Aboriginal Australia and in the main the country has been left untouched and practically unaffected by subsequent progress in the rest of the world.

So much for prehistory, so far as it can be probed archæologically. But a culture does not consist entirely of stones. On the contrary, stone objects constitute only the smallest part even so far as tools are concerned—while they have little to tell us about the social organization and religion. Any attempt to describe the make-up of the present-day culture on the basis of archæological results would be a somewhat hazardous undertaking.

Deep down its roots are late palæolithic and early neolithic—of this there is no doubt, though it underwent change later in the course of independent growth.*

Such characteristic objects as the boomerang and throwing stick, dome-shaped huts, fire drills, fishing by means of poison and the damming of streams with bushes probably belong, if not to the oldest, at least to very ancient strata of Australian culture. The multi-pronged fish spear and the fish hook probably originated in the New Stone Age of New Guinea, and so did platform burial, the mummification of bodies and a special form of youth initiation in conjunction with what are known as bull-roarers: a narrow wooden board which when swung on a long string produces a buzzing sound. There are also grounds for believing that the basic ideas in the curious social system and in the view of life of the Australian Aborigines stem from New Guinea, and this is also true perhaps of the spiral designs which account for a considerable

* The Old Stone Age during the Ice Age is described as palæolithic, the New Stone Age as neolithic and the transition period as mesolithic.

proportion of the decorative art in Kimberley and Central Australia, even if their original home was as far off as the Bronze Ages of China and Indonesia.

But even if it is established that New Guinea was the nearest source, the problem of how Australia's culture developed remains, for it is hardly likely that all its influences arrived at one and the same time. On the contrary, fresh impulses seem to have constantly found their way in. There is no other way of explaining the many similarities between New Guinea and the two regions lying closest to it: harpoons, woven traps, decorated bark belts, etc., in Arnhem Land; bows and arrows, dug-out canoes, and a peculiar form of hero worship on the Cape York Peninsula. There is no denying that some things may even have been introduced direct from Indonesia; at any rate, as late as the sixteenth to nineteenth centuries pearl and trepang fishers from Celebes were of some consequence in Arnhem Land. Nor can we be certain whether, and to what extent, culture waves were brought by new immigrants. This perhaps happened in some cases. Both in Central Australia and on the north coast, legend has it that certain culture elements were introduced by certain groups of ancestors, and sometimes, it is said, they came from across the sea. To what extent such traditions have a historical basis the future must decide.

In these circumstances it is at present very difficult, not to say impossible, to establish definite culture periods or culture strata. Fritz Graebner's pioneering attempt at this half a century ago is now somewhat out of date. More recent investigators, such as D. S. Davidson and Frederick D. McCarthy, have paved the way for more modern ideas by unravelling the chronological development of a large number of elements; but the great work which will knit the past and the present together into a single whole will be written only after many more years of archæological and ethnographical investigation.

If we know little yet of the process of development, we know little either of the course it has taken. Only one thing can be said with certainty: it is from the north that the waves of culture have come. The farther south we go, the poorer the culture becomes.

Various elements are absent, for example, in the extreme south-west. Water craft even in their simplest forms are unknown, there are no examples of stone polishing, no proper axes, and no knowledge of net-making, fish-hooks and so on. South-east Australia, too, seems to be very primitive. There are in fact canoes, but only of the most primitive kind, formed of a single piece of bark. Net- and basket-making are extremely crude. Stone axes are made by pecking, not by grinding as is the case farther north, and the whole social organization is at a much lower stage of development than in most other places on the continent. It is rather more difficult to describe the state of affairs in the central districts. These are the least well endowed by nature: all the same they have been supposed to be the centre of a peculiar type of development which had some influence on surrounding districts. Such an eminent scientist as Father Wilhelm Schmidt has even suggested that the Central Australian tribes were originally on a higher cultural level but were so late in immigrating that they had to be content with the most inhospitable region. This view, however, can hardly be sustained, and the whole idea of a culture emanating from Central Australia seems misconceived. For example, the apparently typical characteristic of dividing the community into four or eight "sections" seems to have started in Kimberley and spread from there, and this to some extent happened in quite recent times.

However that may be, the fact remains that the north is the direction from which the culture waves have flowed, and the Cape York Peninsula seems to have been the principal gateway. Not only is it the point where the distance from New Guinea is shortest: the natural conditions on both sides of the Torres Strait are much the same.

Some indication of their subsequent progress is provided by the trade routes which from earliest times have linked individual tribes. One of them follows the east coast, another runs through the grassland down the Diamantina and Cooper Creek to the country round Lake Eyre and on from there to the south coast. From Arnhem Land and Kimberley there are connexions to Central Australia and the south-westerly corner of the continent;

but the road is long and difficult, making a long detour to avoid the great deserts of the West Australian interior. Natural conditions are thus clearly reflected in the culture: most highly developed in the north, progressively declining southwards through eastern Australia until it reaches its lowest point in Tasmania; but that is beyond the scope of this survey.

* * *

A proper understanding of the culture of the Australian Aborigines must, however, be based on something more than the country as seen by ourselves. Their way of life is so bound up with their own peculiar conceptions that it is necessary to consider these. One of the great ethnographical surprises was the discovery that in many Aborigines there was a belief in a kind of Supreme Being, and this belief was strongest in some of the most primitive tribes, such as the Yuin and Kurnai in the extreme south-east. The name of this sky god was so holy that it could be spoken only in a whisper. He ordered people's lives and watched over their doings. A number of other tribes in Victoria, New South Wales and southern Queensland also believe in this Being. The problem is to know what significance to attach to him. The Central Australian Aranda describe him as an enormous giant with a red skin, emu's feet and a retinue of wives with dogs' legs: a description reminiscent of the ordinary totem ancestors. It has indeed been shown that his exalted position in the minds of the people was brought about by the influence of the Christian religion. This has not happened in every case, however.

In some tribes the idea of this Being is more or less bound up with the moon or with the ancestor of mankind. One thing, however, is common to all these deities: they did not create the world nor do they concern themselves with the welfare of man. Like the totem ancestors of the central tribes, they tend to be mere culture bearers who have instituted holy rites and taught men how to formulate their lives. The female deities, which were discovered in Arnhem Land and in large tracts of Northern Territory a few years ago, intervene more directly in human affairs since, in a manner curiously reminiscent of the ancient Orient, they ensure through initiation rites rebirth after death. This whole conception is so strange and foreign that it postulates the work of some outside influence.

The fundamental idea in the Australian's concept of life is that there is no sharp division between man and nature, between the quick and the dead, nor even in a way between past, present and future. Nature can as little exist without man as man without nature, and yesterday and tomorrow in a manner inexplicable to us merge into today. The whole world is a single entity and its chief characteristic is reciprocity. And so man and nature are indivisibly joined in the fellowship which finds expression in totemism. In some mysterious way man shares a common life with an animal or plant or with some natural phenomenon such as rain or thunder —becomes, in fact, one with it. A man is not only in the closest association with a gray kangaroo, falcon or wild yam, he *is* a kangaroo, falcon or wild yam.

This association occurs in various ways: between the totem and the individual, with one sex as opposed to the other, or with a particular group within the community. In the latter case the group may comprise the local horde (it would never be the whole tribe) or a unit cutting across the horde groupings, in which case it can either be an independent clan within the tribe or it could be identical with other sub-divisions in the form of what are known as tribal moieties, sections and sub-sections. The totemic outlook culminates by embracing the entire universe. The Yualayi in northern New South Wales, for example, classify crayfish, night owls, black swans, eucalyptus, the north-east wind and much else besides as belonging to the emu totem. And not only long-familiar objects are classified in this way. A tribe in Kimberley, which divides the world into two groups, red and gray kangaroos, puts aeroplanes into the former group and lorries into the latter!

Individual totemism is of fundamental importance to the activities of the medicine man. His totem, usually a lizard or a snake, acts as his assistant in the exercise of his calling. Various kinds of group totemism influence the life of the society still more.

They join totem members in everlasting bonds and impose special rights and duties on them. If each sex has its totem it is purely social in character, its influence being confined to such ceremonial occasions as for instance wedding preparations.

Totemism has a more far-reaching influence when there are special totem groups within the tribe. Here too the emphasis is often on their social character, and in such cases they affect the whole system of kinship and the regulation of marriage. In clan totemism, a child is regarded as the mother's "flesh", consequently the line of descent nearly always passes through the mother. But when the totemic idea is linked to other social groups—tribal moieties or sections as mentioned above—the line of descent can pass through the father. The main thing is that all the members of the totem group feel mutually related: they are of the same standing as parents and children, brothers and sisters. Thus any idea of marriage between members of the group is inconceivable—it would be incestuous and is strictly taboo. Even the group's totem belongs to the family and will stand by its brothers and sisters. Consequently they would never dream of harming it or of killing and eating it.

Totem groups which are primarily cult organizations for the purpose of maintaining the equilibrium of the world and the regular course of nature operate in a different way. They are not concerned with marriage laws, and membership depends not on the totem of the parents but on ideas which are difficult for us to grasp. The distant past, "the dream age", saw the creation of human and animal spirits which have taken bodily form in an unending cycle ever since. The spirits live in rocks or water holes: places where the great totem fathers once paused on their way through the world. At the end of their travels they were either transformed or disappeared into the depths of the earth. The mythical ancestor of the kangaroo once stopped and performed the sacred rites which resulted in the propagation of the kangaroo: so here for all time is the spiritual home and cult centre of the kangaroo totem. When the bodies which they have been inhabiting die, the spirits return here and await rebirth. If a woman goes near such a place and suddenly feels the movement of life inside her, then it is a sign that the spirit of a child has made her pregnant. Sexual intercourse is thought to be of no significance.

Sacred places are to be found throughout the horde's district, and since a woman is more likely to pass near one of those in her own horde's district, the horde's laws of descent through the male line usually determine the totem. Sometimes, however, the totem is not determined in this way: the father or possibly the mother has dreamt of the unborn child's totem, and then this will determine which it is to be, but since the father's totem will almost certainly have appeared in the dream, the final outcome will be the same.

More important than the method of acquiring the totem is the fact that only fully grown men who have been through all the initiation rites can belong to the cult association. Women and children are excluded. The cult members are one with the totem and with the totem dream-age ancestor. Painted and clad in various sacred adornments they sing chants describing the adventures of their ancestor and mimic the behaviour of the totem, thereby in some magical way causing rain to fall, grass to grow or animals to multiply, according to the nature of the totem. And thus in the form of a cult drama, with all differences in time annihilated, they re-create and rejuvenate the world.

A typical example of such a ceremony is one practised by the Aranda already mentioned, when the totem group responsible for the propagation of a certain kind of butterfly with edible larvæ performs its rites. At daybreak the larva men, fasting, naked and unarmed, make their way along a path used in the dream age by the totem ancestor to a sacred cave where a big stone surrounded by smaller stones represents the butterfly and its eggs. Led by the totem chieftain carrying a wooden bowl, they file along, a sprig of eucalyptus in either hand. Singing a chant they strike the stones with the bowl and sprigs. Then the chieftain picks up one of the stones and, touching each of the others on the stomach with it, says: "You have eaten much".

After further ceremony, the men proceed to other caves, keeping all the time to the path of the totem ancestor. As they near the camp once more they put on their adornments and paint sacred designs on themselves in red ochre and white clay. Thus arrayed they file along to a small leaf hut which represents the butterfly's cocoon. Some way off the men of other totem groups sit watching, and behind them are the women of the camp. The larva men creep into the hut and as they do so all the spectators throw themselves prostrate on the ground, so remaining throughout the rest of the ceremony.

Meanwhile the men in the hut start chanting once more, and in finally creeping out they are mimicking the fully grown butterfly creeping out of its cocoon. After this they return inside the hut and stay there until evening. They spend the night singing round a big fire. In the morning they remove their adornments and these are distributed amongst the remaining inhabitants of the camp to ward off misfortune; but it is the following sunset before the designs they have painted on themselves are removed.

Similar rites are performed by other totem groups. The emu men, for example, use white clay, charcoal and yellow ochre mixed with fat to paint the picture of an emu on the ground—a highly unconventional painting it is true, not even approximating to a realistic representation of an emu. It consists of an involved design of dots, oblong patches, concentric circles and curved lines representing feathers, eggs in various stages of development, entrails and so on, the object being to include as much detail of the bird as possible so that its magic shall work. Likeness as we understand it is of no significance. In some cases there are special rites connected with rock paintings and engravings.

The pitiless resources of Australia make life hard and relentless, and cult-totemism is the religious expression of the native's adaptation of it. Cult totemism is important in many ways, by no means the least of these being its social aspect. Animals need grass and grass needs rain. All totem groups must therefore work together so that the common objective, the maintenance of life, can be attained. The benefit of such co-operation will accrue in the first instance to other totem groups, for in most cases members of the cult association are forbidden to partake of their totem animal or plant. At most, they may eat it only at special, ritual feasts.

Nothing else influences the life of the Aborigines to the extent that totemism does, and in no other people is totemism so strongly developed. Though it has been possible to give some indication of the interdependence between its form, its function and its method of acquisition—thanks especially to the researches of A. P. Elkin—the fact remains that the boundaries between them are by no means clearly defined. The various forms of totemism can not only merge into each other but can occur within a single tribe—a single individual belonging at one time to three or four different totem groups, each with its own rules and purpose. The whole subject of totemism's form and function, its origin and development is still to some extent unexplored.

Social totemism is to be found in many places of the world and is certainly of ancient origin, though it might conceivably have started spontaneously in separate places. Its occurrence in Australia has doubtless some connexion with New Guinea and other parts of Melanesia, where it is widespread. But cult totemism does not seem to occur in the marginal districts of Australia to the extreme west, south and south-east, which suggests that it is of more recent origin than social totemism; where it does occur, however, it is more highly developed than anywhere else. But it is not a purely Australian phenomenon. Something similar occurs, for example, in New Guinea, and the first seeds doubtless found their way from there to the mainland, where they fell on fertile ground. As for sex totemism, there are signs of this elsewhere, but whether this indicates a connexion is more than doubtful. In Australia sex totemism is mainly found in the central and south-eastern districts, and its occurrence amongst some of the more primitive tribes at any rate suggests that it is of considerable antiquity.

* * *

As mentioned above, certain totemic ideas have a profound influence on the social structure, and the time has come to examine it more closely. When natural resources are so limited and the level of culture is so low, it is not surprising that the population has always been small. Exactly how small is impossible to say with certainty. But it has been estimated that at the beginning of colonization the figure was somewhere between 150,000 and 300,000, a population density of 20-50 per sq. km. The population has not, of course, been evenly distributed. It was densest in the comparatively fertile eastern districts and tapered off to nothing in the West Australian deserts. As there were some 500 tribes in the country, they must have been fairly small, ranging from a maximum of 1,500 down to about 100, with 500-600 the most usual, and even so numbers were to be kept down by voluntary birth control in the form of abortion and infanticide.

Each tribe has its own clearly defined country to which it has an exclusive right. Still more important, the country contains the sacred places of the tribe: the spiritual homes of men and animals and the paths interconnecting them which were used by the dream-age ancestors. Thus the tribe is linked to its country with strong religious ties and it runs the risk of breaking up if they are severed. None the less, it is neither an economic nor a political unit, being split up into small local groups or hordes each comprising a single joint family, or at most a few families consisting of parents, children, sons and daughters-in-law and any grandchildren there may be. Larger amalgamations could not possibly survive. Where the line of descent goes through the female, other subdivisions may occur within the tribe, but male descent always applies within the horde, which is also exogamous, i.e. the man chooses his wife from another horde.

It must, however, be emphasized that the matter of choice is very much circumscribed. It has already been stressed that there can be no question of marriage within the social totem group. Custom further requires that it should take place between certain relatives. Radcliffe-Brown has shown that a " proper " marriage takes one of two forms. In a number of small and widely separated districts near the coast a man marries his mother's brother's daughter or some other woman who stands in similar relationship to him. In the intervening districts, however, a man marries his mother's mother's brother's daughter's daughter or a woman in similar relationship to him. The former custom is evidently the older and an example of marriage between cross cousins (i.e. the respective children of a brother and a sister) which is to be found in many places throughout the world.

In some tribes there is a remarkable system known to the Dieri tribe by Lake Eyre as *pirauru*-marriage. In addition to being married to his real wife, a man can stand in *pirauru* relationship to several women who are already married to other men. This requires not only their consent but the consent of the chief, and comes into force only when the husband is away. It is in fact a form of protection for the wife during the absence of the husband, since a lone woman would run the risk of being raped and killed. Another custom, which is found all over the world, is levirate marriage, which imposes on a man the right and duty to marry his deceased brother's widow. One result of the curious marriage laws is that frequently the old men have the youngest and most attractive wives. Women are frequently betrothed in girlhood and are often given in exchange for another girl. Abduction and wife capture occur, but when they do it is frequently by tacit agreement. It must, of course, be realized that rules are one thing but keeping them is another, for people are but human. An investigation into the marriages in the Kimberley district showed that up to a quarter of them diverged in greater or less degree from the prevailing norm.

All in all, kinship and marriage involve the Aborigines in reciprocal obligations to a far greater degree than they do with us. This results in a system of kinship nomenclature which to us is often incomprehensible. For example, one and the same word describes both father and son, and to describe his son and his brother's son a man uses the same word as a woman uses of her daughter and her sister's daughter. What they express is in fact the behaviour they must adopt to the person in question. Thus there are explicit rules which prescribe who is to receive the gifts of meat which a successful hunter is obliged to distribute: for instance, first his father, then his mother's brother and finally his parents-in-law. The parents-in-law must also be given presents at the time of the betrothal, and this is often misunderstood as mere payment for the betrothed.

Still more curious is a form of behaviour amounting to more or less consistent avoidance of certain relatives. Some may never be spoken to at all; others only with the back turned; with some joking is taboo, with others there must be no reference to their totem. The strictest of all taboos are on contact between mother-in-law and son-in-law; but there must also be the minimum of contact between brother and sister; sometimes one of them may not offer the other so much as a drink of water. Evidence of the lengths to which kinship goes is provided by the Murngin tribe in Arnhem Land which recognizes no fewer than seventy-one kinds of relationship.

Three main types of kinship system occur in Australia, corresponding to the marriage rules previously mentioned. In the first, marriage between cross cousins is permitted. In the second, a man may marry his mother's sister's daughter, but not his father's sister's daughter—an extremely practical arrangement in view of the mother-in-law avoidance, since the father's sister belongs to the same local horde as her nephew. In the third and most widespread system, marriage between cross first cousins is forbidden, whereas marriage is favoured between cross second cousins, i.e. between a man and his mother's mother's brother's daughter's daughter, whereby, of course, he avoids belonging to the same horde as his mother-in-law.

What, then, is woman's position in marriage and society? Superficial observers, with a mixture of indignation and pity, have frequently felt sorry for her in her subjugation. Yet the truth is quite otherwise. A first-class ethnologist, herself a woman, has made detailed investigation into the matter in the Kimberley district and writes as follows:

> "It is true the woman provides the larger part of the meal, but one must not automatically assume that her work is more onerous. Actually it is less so than the men's, as I can speak from experience. Merely to follow them in their hunting over rugged hills in the

blazing sun left me so exhausted that after two attempts I was content henceforth to amble with the women over the plains and along the dry river-beds."

Elsewhere she writes:

"If a girl has little freedom of choice in marriage, at least the young man is in the same position."

And she adds:

"Marriage is more than a sexual union: it involves economic co-operation, the sharing of food and a common hearth, the raising of children. We have found that apart from the choice of residence, husband and wife claim reciprocal privileges, fulfil reciprocal duties."

From other tribes there is similar evidence:

"In general, we should say that the women of Central Australia had a happy life. They are attached to their husbands and children, and if marriage should not always prove a success, nobody wears fetters in the desert—they can always try again."

Certain tribes on the outskirts of the continent—the Kurnai and Narrinyeri to the south-east, the Nanda on the west coast and the Larakia in northern Arnhem Land, for example—recognize no other social unit than the local horde. Mostly, however, the tribe is divided into two halves, and these moieties can be further subdivided into four or eight sections and sub-sections.

The tribal moieties were formerly known as marriage classes because it was thought that their main object was to regulate the man's choice of a wife, since she nearly always had to belong to some group other than his; but this has proved to be a secondary consideration and merely a consequence of the fact that certain relations are preferred in marriage. What really lies behind the division are the separate functions of the two moieties on such occasions as youth initiation and burial, each of them then having its own particular duties. The divisions are also of some significance in the arrangement of the camp, since they are often required to erect their huts a certain distance away from each other. With the peculiar outlook of the Aborigines in mind it is not surprising that this division into moieties and sections is bound up with totemic ideas. Sections and sub-sections are divisions of the moieties, but are in reality independent of them. The moiety division is purely ceremonial, whereas the basis of the sections and sub-sections is marriage regulation. It would take up too much space to go into this in more detail, however.

But whatever the form of sub-division, membership of the group depends on the individual's descent; all local hordes are patrilineal, but this does not apply to the moieties. In almost the whole of Queensland and New South Wales, the greater part of South Australia and southern West Australia they are matrilineal. In the west and north and a small area of Victoria they are patrilineal. When the tribe is only divided into two, no difficulties arise, but the system is more complicated when in addition to the tribal moieties there are four sections; still more so, of course, when there are eight sub-sections.

In such cases membership is by descent, but in a curious indirect way. In the Nyul-Nyul tribe and in many other tribes in West Australia there are four sections, called respectively *panaka*, *burong*, *karimba* and *paldjeri*. A *panaka* man marries a *burong* woman; her son becomes a *paldjeri* and as such must marry a *karimba* woman, whose child again becomes a *panaka*. If on the other hand the man is a *burong* and the woman a *panaka*, the cycle moves in the opposite direction, their child being a *karimba* and must marry a *paldjeri*, the grandchildren again being *burongs*. Among the Arandas in Central Australia there are eight sub-sections. The line of descent can be shown diagramatically as follows (△ meaning man; ○ woman; ~marries, and > becomes):

pananka	△	~	*purula*	○	children	>	*bangata*
knuraia	△	~	*ngala*	○	,,	>	*paltara*
purula	△	~	*pananka*	○	,,	>	*kamara*
ngala	△	~	*knuraia*	○	,,	>	*mbitjana*
kamara	△	~	*paltara*	○	,,	>	*purula*
mbitjana	△	~	*bangata*	○	,,	>	*ngala*
paltara	△	~	*kamara*	○	,,	>	*knuraia*
bangata	△	~	*mbitjana*	○	,,	>	*pananka*

Instead of the cycle being complete in two generations, as is the case with section division, four generations are required for the cycle to be complete. A more detailed explanation of the system, which is linked up with the different positions occupied by men and women in the kinship system is too complicated for detailed discussion here.

Ceremonial bipartition of the tribe and kinship systems reminiscent of those of the Australian Aborigines occur in some places in Melanesia, and there is undoubtedly a connexion between them; but in their more developed form they seem to be found only on the mainland. The section system presumably spread from southern Kimberley by way of the central districts to the greater part of New South Wales and Queensland, so that simple division into two moieties remains only in the most northerly part of Kimberley, on the tip of the Cape York Peninsula, in a large area east of Lake Eyre on the lower reaches of the Diamantina and Cooper Creek and in large parts of Victoria and South Australia. The sub-sections are the least widespread, and certainly the most recent. They are confined to southern Kimberley and most of the Northern Territory.

As already mentioned, each tribe and each horde has its own country; but that certainly does not mean that it is cut off from the outside world. Neighbouring hordes belonging to different tribes meet on the occasion of youth initiation, funerals and totem festivals. Special messengers are sent out beforehand: men or women painted in a manner befitting the occasion. Their visit is often heralded by smoke signals and with them, as a kind of diplomatic credential, they carry a message in the form of a wooden stick carved with signs: these are often an *aide mémoire* for the bearer, though sometimes they are of more general and conventional significance—thus in a sense a kind of primitive writing. Equipped in this way a messenger can safely make his way into a foreign country, all the more so since he—or she—will usually find totem relatives amongst the foreign tribe.

Such meetings are obviously of the greatest importance, first because they help to avoid mutual strife, and second because they result in the exchange of ideas and goods. Quite a considerable degree of trade takes place. Some tribes have a generally recognized monopoly, inherited from the totem ancestors, in the production of certain types of weapons and tools. It is widely believed that foreign things have greater magical force than one's own, so for that reason alone they are sought after. Differences in language cause some difficulty, of course; but it is not unusual for a man to understand the languages of one or two neighbouring tribes, even though he cannot speak them. A highly developed system of signs is a further help.

Among the Narrinyeri of South Australia there is a form of trade linked to the curious institution known as *ngia-ngiampe*. When a boy is born the father will sometimes pack the baby's navel cord in feathers and present it to a member of another tribe. From then on that man's son and the new-born baby stand in mystical relationship to each other; they are each other's *ngia-ngiampe* and may never touch or speak to each other. When they grow up each becomes the trade representative of his tribe. One of them gets sent off with goods to the other's tribe and they exchange products. Business dealings are, of course, somewhat complicated since there is a taboo on their speaking to each other, and everything has to be arranged through intermediaries.

Some far more dangerous journeys are made: through the country of another tribe in search of necessities not to be found in the home territory—red ochre, stones suitable for axe-heads and other tools and, most important of all, the leaves and young shoots of the pitjuri bush (*Duboisia hopwoodi*) which, when fried and eaten with ashes, are one of the most appreciated stimulants. Such journeys are always undertaken by a considerable number of armed men and can range over an enormous distance; members of the Dieri tribe east of Lake Eyre will journey 700 miles to the Herbert River in north-east Queensland to secure this coveted stimulant.

But in addition to such journeys to distant parts, there are other journeys to be made. Even under the most favourable conditions wild life soon gets scared away from the neighbourhood of the camp, and in a drought, when the grass withers and streams dry up, other districts have to be explored for the necessities of life.

It is then that the Aborigines reap the benefit of knowing the resources of their homeland so intimately. Water is the prime necessity and often difficult to obtain. But the camp site must be chosen so that it cannot be attacked without warning. For this reason it is always situated away from closely grown clumps of trees and bushes which would give an enemy cover.

The actual shelter does not cause much trouble, for it is primitive in the extreme. Sometimes no more than a cave provides the alternative to a night in the open, half-shivering in front of the fire. Fire is one of the most important forms of protection, in a way both habitation and dress. The Aborigine usually makes a fire by drilling a stick of hard wood into a piece of softer wood. Another method is to saw the sharp edge of one piece of wood into another —the edge of a throwing board, for example, into a shield. Fire sawing is common in Central and north-west Australia, and probably more recent than fire drilling.

But to return to shelters—geography evidently has some influence on them, for the best huts are found either in the extreme south, where the winter rain and cold make shelter essential, or in the extreme north where a higher level of culture has led to a higher standard of building and where plagues of mosquitoes make it uncomfortable to remain in the open air. Some tribes in Victoria build a cone-shaped framework of long sticks supported by a centre pole, which they cover with bark and grass and a layer of clay. The Dieri and Narrinyeri have dome-shaped huts covered with earth. Elsewhere—in Queensland, for example—the huts are dome-shaped but with no covering of earth and are so small that it is difficult to see how there can be room for all the members of the family inside.

The Aranda and other Central Australian tribes have dome-shaped huts and in addition a simple windbreak consisting of a couple of uprights joined at the top by a cross-bar; against one side of this lean a number of branches, and to increase the amount of warmth they put branches up on both sides. Some northern tribes build their huts in the shape of a barrel vault and cover them with flexible pieces of bark of a kind which provides effective protection against rain and mosquitoes. In parts of Arnhem Land there are even simple houses consisting of a platform on four poles enclosed by walls and a roof of bark. This method has doubtless been copied from Malay fishermen and provides for a smoke fire under the floor as additional protection against annoying insects.

The Aborigines can hardly be said to live in villages, for they are always on the move, seldom remaining more than a few weeks in one place. None the less, it would be wrong to imagine that the huts, wretched as they are, are erected in no kind of system. On the contrary, definite rules consistent with that love of ceremony which permeates the whole of the Aborigines' society are observed. Even among such a comparatively primitive tribe as the Kurnai the camp is arranged so that the huts are a certain distance and a certain direction from each other, according to the relationships of the occupiers. Among the Aranda, the camp consists of a compound of eight groups of huts corresponding to the eight subsections into which the tribe is divided. Two neighbouring groups provide communal meeting centres for men and women respectively; they are taboo to the opposite sex and members of other groups may visit them only if they approach from a certain direction.

Clothes concern them even less than huts. It is quite astonishing how little notice the Aborigines take of the cold, however much they may feel it. And modesty as we understand it is unknown to them. In many places both men and women go about completely naked, unless the fat which they put on their bodies as protection against the wind and rain can be regarded as a kind of substitute for clothes. At most they wear a string of twined human or kangaroo hair round the waist, and sometimes, though by no means always, there are tassels of the same material or of skin hanging from it. Some West Australian tribes adorn the waist string with mother-of-pearl shells etched and coloured with red designs. The broad decorated belts of bark which men in some parts of North Australia wear round the waist are a late importation from New Guinea, and the same probably applies to the grass skirts worn by the women of the same district.

Only in the extreme south and south-east, where the winters are more severe, is there a real garment, though of the simplest kind: a skin cloak wrapped round the body which mothers also use for wrapping newborn babies in. No fewer than 30-40 opossum skins go to a single cloak. The skins are spread out on the ground and dried, carefully cleaned of all traces of flesh with a stone scraper and then rubbed with fat and red ochre. Holes are made round the edges with a bone bodkin and the skins are drawn together by sinews. Some cloaks are painted or drawn with designs.

Though clothes are scanty, adornments are plentiful; but most of them, it must be remembered, are more than mere ornaments: they have some magical significance. This is most evident in the fantastic headdresses which the men wear at totem ceremonies: for instance, long, thin bundles of straw and twigs tightly bound with ochre-coloured hair strings, covered with down and surmounted by a tuft of feathers; or what is known as a thread-cross, consisting of two sticks tied together in the form of a cross, with ochre-coloured or down-covered hair strings stretched between them.

The designs painted on the body in ochre, charcoal or white clay are also of significance, varying according to the occasion. Mutilating the body—inserting a stick in the nose, for example—frequently has some connexion with the initiation rites. We shall be dealing with these later. Nearly all tribes practise a form of tattooing known as cicatrization, which consists of making deep cuts in the skin and rubbing in charcoal or ashes so that, when the wounds are healed, the scars stand out in ridges as thick as a finger. Then there are a great number of other ornaments: headbands of a kangaroo's front teeth, necklaces also of teeth, coloured seeds and snail shells, bracelets of human or kangaroo hair dyed in ochre, tufts of feather for the hair, etc. These, too, often have some deeper meaning than would appear on the surface.

The simple huts and scanty dress can hardly be called an adaptation to the wandering life, however suitable they may be in this respect; they are, rather, a consequence of the generally low level of culture and, in the final analysis, of its isolation. The same applies to weapons and tools; but in one respect there is clear evidence of adaptation in these. When the group moves on everything has to be carried, for the Aborigines have never learned to train their dogs into beasts of burden. So to make their loads as small as possible a single tool must be made to fulfil several functions. An oblong wooden dish serves for collecting roots, fetching water and carrying the baby, and it can also be used as a shovel. The broad, almost trough-like spear-throwers of some of the central tribes have a piece of sharp stone stuck in one end so that they can also be used as chisels. Besides, their shape also enables them to be used as vessels—while by sawing the sharp edge into a shield it is possible to make fire. In Central Australia a boomerang is sometimes used for digging and its edge is sharpened so that it can be used as a knife. Few as the weapons and tools are, they are not common to all tribes.

The sum total of material goods of the Central Australian Loritja amounts to no more than a barbed wooden spear, a simple throwing club, a stone axe, a wooden vessel, a stick for digging up roots and a grinding stone for crushing them, a firedrill and a few ceremonial things; other well-known Australian objects, such as the boomerang and shield, baskets and carrying nets are completely lacking. A quick survey of the more important kinds of tools, weapons and household implements might well be in place here.

The Aborigines' culture is an entirely Stone Age one and it is instructive for archæologists to see stone objects belonging in theory to different stages of development in use by a single tribe. Ground stone axes occur alongside flaked tools and casual stone chippings. Axes are made from fine-grained rock such as diorite, diabas and prophyry, while knives and spear-heads are made from quartzite and similar stones which are worked by chipping and pressure. Australian flint is generally poor and unsuitable. Sharp-edged clam shells and the teeth and bones of animals are used to a limited extent. Two new materials available to the Aborigines since colonization are bottle glass and technical porcelain, which have the qualities of best flint. This led to some difficulty in maintaining the first telephone lines, for the natives stole the insulators.

The axe is an important tool, but, as already mentioned, it does not occur everywhere. Sometimes the native is content to shape a stone with a couple of deft blows with a hammer stone so that a useful edge appears. At others he will shape it by pecking or pressing, then carefully polishing it on the grindstone used for crushing seed. An interesting point is that though the axe is frequently ground both along the edge and over the greater part of the surface, the native does not really comprehend why polishing makes it into a more satisfactory tool. Actually grinding does not make the edge sharper, it merely makes the tool more durable so that it can be wielded more powerfully. But this presupposes a strong hafting and at this point comprehension falters. A common form of shaft in north-eastern Australia consists of no more than a branch bent round the axe-head and bound together. Obviously this does not permit of really powerful blows. West Australian axes are even less effective; the head consists of solidified resin from porcupine grass or grass trees with a couple of stone chips and a shaft stuck into it.

Wooden vessels are hollowed out with a kind of chisel which is actually no more than a rough chip of quartzite fastened to a long wooden shaft or to the end of a spear-thrower. For finer woodwork there is a small, triangular-pointed blade the sides of which are formed by a pressure flaker.

No less important than the axe, and equally simple, is the knife. In south-western Australia the knife consists, like the axe, of a number of sharp stone flakes fastened with resin into the side of a wooden shaft. But throughout Northern Territory, Central Australia and the adjoining districts of Queensland and West Australia, the commonest form of knife is a roughly chipped blade of quartzite. The stone is supported against the earth and then with a few smart blows of a hammer stone a long flake is chipped off; then another flake alongside the first is removed in the same manner, and a final blow releases the whole blade which now has the appearance of a crude three-sided point. It is bound with skin, or a lump of beeswax is stuck round it for a handle, or, more rarely, it will be provided with a wooden haft. Simple stone scrapers and a bone needle more or less complete the entire list of tools available to the Aborigines.

Apart from stone, the chief materials are wood and bark. Obviously with tools as crude as those described, the products are seldom of any quality. Shafts of spears and axes often show all the defects of the original tree and wooden vessels are lop-sided and twisted. When a Pitjendadjara man wants to make a spear-thrower he first of all finds a sharp stone weighing anything up to 6 lb. or more. With this he cuts three deep furrows to form a triangle into the wood of a suitable tree. When he has gone deep enough he gives the tree a few powerful blows so that it splits. Then he loosens the triangular piece by means of wooden wedges, peels off the bark and gives it its first rough form with sharp stones. He finishes it off with a stone chisel stuck in the end of a spear-thrower.

In spite of their crudity, these wooden objects are usually carved or painted with designs which, simple as they are, serve to give the object some supernatural force. Apart from naturalistic figures directly connected with totemic or magic rites, the designs are usually geometrical. There may be some significance behind them, but it is impossible to lay down rules for the meaning of the patterns, for the same lines, curves and circles sometimes mean one thing, sometimes another, according to the context. Concentric circles can signify wild yams, emu meat, etc. This is not the place to go into the five or six different style-groups which have been observed. The commonest and probably oldest designs consist of parallel fluting, zig-zag lines and V-shaped figures. Rather more recent, though none the less of considerable antiquity, are the diamond-shaped patterns which appear to have been introduced from New Guinea together with certain initiation rites and which later became widespread. Concentric circles and U-figures are specially characteristic of the northern and central regions and would also seem to derive from New Guinea—as do the painted and quasi-realistic designs of north-east Queensland and northern Arnhem Land.

There is no Australian weapon so famous as the boomerang, although its fame is to some extent undeserved, for it is not peculiar to Australia and it is not found even in all parts of the continent.

In the Cape York Peninsula it has been superseded by bows and arrows from New Guinea; furthermore it does not occur in northern Arnhem Land or on the coast of Kimberley or, most probably, in other scattered places in the extreme south. The boomerang is widely known as a weapon made of a curved or angled piece of wood with sharp edges, and most people believe that if it does not hit its target it returns to the thrower. This is only true of boomerangs with ends twisted slightly out of the same plane, and as a matter of fact they are sporting implements rather than offensive weapons and do not occur in all districts of Australia. The Norwegian explorer Carl Lumholtz observed the flight of a boomerang thrown by a native of Queensland and described it as follows:

> "As it leaves the hand it turns on its side and rotates round a vertical axis humming like a spinning wheel. As it moves rapidly forwards this rotary movement causes it to climb obliquely into the air. It returns not by the way it went but in a left-hand curve, thus describing an ellipse. As it slowly loses momentum it gradually falls to the ground, often no more than a couple of steps from its point of departure. . . . The natives often make it hit the ground 10-12 steps from the point where it was thrown; but far from reducing the speed this increases the velocity. After hitting the ground the first time the weapon can even repeat it and fly on again, describing a circle from right to left."

There are in fact several different kinds of boomerang. In northern and Central Australia some have one long and one short, beak-like end, and in parts of the eastern districts they are sometimes of considerable size and sword-like—intended for striking instead of throwing.

The boomerang is a development of the throwing club. A slightly curved and pointed stick which was perhaps its forerunner occurs throughout Western Australia and in scattered places farther south, i.e. in the most isolated districts. More advanced forms with a cylindrical, elliptical, or ball-shaped club head are found farther east. In northernmost Queensland the head is pineapple-shaped, as it is in parts of New Guinea. But not all clubs are intended for throwing; a simple cudgel for striking is widespread throughout the continent.

The principal weapon of the Aborigines is without doubt the spear. A widespread type of great antiquity, particularly in the south-west, is little more than a sharp-pointed wooden stake. Scarcely more recent is a spear with a lump of gum on one end with sharp stone flakes stuck into it. Nowadays these only occur in scattered parts of the north, though they are widespread in the south. The probable reason for this is that they have been to some extent superseded by later types with barbs either carved out of the wood or made of bone splinters which are bound on. Stone heads are far rarer. In Arnhem Land and northern Central Australia they are crude three-sided blades rather like the knives already mentioned; the best ones are made in the Kimberley district. After some preliminary chipping the stones are laid on a base of several layers of soft bark; then flake after flake is chipped off, first with a wooden stick, then with a thick and finally with a fine piece of bone until the form desired is achieved: a thin, oval point which in beauty is the equal of any of its kind in the world. In addition to the usual kinds of spear in some parts there are multi-pronged fishing spears and, in Arnhem Land, harpoons with detachable heads for catching dugongs.

Spears are frequently thrown by hand; this applies in Arnhem Land and some districts of Queensland. Elsewhere they are more usually thrown with a spear-thrower: a stick or narrow board with a barb at the rear end against which the base of the spear rests. The spear-thrower is retained in the hand after the spear is thrown and gives the spear greatly increased force. A throw of fifty to sixty yards is quite usual and over 100 yards is possible. Spear-throwers are of many types. In the south-east they take the form of a stick with a flat extension in the middle to protect the thrower in close combat. In many parts of West and South Australia they tend to be leaf-shaped, and on the Cape York Peninsula they have a flat mussel shell at the rear as a support for the hand. Altogether there are reckoned to be at least seven main types.

The only weapon of defence is the shield which is made in two forms: one is thick and narrow to ward off club attacks and the other is broader to give protection against spears. Strangely enough the shield is found neither in the Cape York district nor in Arnhem Land.

The Aborigines' culture is thoroughly continental. The coasts provide no incentives for seafaring, and the paucity of water in the rivers makes the use of craft impossible in most parts. Throughout the enormous stretch from the Murray to Shark Bay on the west coast one seeks in vain the simplest kind of craft, while both at the mouth of the Murray and on the north-west coast only the most primitive kinds of timber raft are to be found. In the south-eastern districts the natives have gone so far as to make canoes of a single piece of bark stopped at either end with clay or—on the coast of New South Wales—with lashing, and in some places farther north they have gone a step farther and made them with ribs, with poles along the gunwales and thwarts. Along one stretch of the coast of Queensland the hull consists of three pieces of bark sewn together. Outrigger dug-outs equipped with sails are found on the Cape York Peninsula, but they must be regarded as a loan from nearby New Guinea just as corresponding craft on the coast of Arnhem Land and Kimberley—though minus the outriggers—are copies of Malay fishermen's craft. This again is an example of the gradual rise in the level of culture from south to north which is so characteristic of Aboriginal Australia.

More important than the types of craft are the means of transport available on land. These are simple and few and thus adapted to the wandering life: bags, vessels and baskets of one sort or another are essential for fetching water and gathering wild roots and fruits. Most widely used are big wooden trays or trugs which the women bear supported on the hip, while to protect the skin from chafing a piece of soft bast is laid between hip and trug. Evidence of the importance attached to this gathering is the fact that among the Worora in Kimberley a woman is called *ngalinja*, a derivative of the word for this kind of bast, *ngali*. String bags, some knotted, others made of rows of loops linked together, are widespread. Baskets are made either by plaiting or coiling, the latter technique being peculiar to the eastern districts. Bark is also used in various ways for vessels and pails, and the primitive tribes of the south-east are said to use human skulls as water containers.

With such scanty equipment the Aborigines obviously cannot be too fastidious in the matter of food, and very little which is edible, from ants' pupæ to stranded whales, is left untouched. "There is no sight more disgusting than that of a shapely young native girl creeping out of the rotten carcass of a whale" wrote George Grey, a British officer who travelled through West Australia over a hundred years ago. With the intimate knowledge the Aborigines have of food resources in their country, real famine is exceptional, even though it may be difficult at times to find enough for the next meal. Among the commoner items of food, Grey mentions three species of kangaroo, two kinds of opossum, dingoes, emus and other wild birds, three kinds of tortoise, eight snakes, seven iguanas, eleven frogs, many sorts of fish, and shell-fish of all kinds, to which must be added different kinds of roots, seven fungi and a number of seeds and fruits. But this abundance is more apparent than real, for by no means all these foods are in plentiful supply and the list is more an expression of what the Aborigines have to hope for. It must also be remembered that totemic ideas and food taboos depending on sex and age may result in the individual's choice being by no means unlimited.

It is the women's task to provide the family with food in the form of plants and small animals which can be easily caught. They leave the camp in the morning taking with them a digging stick, the point of which has been hardened in the fire, a stone axe and a wooden trug or basket, perhaps a baby on the hip, a larger child on the shoulders and some dogs to sniff burrowing animals out of their holes. The dogs often get spoiled and it is not uncommon to see a woman breast-feed a motherless pup as well as her own children. Wild yams are a nourishing form of food but digging them up is no light task. Grey writes that in order to get one single tuber a hole must be dug some ten inches across and twice as deep, the method being to loosen the earth with the digging stick in the right hand and shovel the earth out with the left. Though the

Aborigines have never raised themselves beyond the level of food gatherers and hunters, there is said to be something in the nature of cultivation in Western Australia where the women put a piece of yam back into the earth to ensure a further crop.

Another important item of food is the fruit of a species of araucaria, and when it ripens all the neighbouring hordes join in feasting and dancing. In addition there are the sporangium of a kind of water-fern and the fruits of the cycas—although the latter eaten raw have a somewhat disastrous emetic and purgative effect. Among the Aranda and Loritja the tubers of a kind of cyperaceæ, ground and roasted, are almost their daily bread.

While they are out food-gathering the women are, of course, continually on the lookout for small animals of all kinds. If their eyes light on a tree showing the fresh claw marks of an opossum, or on one where the delicious tree iguana lives, not to mention trees harbouring the wild stingless bee, whose honey—even though it may be mixed with insects or wax—is a particular delicacy, they will be up the tree in no time. And, of course, the same applies to the men. The tall, smooth stems of the eucalyptus do not deter them. If the trunk is slim enough for them to get their arms round, they cut a succession of notches in it large enough for their big toes and, axe in mouth, climb step by step to the top. If this is impossible they sling a stem of rattan round the tree and, leaning back, simply walk up the side of it, moving the sling up in a series of sharp jerks.

The women's food-gathering is a daily task. Hunting larger animals is the men's job—equally strenuous though more exciting. Various kinds of kangaroo and emu are the finest game, and the skill of the Aborigines in finding and following a trail of man or beast has continually astonished white observers. The ethnographer Lloyd Warner remarks that even girls of eight or nine years old can distinguish the footprints of their own horde from hundreds of others.

Dogs are a valuable aid in tracking game. Kangaroos are very timid and to get near to them by long detours while keeping down wind is a test of both skill and endurance. To prevent the kangaroo from picking up their scent men rub their bodies with clay, and for cover they often hold foliage in front of them. Once they get near enough they must throw their spear so that it hits the creature's hind legs, otherwise it will get away. In the drought, when the grass withers, there are big communal hunts. The men divide into two groups. While one group creeps behind the herd of kangaroos and sets fire to the grass, the hunters wait in front and kill the animals as they run away from the flames. The women follow behind the men and deal with the smaller animals.

There are many other methods of hunting: lying in wait at water holes, chasing the animals over the rocks for days until they are exhausted, or using dogs to drive them into marshes. In some parts they are driven towards large outstretched nets. The emu is easier than the kangaroo to deal with, for in spite of its timidity it is inquisitive and fairly easy to outwit. It can be driven into a pitfall, surrounded, or caught in nets. The Yualayi have nets as much as 300 yards long. Before a hunt the Waramunga of Central Australia dope the emu by putting pitjuri twigs into their water holes. The Yualayi lure the emu towards them with simple wooden trumpets and catch them in snares hung from trees.

Near the coasts and lakes fishing is an important source of food. Usually the fish are speared, sometimes at night by the aid of flares. Towards the end of the dry season when the water level falls, fish are caught by means of dams made of branches or stones. In the upper reaches of the Darling River there is said to be a maze of stone barriers or dams stretching a hundred yards up river where the fish are taken with the bare hands. In some places woven fish traps are used. This is, for instance, the method used to catch eel. A method used in stagnant pools is to poison the water with certain parts of plants. Another method is dredging by long seines or catching the fish in small bag nets fastened to a long stick. But, as mentioned earlier, net-making is a culture element unknown in the south-west. The same applies to fish hooks, which are elsewhere made of bone, shell and wood.

Women are given only a modest share of the hunt, most of it falling entirely to the men, though it is divided amongst relations in accordance with prescribed rules. The preparation of food is simple enough. Such things as roots are crushed on the grinding-stone and baked in hot ashes. If they are poisonous they are first well soaked and then dried. Bigger game are usually cooked in an earth oven. This is merely a trench with stones in the bottom in which a fire is lighted. When the fire has burned itself out the animal is laid on the glowing stones with perhaps other stones inside its carcass, the trench is filled in, and in course of time the meat is cooked. In this way, a spiny anteater complete with skin and quills is transformed into a fat and juicy steak—*crede experto!*

This sketch of the way the Aborigines provide for themselves would be incomplete without reference to what in their view is probably most important of all: magic. Without magic all their efforts would be in vain. Among the Ungarinyin in Kimberley a speech has to be made by the horde's chieftain to give the hunters strength and to ensure that the game will appear in adequate numbers. And when the quarry is killed it must be swung round so that its blood spatters the ground, for this will cause animals to breed more copiously. And the endless and periodically recurrent ceremonies to ensure the continued balance between the forces of nature are a burden devolving on the fully initiated men. The well-being of the tribe is dependent on them, and so sacred are the mysteries involved that only gradually may they be revealed to the youngsters.

Acceptance into the society of adult men is one of the most important events in a young man's life, and this is another respect in which development is more advanced in the north than in the south, for the most intricate and prolonged rites are in Central and North Australia while the simplest are in the south. Indeed, among some of the Kurnai hordes in Victoria there seems to be no initiation rite at all, and for this reason these hordes are never allowed to take part in the ceremonies of other tribes. Otherwise it is an unvarying rule for neighbouring groups to be invited to the festivities, and these often start by disposing of old quarrels in more or less serious combat so that afterwards everyone may enter into the solemn rites in a peaceful frame of mind.

There are Kurnai hordes, however, in which the young men must undergo initiation lasting as much as two or three weeks. One evening, after two or three days of introductory ceremony, the novices have to lay themselves down in an enclosure of bushes, while all night long the men and women dance monotonously round them, mimicking the call of the emu-wren—which is their particular male ancestor and sex totem. The novices may not speak: they must twitter like emu-wrens, for they are about to be transformed into emu-wrens. The continuous dancing sends them into a trance and when they awaken out of it they have assumed their new character. At daybreak all the women leave and the men lie down to rest. When night falls once more the great miracle takes place and the heavenly emu-wren appears. A low-pitched hum made by whirling the sacred bull-roarers round on a line heralds its approach and gets nearer and nearer, while the youths await its arrival with covered heads. Finally the covering is removed from the novices' eyes and the chieftain standing before them points up to the sky with his spear and shouts three times: "Look up!" The other men point their spears at the novices and threaten to kill them if they reveal the sacred mysteries to women or to anyone else not initiated. Then, solemnly, the chieftain recites the myth of their descent from the emu-wren and shows the sacred bull-roarers in which the voices of the totem ancestor and his mate are concealed. Finally, rules of behaviour are implanted: the young men must obey their parents, share with their friends, keep away from young girls and married women and observe the food taboos until the old men lift them. After the actual ceremonies and before they can enter as fully-fledged members of the tribe, the initiates must spend a month at least in the bush isolated from the rest of the tribe. Among most tribes the initiation rites are far more complicated and combined with more or less crude surgical operations.

In the remotest parts of the continent the septum of the nose is perforated; in other regions there is cicatrization or the removal of a finger joint. Among the Yuin in south-eastern New South Wales the young men have to sit so close to a blazing fire that they are nearly roasted. The climax of the ceremony occurs when a man suddenly jumps up out of a covered grave, ten men in fantastic disguise perform a dance and the initiates are taken one by one to have one of their front teeth knocked out. Here, too, the humming of the bull-roarers is believed to be the voice of the Supreme Being. The knocking out of one, two or even all four front teeth occurs throughout the whole of Australia, except for the coastal districts to the west and south and a small area of Queensland.

In the central districts the practice has lost its original connexion with the initiation and can also be practised on women. The circumcision of young men is, however, the most important feature here, and this is true also of many tribes where tooth-knocking is still part of initiation. With most of them circumcision is succeeded sooner or later by a barbarous practice of subincision, which consists of splitting the urethra.

In a typical tribe such as the Aranda the ceremonies are so protracted that only some features of them can be mentioned. As soon as a boy reaches the age of ten or twelve the ceremonies are inaugurated by his being repeatedly tossed into the air by the men of the camp, much as we toss children in a blanket. From then on the boy avoids the company of women and gradually starts to join the men on their hunting expeditions. At the onset of puberty more serious rites follow and these last several days. First he attends some of the secret totem ceremonies and listens to the myths that tell of the journeys of the totem ancestors. Then circumcision is performed and after that the sacred bull-roarers, the *tjuringas*, which are usually stored in sacred places, are revealed. In addition to the actual bull-roarers there are objects of similar shape but made of stone and up to three feet long. In many of the central tribes each man has his own *tjuringa*, and his soul is believed to stand in mystical relationship to it. Among the Aranda, circumcision is succeeded some weeks later—to the accompaniment of more totem ritual—by subincision. When the wound is healed the young man undergoes a ritual cleansing by lying on a fire covered with leaves. After that he takes part in still more seemingly endless ceremonies and these are rounded off by a period of isolation in the bush.

The districts over which the different rites are distributed reflect their relative ages. Such things as nose perforation and cicatrization are clearly the oldest, followed by tooth-knocking, circumcision and finally subincision. Everything points to the probability that circumcision and many of the other operations came from New Guinea. Whether this is also true of subincision is more doubtful, though the possibility cannot be ruled out.

* * *

What is the reason for all this? First and foremost there is the separation of boys from women. Women are not debarred from all sacred rites: in some they take part in the introductory ceremonies while in others there are certain rites which are performed only by women; but, to use a biblical analogy, women are not allowed farther than the court of the shrine. Secondly, there is the emphasis on the transition to a new life. This often takes the form of resurrection after ritual death, the novice having to live for a time in the bush unseen by women; during this time he is even said by some tribes to have been devoured by a spirit. The significance of tooth-knocking and circumcision is less certain. Subincision is obviously connected with the belief in the life-giving and strengthening power of blood. Blood is sacred and there are many totem rites and other solemn occasions when the men gash their arms and genitals. But all this is only the outward sign of the achievement of manhood. The decisive factors are participation in the rites, which are the basis of life and ensure the well-being of society, and the revelation of the sacred symbols, the sight and touch of which are like receiving a sacrament. Nothing is more impressive, says Elkin, than to see the reverence with which the old men contemplate these sacred symbols, as they solemnly chant the song versions of the myths appertaining to them.

Initiated adult men wield all the authority. Nowhere else in the world have old men so much say in affairs. Though there is no strictly organized form of government, they do in fact form a gerontocracy. The old men comprise the council of the horde. In northern Queensland they are all members of the council and there is no individual chieftain. The Dieri have an elected chieftain who is the leader of the council; but matters under discussion are not put to the vote of the council. All the members have to be unanimous, otherwise the matter is dropped. In Central Australia there is a third kind of council. This consists of the head men of the totem groups, usually not more than five or six, though in rare cases there may be up to ten or twelve members.

Whether they belong to the same tribe or not, relations are by no means always peaceful between hordes. Lloyd Warner says of the Murngin that war constitutes a large part of their existence. But it is never very bloody and seldom amounts to more than nocturnal raiding. The main sources of strife are the abduction of women and revenge.

Revenge is an important factor, for any sickness or death which cannot be readily accounted for is blamed on witchcraft. Witchcraft takes many forms. You can secretly point a stick or a pointed bone in the direction of your victim singing a charm as you do so. The power of the stick or bone will then be transmuted into an invisible, fatal dart. Alternatively you can creep up beside your victim while he is asleep, make an incision in his loins and without his being aware of it, steal his kidney-fat. Then in the course of a couple of days he will die!

Aided by his individual totem the medicine man has to find the cause of sickness and death and do what he can to prevent it. The usual method of healing is to rub the victim's body or suck it and make the sickness disappear in the shape of a stone or a piece of bone. To our minds there might seem to be more than a dash of conjuring mixed up in this, but in the mind of the medicine man the object he removes really is the visible sign of the sickness and therefore the sickness itself.

If all aid proves unavailing and death occurs then the matter is serious and concerns the members of the entire horde. They give vent to loud wails, gash themselves with knives and bang their heads till they bleed, directing the most dire threats at the person whose witchcraft brought about the death. In addition they take a number of precautions to prevent themselves from coming under the influence of death. The deceased's belongings are smashed up or destroyed; the corpse is carried to its final resting place by a round-about route so that the dead man's spirit cannot find its way back; for months or even years his name must not be mentioned; the mourners are cleansed by sweeping with smouldering branches, the camp is abandoned and various items of food, among them the deceased's totem, are taboo until by special rites the taboo is lifted. Last but not least, by special portents the person who perpetrated the magic which caused the death is sought out.

Methods of disposing of the corpse vary more in Australia than in most other places in the world and often depend on the deceased's sex, age and position in society. In some tribes burial takes place in hollow trees, in others the corpse is burned. Throughout the north-west part of the continent the corpse is laid on a platform until it has decomposed. Its spirit is now liberated and the bones are buried. In some eastern and south-eastern districts the intestines are removed, the corpse is dried in the sun or by a fire, then either burned or put in the crown of a tree. The object of such mummification is not to preserve the body for all time—merely until the period of mourning is past and possible revenge achieved. The most remarkable custom of all is that of eating the deceased.

In bygone times the Aborigines have had the—to some extent unjust—reputation of being inveterate cannibals; but in this respect they are not to be compared with many other peoples. In their case, as indeed everywhere, religious ideas are responsible for the practice. By eating a person you unite yourself with him and acquire his characteristics. Therefore even where cannibalism is generally practised, by no means everyone who dies is eaten. In Queensland, for example, this only happens to fallen warriors, medicine men, and women who have suffered a violent death. Often only certain persons take part in the meal—in Victoria, for example, only certain relations. Among some tribes only a small part of the kidney fat is eaten. The fact that the practice is often associated with mummification and platform burial indicates that cannibalism has a ritual significance. Not until the burial rites have been performed is the spirit liberated and reunited with the totem ancestors. In the greater part of eastern Australia and in certain other parts this means that it ascends to heaven; in other regions it is supposed to find its way back to the spiritual home of the totem group and thus the cycle of life is completed.

* * *

In retrospect, the Aborigines' culture shows pronounced uniformity. This does not, of course, mean that it is the same everywhere. After carefully studying its material products McCarthy has distinguished no less than eleven individual districts. If social and religious ideas were taken as a basis a number of other cultural districts could be listed. And finally natural conditions would be reflected in the annual cycle in which occupation, wandering and totem ceremonies move. But all this does not alter the fact that uniformity is characteristic of the culture. The same aids to survival are found with certain variations everywhere. They provide a theme which is played in variations. This is typical of a culture still at the level of food gatherers and primitive hunters and yet to attain the degree of specialization which finds expression in adjustment to changing environment. This accounts for the fact that the same culture can thrive both in the rain forests of Queensland and in the bush steppes of Central Australia.

The influence of natural conditions must be sought in other spheres: in the accessibility of outside cultural influences and the routes taken by these influences once they have made an entry. The Australian Aborigines are what Ratzel has called a marginal people, and as such are condemned to the poverty of isolation. It has already been stressed many times that influences emanated from New Guinea and—obviously to a much smaller extent—direct from Indonesia, and that these influences become less and less pronounced the farther south one goes. But here is an interesting point. A conscious choice was evidently made. None of the Australian Aborigines use earthenware vessels. Yet from native songs it appears that Indonesian fishermen, who used to visit

Arnhem Land down to the last century, taught the natives to make pottery for them. The natives never made it for their own use, however. And the explanation is simple: a wandering life makes such vessels extremely impracticable. But the position with regard to agriculture is somewhat different. In view of the intercourse which took place from the earliest times across the Torres Strait it is inconceivable that the Australian Aborigines would have had no opportunity of learning the simple form of agriculture which is found in New Guinea. And in northern Australia the natural conditions are not unfavourable to it. Only one explanation seems possible. While the Papuans of New Guinea and the Aborigines of Australia were at the same stage of development the door was open to new influences; but by the time the inhabitants of New Guinea had risen above the level of mere hunters the culture of the Aborigines had become so stabilized that it could no longer suffer any fundamental change. If it were not to disintegrate it had to continue on the lines it had taken thousands of years before, and from then on only a few relatively unimportant new features found acceptance.

BIBLIOGRAPHY

There are two excellent surveys of the culture of the Australian Aborigines —A. P. ELKIN: *The Australian Aborigines*, 3rd ed., Sydney and London, 1954; F. D. MCCARTHY: *Australia's Aborigines*. Melbourne. 1957

Among older works giving information about the inhabitants are: DAVID COLLINS: *An Account of the English Colony in New South Wales*, London, 1798. GEORGE GREY: *Journals of Two Expeditions of Discovery in North-west and Western Australia*, i-ii, London, 1841. EDWARD JOHN EYRE: *Journals of Expeditions of Discovery in North-west and Western Australia*, i-ii, London, 1841. EDWARD JOHN EYRE: *Journals of Expeditions of Discovery into Central Australia*, i-ii, London, 1845. CARL LUMHOLTZ: *Blandt menneskeædere*, Copenhagen, 1888.

There is such a wealth of ethnographical works proper that only a few, of widely differing scope and value, can be noted here. J. BISCHOFS: "Die Niol-Niol, ein Eingeborenen-Stamm in Nordwest-Australien" (*Anthropos.*, iii, Mödling, 1908). A. R. BROWN: "Three Tribes of Western Australia" (*Journ. R. Anthrop. Inst.*, xliii, London, 1913). ALBERT F. CALVERT: *The Aborigines of Western Australia*, London, 1894. ERHARD EYLMAN: *Die Eingeborenen der Kolonie Südaustralien*, Berlin, 1908. A. W. HOWITT: *The Native Tribes of South-east Australia*, London, 1904. ANDREAS LOMMEL: "Die Unambul" (*Monograph. z. Völkerk*, ii, Hamburg, 1952). JOHN MATHEW: *Eaglehawk and Crow*, London, 1899. K. LANGLOH PARKER: *The Euahlayi Tribe*, London, 1905. HELMUT PETRI: *Sterbende Welt in Nordwest-Australien*, Braunschweig, 1954. STANLEY D. PORTEUS: *The Psychology of a Primitive People*, London, 1931. WALTER E. ROTH: *Ethnological Studies among the North–West–Central Queensland Aborigines*, Brisbane and London, 1897. BALDWIN SPENCER: *Native Tribes of the Northern Territory of Australia*, London, 1914. BALDWIN SPENCER AND F. J. GILLEN: *The Arunta*, i-ii, London, 1927 (2nd improved ed. of the same authors' work: *The Native Tribes of Central Australia*, London, 1899). BALDWIN SPENCER AND F. J. GILLEN: *The Northern Tribes of Central Australia*, London, 1904. R. BROUGH SMYTH: *The Aborigines of Victoria*, i-ii, London, 1878. CARL STREHLOW: "Die Aranda- und Loritja-Stämme in Zentral-Australien," i-v (*Veröffentl. a. d. Stadt. Völker-Mus., Frankfurt am Main*, Frankfurt, 1907-20). GEORGE TAPLIN: *The Narrinyeri*, Adelaide, 1874. W. LLOYD WARNER: *A Black Civilization*, New York and London, 1937.

Individual subjects are treated, *i.a.*, in the following works—RONALD M. BERNDT: *Kunapipi*, Melbourne, 1951. D. S. DAVIDSON: *The Chronological Aspects of Certain Australian Social Institutions*, Philadelphia, 1928. D. S. DAVIDSON: "Australian Spear Traits and Their Derivations" (*Journ. Polyn. Soc.*, xliii, New Plymouth, 1934). D. S. DAVIDSON: "Archæological Problems of Northern Australia" (*Journ. R. Anthrop. Inst.*, lxv, London, 1935). D. S. Davidson: "Australian Throwing-Sticks, Throwing-Clubs, and Boomerangs" (*Amer. Anthrop. N. s.*, xxxviii, Menasha, 1936). D. S. Davidson: "Australian Netting and Basketry Techniques " (*Journ. Polyn. Soc.*, xlii, New Plymouth, 1933). D. S. Davidson: "The Chronology of Australian Watercraft" (*Journ. Polyn. Soc.*, xliv, New Plymouth, 1935). D. S. Davidson: "The Spearthrower in Australia" (*Proceed. Amer. Philos. Soc.*, lxxvi, Philadelphia, 1936). D. S. Davidson: "Transport and Receptacles in Aboriginal Australia" (*Journ. Polyn. Soc.*, xlvi, Wellington, 1937). D. S. Davidson: "A Preliminary Consideration of Aboriginal Australian Art" (*Mem. Amer. Philos. Soc.*, ix, Philadelphia, 1937). D. S. Davidson: "Fire-Making in Australia" (*Amer. Anthrop. N. s.*, xlix, Menasha, 1947). D. S. Davidson: "The Thread Cross in Australia" (*Mankind*, iv, Sydney, 1951). Maria Frank: "Botenstäbe in Australien" (*Zeitschr. f. Ethnol.*, lxxii, Berlin, 1941). Christoph von Fürer-Haimendorf: "Zur Urgeschichte Australiens" (*Anthropos.*, xxxi, Mödling, 1936). Fritz Græbner: "Kulturkreise und Kulturschichten in Ozeanien" (*Zeitschr. f. Ethnol.*, xxxvii, Berlin, 1905). Josef Hækel: " Ethnologische und prähistorische Probleme Australiens" (*Wien. völkerkundl. Mitteil.*, ii, Wien, 1954). Ethel Hassell: "Notes on the Ethnology of the Wheelman Tribe of South-western Australia", ed. D. S. Davidson (*Anthropos.*, xxxi, Mödling, 1936). Frederick D. McCarthy: "Aboriginal Australian Material Culture" (*Mankind*, ii, Sydney, 1940). Frederick D. McCarthy: "The Stone Implements of Australia" (*Austr. Mus. Mem.*, ix, Sydney, 1946). Frederick D. McCarthy: *Australian Aboriginal Decorative Art*, 2nd ed., Sydney, 1948. Frederick D. McCarthy: "The Oceanic and Indonesian Affiliations of Australian Aboriginal Culture" (*Journ. Polyn. Soc.*, lxii, Wellington, 1953). W. Milke: "Totemismus und Totemzentren in Ozeanien" (*Veröffentl. d. Mus. f. Natur-, Völker- u. Handelsk.*, xiii, 1, Bremen, 1950). D. J. Mahony: "The Problem of Antiquity of Man in Australia" (*Mem. Nation. Mus.*, xiii, Melbourne, 1943). S. R. Mitchell: *Stone Age Craftsmen*, Melbourne, 1949. Helmut Petri: "Zum Problem der australischen Dualsysteme" (*Jahrb. d. Linden-Mus. N.F.*, i, Heidelberg, 1951). J. Stokes: *Discoveries in Australia*, i-ii, London, 1846. Northcote W. Thomas: "The Disposal of the Dead in Australia" (*Folk-Lore*, xix, London, 1908).

Wilbur S. Chaseling: *Yulengor*, London, 1957. L. Fison and A. W. Howitt: *Kamilaroi and Kurnai*, London, 1880. C. P. Mountford: *The Tiwi*, London and Melbourne, 1958. Ronald M. Berndt: *The Djanggawul*, Melbourne, 1952. R. M. and C. H. Berndt: "Sexual Behaviour in Arnhem Land" (*Viking Fund Publ.*, xvi, New York, 1951). D. S. Davidson: "The Family-Hunting Territory in Australia" (*Amer. Anthrop. N.s.*, xxx, Menasha, 1928). D. S. Davidson and Frederick D. McCarthy: " The Distribution and Chronology of Some Important Types of Stone Implements in Western Australia" (*Anthropos*, lii, Posieux, 1957). A. P. Elkin, C. and R. Berndt: *Art in Arnhem Land*, Melbourne and London, 1950. Josef Hækel: "Zum Individual- und Geschlechtstotemismus in Australien" (*Acta Ethnol. et Ling.*, i, Wien, 1950). Phyllis Kaberry: *Aboriginal Women, Sacred and Profane*,

London, 1939. FREDERICK D. MCCARTHY: "Culture Succession in South-eastern Australia" (*Mankind*, v, Sydney, 1958). H. PETRI: "Der australische Medizinmann" (*Ann. Lateran.*, xvi-xvii, Città del Vaticano, 1952-53). A. R. RADCLIFFE-BROWN: "Notes on the Social Organization of Australian Tribes" (*Journ. R. Anthrop. Inst.*, xlvii, liiii, London, 1918, 1923). A. R. RADCLIFFE-BROWN: "The Rainbow-Serpent Myth of Australia" (*Journ. R. Anthrop. Inst.*, lvi, London, 1926). G. RÓHEIM: "Women and their Life in Central Australia" (*Journ. R. Anthrop. Inst.*, lxiii, London, 1933). On modern problems of the Aborigines, see D. BATES: *The Passing of the Aborigines*, London, 1938. R. AND C. BERNDT: *From Black to White in South Australia*, Melbourne, 1951.

Numerous articles on the ethnography of Australia, including those by Radcliffe-Brown on social conditions and by A. P. Elkin on totemism, are to be found in the journal *Oceania*, published by the Australian National Research Council, Sydney, 1930 onwards.

PLAINS INDIANS

An Advanced Hunting Culture

Horse and Bison

IN THE autumn of 1528 a number of boats filled with Spanish soldiers were stranded on an island off the coast of the Gulf of Mexico, not far from what is now known as Galveston. Only a few of the company were saved, among them Núñez Cabeza de Vaca, who was later to become famous for his travels to Paraguay. The Indians received the survivors hospitably though they made them work for their living. Cabeza de Vaca complains that he had to search for edible roots among the water rushes until his hands were cut and bleeding. This was too much for the proud Spaniard. He escaped to the mainland and became a pedlar.

From the sea coast into the interior he carried snails and mussel shells, and from the interior out to the sea coast he brought such things as skins, red ochre for painting the body, stones for arrowheads, etc. In this way he travelled far and wide. He spent six winters among the tribes of south Texas before finding his way to the Spanish settlements in Mexico. It is from Cabeza de Vaca that we have the oldest known description of a remarkable kind of "cow" as large as Spanish cattle though with small horns and an enormous mane. What he described was the American bison, and it played such an important part in the life of the natives that, though the bison were never domesticated, the Spaniards called them *vaqueros*, cowherds. The Indians lived off the creatures' meat and made cloaks, shoes and shields of their skins

Some twenty years later, lured by tales of riches to the north-east where kings were said to be lulled into midday sleep to the chimes of golden bells, Coronado's expedition made its way up from Mexico. The expedition penetrated beyond the Arkansas River, but, far from finding an El Dorado, all they discovered was a collection of wretched bison hunters. Of course, these hunters had no horses as their successors were to have. When they shifted camp to a fresh hunting ground their loads were carried, and their tent poles were drawn, by dogs. "They are a friendly people and not cruel. They are steadfast friends," runs an old account. Another expedition which found its way to the plains from Florida under the leadership of de Soto, saw how the Indians scalped their victims—a custom never before observed in the New World.

Now the chief thing about all this is not the fact that the plains were inhabited before the arrival of Europeans. It is that the inhabitants possessed a culture which was essentially much the same as that found there later. There was, however, one important difference: there were no horses. And in spite of all other similarities this was sufficient to bring about a material difference in their mode of life.

A characteristic feature of North America, in contrast with Europe and Asia, is that the principal dividing lines run from north to south. In the west the Cordilleras follow the Pacific coast. In the east there are the Atlantic highlands, and between the two there are low hills and plains. These surface conditions affect climate and vegetation and also human life, since they render communication easy between north and south but difficult between east and west.

West of the Mississippi the prairies rise almost imperceptibly until, at the foot of the Rocky Mountains, they are higher than the peaks of the Appalachian Mountains in the east. The straight line of the horizon is broken in only two places: by the Ozark Plateau in Arkansas and by the Black Hills in South Dakota, which rise like well-wooded islands out of a surface as endless and monotonous as that of the sea. In the lower-lying districts down towards the Mississippi open grassland alternates with deciduous forest and nowadays all this has been put to the plough by enterprising farmers. But all this lushness gradually disappears the farther one goes west. Mere strips of willow and cottonwood follow the line of deep river valleys. Between them is steppe—tufts of coarse grass which grow rapidly while the earth is damp from the melted snow, but which wither in the summer and turn into natural hay. "A country of grass and sun and wind" it has been called, with freezingly cold winter storms and blistering summer heat, what rain there is pouring down in heavy thunder showers.

Agriculture is feasible only by means of modern irrigation or dry farming, neither of which was known to the plains Indians. One form of wealth alone existed: the great herds of wild bison. As an American zoologist put it: It would be as easy to count the leaves of the forest as to count the numbers of bison existing prior to 1870.

There was other game, too, which the Indians could hunt. Herds of prong-horned antelope wandered across the steppes, and in the wooded valleys there were deer. Of carnivores there were bears and prairie wolves. But the bison was the most important animal of them all. Now, if a population of any size is to base its whole existence on bison hunting without the support of agriculture, it needs mobility which only the horse can provide. It follows then that the high plains can have afforded a home for no more than small wandering tribes. So the plains formed a barrier between east and west similar to the barrier which the European Alps have provided between north and south.

But were conditions always so uninviting? The question arises because there is no doubt that during the period of thaw following the Ice Age rainfall was more abundant and conditions were more favourable to vegetation. Later, i.e. from 7000-4000 B.C., the climate became warmer and also drier than nowadays. At Lindenmeier, Colorado, on the high plains, a number of important finds from the period have been made. The index form is what is known as the Folsom point, which takes its name from the place in New Mexico where it was discovered. Chipped out of flint-like material, it has a characteristic appearance, with a concave base and a groove on both sides running down two-thirds of its length. In addition there are scrapers, knives and choppers, etc., all of chipped stone, and needles and bodkins of bone. Most important of all: these artifacts occur in conjunction with the bones of extinct species of bison and mammoth and of other animals such as caribou and musk-ox which no longer exist in the area. These are some of the oldest indications of the presence of human beings in the New World.

With the aid of radioactive carbon it has been possible to put the period of these discoveries at *circa* 8000 B.C. From approximately the same time there are tanged projectile points without longitudinal grooves. Somewhat later, as in the important find at Cody, Wyoming, which is put at *circa* 5000 B.C., there occurs a peculiar kind of knife with a transverse edge. All these derive from primitive hunting cultures amongst which even dogs were unknown. Considerably more recent, though still from as far back as 2000 B.C., there is what is known as the older Signal Butte culture in western Nebraska, where bone objects occur in conjunction with new kinds of stone tools, some of them even having been ground. Pottery is still completely lacking and, as in earlier times, the basis of livelihood was hunting. In this period, when the climate had again become rather colder and damper, the gathering of wild seeds seems to have been of some importance, as evidenced by the number of grindstones which have been found. The mode of life must have been very much like that of tribes in the Great Basin within historical times.

Here and there on the high plains proper, and of more recent date, there are "workshops" for fashioning stone objects—what are known as the Spanish Diggings in Wyoming, for example. There are also the remains of ancient camp sites, stone circles where tents once stood; arrowheads, clubheads and scrapers—nothing in fact that might not be expected of a few scattered hunters. But things were different in the valleys and the more fertile, low-lying regions to the east, where there are traces of several early farming cultures with evidence of the cultivation of gourds and, later perhaps, maize and beans. The houses were partially underground and simple pottery occurred. The culture seems to have been connected primarily with the forest country east of the Mississippi and to have spread from the low prairie up through the Missouri Valley.

From time to time agricultural tribes also made their way on to the high plains; the village sites, however, are not only small but show no trace of fortification—striking evidence that the population was of insufficient size to produce hostile clashes of any consequence. There could have been no question of prolonged settlement. On the fringe of primitive agriculture, settlement must always have been transient. Farmers of today know only too well from bitter experience the devastating effect of sudden drought and dust storms. To the Indians such catastrophies must have been even more disastrous.

The evidence of language confirms the findings of archæology and both indicate that towards the east and in the Missouri Valley tribes have inhabited the prairie for so long that the date of their arrival is lost in antiquity. Two different linguistic stocks have their centre of gravity here—the Caddoan and the Siouan. In the first group, the Wichita are the most southerly tribe or rather tribal federation. Their country stretches approximately from the middle of the Arkansas River into Texas and their culture approaches that of the tribes round the Gulf of Mexico. In language they are related to the Pawnee, a federation of several tribes in the area of the Platte River. Farther north, on the middle reaches of the Missouri, live the Arikara, who apparently separated from the Pawnee as recently as the seventeenth or eighteenth century. The Siouans seem largely to have congregated round the Missouri, having in the first instance followed its valley to the north-west.

Round the lower reaches of the river live the Chiwere. After their arrival, they sub-divided into three mutually independent tribes, the Iowa, Oto and Missouri. In an arc south-west of them are a number of other tribes (the Osage, Kansa, Omaha and Ponca) who also came into existence by the sub-division of a single people, the Dhegiha. Finally, on the upper reaches of the Missouri there are two smaller Siouan tribes, the Mandan and Hidatsa; the Mandan at any rate would seem to be among the oldest inhabitants of the region.

Hunting tribes with no knowledge of agriculture which wandered across the high plains were far fewer before the introduction of the horse. It is significant that of all the linguistic stocks now represented in the area, only one belongs exclusively there, and that, moreover, is a language spoken by a single small group, the Kiowa, who lived originally on the headwaters of the Missouri, whereas they were subsequently driven south to the region lying between the Arkansas and Canadian Rivers. They have incidentally the doubtful honour of being reckoned the most bloodthirsty brigands of all plains Indians, and in proportion to their numbers are said to have killed more white men than any other.

There is no doubt that the tribes which the original Spanish expeditions found farthest south included the Apache. In the far distant past they must have found their way down from the north, where their Athapaskan relatives in Alaska and western Canada still live. By far the majority of the Apache, however, are distributed farther west in New Mexico and Arizona and cannot be considered plains Indians.

The nearest relatives of the Comanche are also to be found in the west. The Comanche belong to the great Uto-Aztecan stock and both their language and traditions show that they separated from the Shoshone of Wyoming comparatively recently.

But while the Shoshone never completely broke the cultural connexion with the Pacific plateaux, the Comanche were a genuine plains tribe. Later they were driven south to Texas and the Mexican border, where for 200 years they were a scourge to the Spanish settlers. On the northern plains the Blackfoot or Siksika constitute a somewhat loose confederacy of three different tribes belonging to the Algonkian stock. In the middle of the eighteenth century their hunting grounds stretched from the foot of the Rocky Mountains in the west far into Saskatchewan in the east, and from the Saskatchewan River in the north nearly to the headwaters of the Missouri in the south. They probably once lived farther east on the edge of the woodlands, and an old account mentions a Blackfoot group which lived entirely there and existed largely on hunting the beaver. In their heyday the Blackfoot were a powerful and warlike people fighting and being fought by enemies on pretty well all sides.

Whether other tribes existed on the high plains in olden times is not known. Suffice to say that the coming of the white man brought about a radical change. Repercussions of the mighty Iroquois battles in the neighbourhood of the Laurentian lakes made themselves felt out west. Advancing Algonkian tribes added to the pressure, and the French, who settled on the lower St. Lawrence, not only gradually increased the area under their sway there but also supplied the surrounding population with firearms, giving them a terrifying superiority over people living farther west. For many of these latter, the high plains became their refuge and the horse their salvation.

Horses were introduced into Mexico by the Spaniards. From the Spanish settlements around Santa Fé they spread rapidly northward on both sides of the Rocky Mountains. This was largely brought about by peaceful trading. It was only later that horse-thieving became a factor, while the capture of horses run wild was never of any consequence. It was not until the second quarter of the seventeenth century that the Indians seriously took to horsemanship, but by the end of the following hundred years the horse had penetrated as far north as the Red River in Canada.

As might be expected, horses became most numerous among tribes in the south. Strangely enough, however, certain tribes on the plateaux west of the Rocky Mountains, where true plains culture never became established, were among those to own most animals—partly because they were not subject to such plundering as the plains tribes proper were, partly because fodder was more plentiful.

However that may be, new groups streamed across the high plains from the east and north. The Cheyenne, Arapaho and Atsina (Gros Ventre) belong to the Algonkians. As late perhaps as the seventeenth century the Cheyenne and Arapaho lived in the woodlands of the upper Mississippi and Red River. But under pressure from the east they were driven out into the open country, first to the Black Hills and then from there on to the plateau at the foot of the Laramie and Park Mountains. As late as *circa* 1800 some of the Cheyenne had still not completely abandoned their old methods of farming. One Arapaho group attached itself to the Blackfoot; this group is now known as the Atsina. Only small sections of two other tribes, the Cree and Ojibway, tried their luck out on the prairie. The main body stayed in the forest country. Two small Athapaskan tribes also came from the north. One of them, the Kiowa-Apache, were probably carried along on their wanderings south by the Kiowa proper (with whom, in fact, they are in no way connected), while the other, the Sarsi, joined up with the Blackfoot.

Still more important are the Siouan tribes. It was not until the second half of the eighteenth century that the Crow emigrated to the region of the upper Missouri. Their language is closely related to that of the Hidatsa, and at Glendive, eastern Montana, in the upper Missouri region, remains of hoes and potsherds similar to those used by the Hidatsa have been found. Not long previously the largest of all Siouan tribes, the Dakota, had been driven out on to the grassland.

The eastern Dakotas between the upper Mississippi and the Missouri still show clear traces of an earlier woodland culture, whereas the western groups have entirely adopted the horse-riding life of bison hunters. The Dakota have always been numerous and nowadays they comprise nearly half of all plains Indians. Closely related to them are the Assiniboine. They were forced to leave their homelands west of Lake Superior about the same time and seek refuge on the high plains.

The high plains thus became the arena of a welter of horse-riding tribes fighting endlessly over what each regarded as its individual territory. And so the characteristically warlike attitude developed, to be subsequently intensified by resistance to the white settlers advancing from the east, until at length the power of the tribes was broken and the bison brought almost to the point of extinction. The horse was not responsible for creating plains culture, but life in the saddle brought it into full flower. Like the spring grass, it grew rapidly and withered all too soon.

The origin of most of the tribes being what it was, roots naturally go down deepest in the eastern woodlands. This applies to agriculture, which provided the basis of the older population's life on the low prairie and in the Missouri Valley, and also to a number of characteristics of their warrior life. Other aspects, such as the well-defined military hierarchy, the distinctions connected with it, and religious self-torture all point in the direction of Mexico; but to what extent they amount to an immediate connexion is difficult now to decide. It is possible that they found their way in from the east, where Mexican influence was strong in the late pre-Columbian period. Human sacrifices and star worship in the Caddoan tribes are also strongly reminiscent of Mexico.

In addition there are all the paraphernalia that followed the introduction of the horse: saddles, stirrups, lassoes, castration, all of them seemingly adopted from the Spaniards; spurs and bit on the other hand never won acceptance. In contrast with Europeans, Indians always mounted from the right, but this is possibly an old Spanish custom originating with the Arabs. Some culture elements which were Indian originally were adapted to meet the new conditions. There were a few aboriginal inventions connected with the horse complex and certain older characteristics disappeared; but more of this later.

* * *

In comparing two such forms of culture as those which existed on the north-west coast of America and on the plains, one cannot help noticing that differences permeate them both on the surface and deep down in the structure of society, in morals and in outlook on life. On the north-west coast there was a society without any attempt at political unity, supported by a jealous and exclusive plutocracy whose only concern was to dazzle their fellow-tribesmen by the performance of hereditary ceremonies and to assert an imagined superiority by alternately collecting, and ruthlessly destroying, treasures—a society which with some cause has been described as lacking in potentialities for healthy growth and stuck in a blind alley. By contrast there was the bellicose democracy of the plains Indians, in which all were equal in the sense that each by personal endeavour had the opportunity of achieving the highest distinction, a society containing the germs of a political development which already to a certain degree extended beyond the tribe.

With the plains Indians the tribe really was a political unit, even if it appeared as such only on certain occasions—at the Sun Dance in particular, and also by virtue of the fact that its individual groups never went to war against each other. More rarely, as was the case with the Crow, there was a common tribal council. It was more usual to form independent groups. Thus the Teton Dakota split up into seven "council fires". In certain special cases several tribes federated, though the Pawnee, Blackfoot and one or two others of whom this was true never achieved the close organization of the Iroquoian League, for example.

Among the typical hunters of the high plains, the tribes were divided geographically into bands, but there was no division apart from this. The only exception were the Crow since, as already mentioned, they had separated from the Hidatsa not long before, and so the old social organization remained. On the other hand, the agricultural Siouans of the Missouri Valley and eastern area had a fully developed clan system which cut across geographical divisions. Its roots are almost certainly to be found in the great clan region east of the Mississippi.

With the Mandan and Hidatsa—as well as the Crow—descent went through the female; with the Chiwere and Dhegiha, on the other hand, it was patrilineal; but in both cases its purpose was the same, i.e. the regulation of marriage, it being permissible to marry only a member of another clan—in a word, exogamy. Linked to this among the southern Siouan were certain totemic notions. The Omaha, for example, were divided into ten clans, each with its totem animal which the clan members were prohibited from killing or eating.

Two Ponca clans were dedicated to thunder and conducted a thunder cult; two others were in command on the warpath, while three separate bison clans looked after both the practical and ceremonial aspects of bison hunting. Among the Mandan and

Hidatsa, the designations of the clans were more in the nature of nicknames or place names. The clans were further classified into two large groups or phratries. These too were exogamous, but otherwise they had more of a ceremonial than a social character and were an expression of what might be called a cosmic antithesis, with the sky and the male principle on one side as opposed to the earth and the female principle on the other.

Originally the clan and phratry systems probably had little to do with each other. In any case the clans would seem to be the older. Clans are as little known to the semi-agricultural Caddoans (the Pawnee, Arikara and Wichita) as they are to the hunters of the plains. None the less, among the Pawnee the tribe divided into two matrilineal moieties, though exogamy did not apply. As with the southern Siouans, their names were related to a cosmic antithesis, in this case to "summer" and "winter" people; and the course of nature depended on their co-operation in religious ceremony.

Whether a man had to find his marriage partner outside the clan or not, a rich man always tried to have as many wives as possible, and preferably sisters, for they were most likely to get along together without quarrelling. But the number of wives seldom exceeded three. Among a people where so many of the men died on the warpath, polygamy was, of course, a practical arrangement. Where marriage between members of the same clan was prohibited, the reason was that all its members regarded themselves as being related. Uncles were equivalent to parents and thus cousins were regarded as brothers and sisters. Among the matrilineal Crow and Hidatsa one's father's brother's son and every masculine clansman of the father's generation was one's " father", just as, conversely, among the patrilineal Omaha one's mother's sister and mother's sister's daughter was one's "mother". On the whole, these designations are not so much an expression of what we understand by relationship as of the manner in which a well-brought-up Indian should behave towards a fellow clansman. A man must show the utmost reserve towards his mother-in-law and a woman must do the same towards her father-in-law, while brothers and sisters—using the terms in their widest sense—must avoid each other.

On the other hand, brothers-in-law and sisters-in-law were allowed to joke with and tease each other in the most intimate way. A similar state of affairs is found in quite a few places round the world—we shall come across it later among the Tuareg of the Sahara—and it is in fact two aspects of the same thing, namely, a means of avoiding conflict between near relatives.

In spite of certain differences between the kinship systems of the Crow and Omaha, they agree on one point—in emphasizing the family, whether it is reckoned through the female or the male line. Corresponding systems occur not only among other village-inhabiting Siouans but also among the Pawnee and Arikara, who are also more or less settled agriculturists. In direct contrast are the kinship systems among the hunting tribes proper on the high plains (except for the Comanche who in this respect agree with the tribes of the Great Basin); here the emphasis is not on the family but on the generations. Fred Eggan has drawn attention to the fact that this applies to tribes of widely differing origins and widely different historical backgrounds and sees in it, certainly correctly, evidence of adaptation to the highly developed hunting life, where mutual help between people of equal age is essential.

The families comprise not only parents and children, but sons and daughters-in-law, grandchildren and perhaps more distant relatives. They are in fact joint families. Among the hunting tribes each local group consists of a number of joint families and generally the wife joins the husband's group. Only among the Arapaho and Cheyenne is it the man who moves into the wife's camp. This is presumably a survival from the time when they had not yet given up life in permanent villages, for it is among just the agricultural village tribes that the same custom (matrilocality) occurs. Among the Omaha matrilocality is the rule so long as they keep to the villages; but during the hunting season it gives way to patrilocality. The separate local bands are to a certain extent exogamous, even if there is no strictly observed rule. Among the Pawnee and Wichita the wife is chosen inside the village, which is thus endogamous.

The plains Indians had none of the exaggerated respect for a man's birth or riches which was so characteristic of the north-west coast Indians. Like a Nordic Viking chieftain, the chief had to be as generous as he could, and would never deny aid to a poorer clansman in need of food and a horse to ride; but riches were no entitlement to respect, and it would have been difficult to gain general acceptance of such a view, for the idea that an individual could acquire the rights of hunting territory or of clan ceremonies was something quite foreign to the minds of these Indians.

Distinction could be gained only by personal achievement—in some warlike capacity of course. To steal a horse from the enemy was commendable for a start; but in the eyes of the Blackfoot there were three particularly meritorious deeds: to acquire an adversary's weapon; to gain a scalp and to touch a live enemy. The order of merit of such exploits varied from tribe to tribe. The Kiowa thought that the most meritorious of all deeds was to go to the aid of a comrade during a retreat. Those performing deeds of valour were awarded the right to wear certain distinctive marks.

The Dakota had carefully worked out rules for these marks of distinction—and an eagle's feather might be as well-earned as a knighthood. Since a man's deeds alone gave him the right to public office, it was customary for him to paint all his exploits on his great robe of bison skin, or somctimes on his tent. Before he took over a new office he would stand forth and solemnly recite the list of his achievements. In some tribes it was customary at the mention of each item for him to aim a blow at a pole with an axe—from this derives the French-Canadian expression "to count coups"—and this was evidence not only of the Indians' contempt of death in battle but equally of their sense of the picturesque in boasting of it. Red Cloud, a famous Dakota chieftain of the 1860s, who was one of the most dreaded enemies of the United States, reckoned no fewer than eighty "coups" to his credit.

The leading men of the various bands or clans made up the tribal council which looked after common interests, and one or more of them were usually regarded as chieftains whose task it was to implement the findings of the council. Sometimes this arrangement was extremely loose, sometimes the reverse, as for example among the Cheyenne who elected an assembly of forty members and four chiefs of equal standing. A similar number of chieftains was the rule with the Dakota, four being a number sacred to the plains Indians, corresponding to the four corners of the earth.

Real power, however, lay with the brotherhoods. These were in many respects reminiscent of medieval guilds and were one of the most characteristic features of Indian society. Each brotherhood had its own leader and always showed a united front to the outside world. The brotherhood by sticking together could by its unanimity therefore not only carry the council with it, so that no resolution could be carried without its consent but was often entrusted by the chieftain with the task of seeing that the resolutions of the council were carried out. For instance, it was usual for one of the brotherhoods to be appointed to police the camp or the hunt, the appointment ending when the allotted task was completed. There were, however, differences in the character of the brotherhoods in individual tribes. In some the religious element was stronger than in others, though it was never entirely lacking, for respect for the supernatural permeated existence. This was particularly true, for example, of the Iowa, Omaha, Ponca and Kansa, where the brotherhoods never did police duty. With the Pawnee the strength of the religious element varied depending on whether the brotherhoods were shamanistic in character, were connected with the tribe's sacred bundles or were organized on the basis of the religious experiences of the members in question. In such circumstances the ties of brotherhood amounted to little more than the performance of special ceremonies often of some magical kind; but purely humanitarian ends such as attendance on the sick were also served.

A special kind of development occurred among the Hidatsa, Mandan, Arapaho, Atsina and Blackfoot. Not only was the military character predominant, but the brotherhoods also were arranged in a fixed order in accordance not with rank but with age, members moving from one class to another like children at school. With the exception of small boys, nearly every male in the tribe was a member of one of these brotherhoods. Admission took place by the members as a whole buying for themselves the right of the next eldest brotherhood, though each individual chose his own seller—preferably one belonging to his own father's clan. A curious custom, which doubtless had some magical background, required that as part of the payment the buyer should relinquish his wife to the seller for a time, and if the buyer was unmarried he had to borrow the wife of a fellow clansman. In order to maintain some sort of continuity with the past a few individual members after such a general sale always remained in the brotherhood. If a member for some reason or other did not sell his membership, then the term of his membership became unlimited, so that even though the members of the brotherhood were usually of the same age, there could at times be both old men and youngsters in its ranks.

These age-class associations would appear to have come into existence among the Mandan and Hidatsa as a result of their putting the older co-ordinate brotherhoods into order of seniority and then passing on the system to the Arapaho, Atsina and Blackfoot. The co-ordinate brotherhoods are therefore the first stage of development. They, too, have a common origin—a fact which is apparent in several ways: names such as Bulls, Crazy Dogs, Young Foxes, etc., are the same in the most widely differentiated tribes, while ceremonies and equipment are remarkably similar. The Hidatsa "Dog" association, which has a mythological basis and name, held dances at which members performed stripped to the waist, painted themselves red and wore headdresses of owl and magpie feathers. Round their necks there hung whistles made from birds' bones and in their hands there were bows and arrows and rattles of hoof. They had certain rules and privileges in the matter of food, and before the dance they howled like dogs. In battle they had to display particular bravery, and this applied particularly to the chieftain of the brotherhood who was called "the real dog".

A curious feature was that what was said to him always had to be the opposite of what was meant. "Come", for example, meant "Go", and so on. The Bull-brotherhood wore headdresses decorated with horns and carried shields and lances decorated with feathers. They danced under the direction of two leaders in bison masks, to whom a woman clothed in a brand new dress of antelope skin offered drinking water. The magical significance of this is obvious. But the " Bulls " also had a warlike character, and the two leaders could never surrender in battle. The Hidatsa and Mandan also had women's societies in which the magical aspect was prominent, one of the main objects being to summon the bison herds and promote the growth of maize.

* * *

The military spirit which was characteristic of the most highly developed brotherhoods found an outlet in endless tribal feuds. Hunting and warfare were the two great passions of the plains Indians, and from earliest childhood the upbringing of boys concentrated on training in toughness, self-control and contempt of pain. Any suggestion of taking up the war-hatchet certainly could not originate with the chiefs: they were in duty bound to strive for the maintenance of peace. So large-scale actions involving the whole tribe as such were rare. Most wars were as it were private ventures, but no less frequent on that account, for ambition and revenge were always uppermost in youthful minds. Even if they did sometimes have to steal out of camp at night in order not to rouse the disapproval of the older and more experienced, the urge to acquire an extra scalp or two was all too often sufficient to lure adventurous youngsters on to the warpath. To a large extent also there were magical notions of revenge behind these adventures, the gaining of a scalp meaning the acquisition of the victim's "power". In this connexion it is significant that even simple horse-thieving was organized on the pattern of a campaign of revenge.

Larger ventures with up to a hundred or two participants took place only exceptionally; but when they did, a number of solemn preparations preceded them. Some Omaha warriors, for example, decide to launch a large-scale attack on the Pawnee. A man with a face covered in mud makes his way round the camp shouting, "O mighty Spirit! Strangers have affronted me but I count on your aid!" Then that evening four of his friends shout outside each tent: "My friend! So-and-so invites you when the time is come." The guests foregather in the host's dwelling, each bringing a food bowl and spoon. "My friends!" says the host, "we have invited you to this feast because we wish to set out on the warpath." The young warriors then ask: "Friend! Which direction do we take?" "The direction of the Pawnee" is the answer. Then all those willing to take part promise their help. They are given maize and dried meat to eat, and when they have done so they throw the grass which they have used to wipe their hands and bowls on to the fire and bang their bowls against each other in the smoke crying: "I have come home with horses as my prize!", "He fled but I seized him!", and so on. These are in fact appeals to the gods of war and thunder for aid in performing the deeds mentioned.

If a large-scale enterprise is envisaged, the goodwill of the god must also be secured in other ways, and this is done by opening his sacred bundles which contain the skins and feathers of certain birds. The bundles are laid down in the centre of the tent and those guarding them chant sacred songs—so sacred that the contents of them have remained secret to this day. They are usually repeated four times, and the warriors perform their dance a similar number of times. At a later ceremony the bundles are opened with great solemnity and the beaks of the birds are turned to point in the direction of the enemy. For four nights in succession there are similar celebrations. Meanwhile, hasty preparations are made: weapons are got ready, food and footwear collected, etc.

Though war and hunting play so large a part in the plains Indians' life, their weapons show no evidence of much inventiveness. They usually consisted of lances, which originally had blades of stone, bows and arrows and clubs. The bow was comparatively short, capable of being used on horseback, and was either a simple wooden stave or was strengthened by a layer of animal sinews gummed on one side; this latter type came from the west where similar bows occur, though going right back they derive from the compound Asiatic bow. Further evidence of this is that it was sometimes double-curved, like Cupid's famous bow. Specially costly bows to be found amongst the Crow, Hidatsa and Mandan were made of deer antler. Bows continued to be used long after the introduction of the gun, for according to the statements of old frontiersmen, in speed and accuracy they were not surpassed until the arrival of the modern magazine rifle. The arrows, only on rare occasions poisoned, were kept with the bow in a quiver made of skin.

A club, which originated in the eastern woodlands, had a flat, broad, angled shaft, and in more recent times it also had a sharp steel blade let into it. But more characteristic of the plains was a war hammer which consisted of an egg-shaped head of stone and a springy shaft: a terrible weapon in a strong hand. When colonization took place, the steel or brass hatchets widely introduced in great numbers by the settlers were, of course, also used. The only defensive weapon was a round shield of bison skin painted with symbolic and magical figures. Leather armour was possibly used in olden times by the Pawnees.

But to return to the Omaha: no sooner have they left the camp than they are obliged to fast for four days. After that they all take on fresh names in order to confuse unfriendly spirits. Some men are appointed police and the strictest discipline is observed. The scouts go out in front, and some distance behind them the main force follows, headed by the bearers of the sacred bundles and the leaders of the expedition. Each evening guards are set up, and if danger threatens they howl like coyotes. Every morning at daybreak the party strikes camp. The assault on the enemy is sudden and ruthless. An infernal hullaballoo fills the air as war cries sound from a hundred throats. Seldom are either women or children spared. Chivalry in combat was even less known to the Indians than it is to the Great Powers of today. Their object, it has been said, was to "steal up to the enemy like a fox, charge like a tiger and fly away like a bird". The visible sign of victory was the scalp: a swift stroke of an ordinary butcher's knife and the skin of the crown was parted. Then with a sharp tug it was fleeced, raised aloft with a roar and then, bloody and smoking, fastened to the belt. The ideas, though, that all Indian tribes were scalp hunters and that the scalp is an exclusively American trophy are delusions. Herodotus, in fact, mentions them in connexion with the ancient Scythians, while in South America they are practically unknown. Originally scalp-taking occurred only in the area east of the Mississippi, while in New England actual head-trophies occurred. The fact that scalping later spread over almost the whole of North America, excluding the Arctic regions and the Mackenzie district, is owing largely to the barbarous premium which white men were ready to pay for scalps as tangible evidence of the death of a red adversary.*

In these circumstances it is not surprising that the Indians nursed an implacable hatred of the white invaders. It is well to remember that references to the bloodthirstiness and treachery of the Indians date from a time when they were waging a desperate battle in defence of the land of their fathers.

The fate of the Teton Dakota was typical. Until the year 1876 they were in undisturbed possession of extensive hunting grounds. Then gold was discovered in the Black Hills, and, in spite of the U.S. Government's promise, the country was flooded with gold prospectors. Finally the Dakotas lost patience and in the course of their subsequent resistance they annihilated General Custer and his entire force at Little Bighorn River. The outcome of the war was, however, never in doubt. The Dakotas were deprived of a third of the territory which had been guaranteed them, and what remained was insufficient for hunting and too infertile for profitable agriculture. Smouldering discontent burst into flame again during the Ghost Dance movement (see page 95) when in 1890 American troops took bloody revenge for their defeat, butchering at Wounded Knee some 300 Indians, including numerous women and children.

At the end of a successful expedition, when the warriors had returned home, there remained the sharing out of the rewards of victory. Among the Omaha, this took place by the members of the expedition forming up in ranks in front of the sacred bundles. Then each of them in turn solemnly promised to tell the truth and having told his story he dropped a stick on to the bundles. If it

* In Pennsylvania in 1764 the price fixed by the Government for a male Indian scalp was $134 and for a female $50.

remained where it fell, this was taken as confirmation of his story and he was allowed to wear the traditional mark appertaining to his deed. In the evening all the new scalps were hung up on a tall pole and the women danced round them while the men provided an accompaniment of singing and drumming. Eventually the scalps were put in some remote place, presumably as a sacrifice, or they served as decoration on the horses' harness.

From this somewhat lengthy description of the warlike tendencies of the Indians it must not be imagined that peaceful co-existence between tribes was unknown. A substantial measure of trade was conducted between them, and the big pipe-stone quarry at Coteau des Prairies on the upper Mississippi, which provided the red catlinite for the bowls of pipes, was sacred ground where deadly enemies could meet without fear of treachery on either side. Between tribes speaking different languages there was a well-developed sign-language which made it possible to "discuss" day to day matters. Tribes such as the Crow, Kiowa and Blackfoot were famous for their skill in this respect.

* * *

In such matters as economy and housing, it has already been remarked that there was a considerable difference between the tribes in the lower lying eastern regions and the Missouri Valley on the one hand and the wandering huntsmen of the high plains on the other. The former lived for part of the year in villages and in addition to hunting carried on some sort of agriculture. The latter chased bison the year round and knew no other home than their tents.

Agriculture was located in the river valleys for the reason that the soil of this one-time forest country was more easily cultivated with the simple tools available to the Indians. The soil was cleared and worked with the aid of a hoe made of a bison's shoulder blade; but manuring was unknown and when a plot was worked out a new plot was brought under cultivation. The crop consisted of maize, beans, gourds and sunflowers. Maize was the chief crop and was known to the Omahas as "mother", while the bison was "grandfather". Tobacco was also grown, not only by the farming tribes but also by such hunting tribes as the Crow and Blackfoot, the principal reason being that it was a sacred plant, indispensable to religious rites. In fact, one of the greatest tribal treasures of the Arapaho was their sacred pipe. The pipes usually had a ⊥-shaped bowl carved out of soft stone (catlinite) and a long and often flattish stem decorated with feathers or the split and painted quills of tree-porcupines. This, of course, applied especially to the big ceremonial pipe, the "calumet" (local dialect for the French *chalumet*, from the Latin *calamellus*, a little tube) where every single item of decoration and each separate colour had some symbolic meaning. It was smoked when the gods were invoked in connexion with some ceremony such as adoption, declaration of war or declaration of peace, etc. Curiously enough many of these pipes were no more than dummies, for it was the solemn motions rather than the smoking itself that mattered. The pipes were kept in beautifully beaded and fringed leather pouches or in the skin of a deer or antelope.

So long as there was sowing and reaping to be done, the farming tribes lived in villages which often stood on inaccessible cliffs surrounded by stockades some distance from the fields. The building of the houses was left mainly to the women. In the extreme south the houses were something like old-fashioned bee-hives. The Wichita covered them with straw, and the Osages with mats or bark. In the Wichita house there were originally as many as four entrances, one facing each point of the compass and from the top of it there were four poles pointing in the same directions—another example of the plains Indian symbolism connected with the number four.

Farther north there were round houses with conical roofs covered with earth. These were mainly found among the tribes on the Missouri (the Hidatsa, Mandan and Arikara) but houses rather like them occurred among the Pawnees, Omaha, Ponca, Missouri and Oto.*

* In the late pre-Columbian cultures on the northern plains—the Upper Republican and Nebraska cultures—the earth lodges often had a rectangular ground plan, sometimes with the entrance through the roof instead of a passage.

When the Hidatsa set about building one of these earth lodges they began by erecting the four centre posts which were connected at the top by horizontal beams. To the minds of the Indians the centre posts were living beings and they held them sacred. It was therefore permissible for them to be chopped by certain people only. After completion of the house sacrifices were brought to them. Round the centre posts were erected a circle of outer posts, half their height, and these, too, were joined by horizontal beams. A sloping wall of closely packed logs leaned against these beams which also supported the roof rafters, which sloped up to the beams joining the centre posts and left a space in the middle of the roof for a smoke hole. The actual roof consisted of willow branches and a thick layer of prairie grass, while the whole building was covered with sods. It was so solidly built that in fine weather the inhabitants often spent their time on the roof.

The entrance was by way of a short side passage of earth-covered timber shut off by a door of skin. In the middle of the house was the hearth and behind that was the place where the sacred bundles were kept. Round the walls there were low bedsteads and the blankets and pillows were of skin. To provide comfort for sitting there were peculiar triangular supports for the back formed of sticks bound horizontally together. The dwelling was often so roomy that a dome-shaped bathroom and a stable for ten or twelve horses were accommodated under the one roof. Among the Mandans the house belonged to the clan of the women who lived in it and they also jointly owned the household goods, the fields and the mares, while weapons, stallions and geldings belonged to the men.

Probably all the village tribes knew how to make simple pots, and tradition among the Cheyenne, for example, indicates that they made them before hunting became their exclusive interest. The method is the same as that of the older ceramic periods in eastern North America; the vessel was formed out of a single lump of clay, not, as was the case with many other Indians, by coiling. The former method, which was known to the inhabitants of the western plateaux, to a single tribe in California and even to the

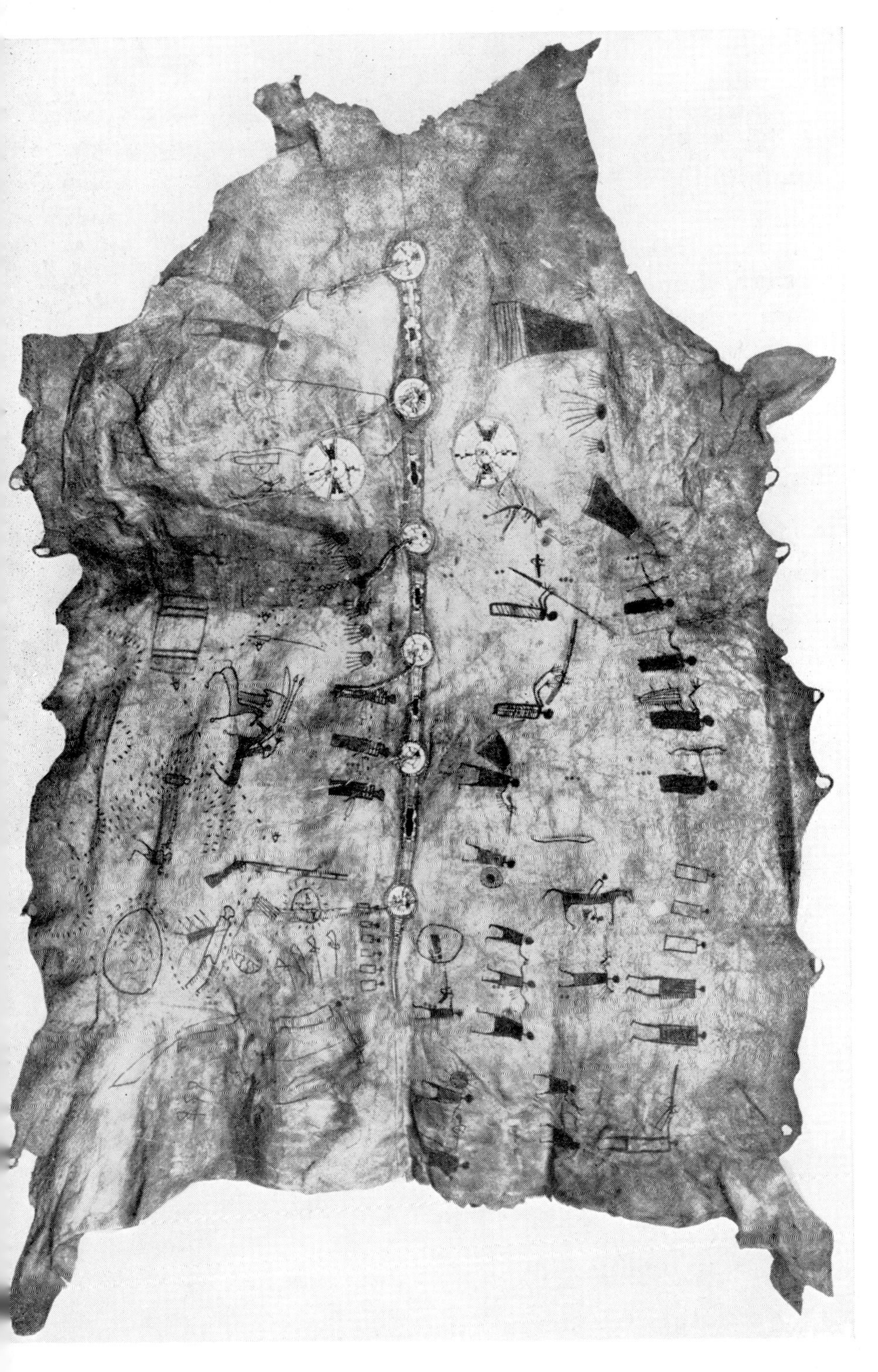

The decorations on this bison robe, which belonged to a warrior of the plains Indians, record the exploits in war of its owner. (National Museum, Copenhagen.)

Above: A bison dance by Mandan tribesmen.

Below: Indians on the plains hunting bison.

Above: A Mandan village on the Missouri River. In the foreground are bull boats.

Below: Scalp dance by men of the Minitari tribe.

Above: These paintings by C. B. King show (*left*) a young chieftain of the Pawnee and (*right*) an Oto chieftain. Both pictures date from 1825 and are in the National Museum at Copenhagen.

Below: Of this war equipment of the plains Indians the hide shield is Comanche, the sinew-lined bow and stone club are Blackfoot and the quiver and arrows are of the Dakota tribe. A scalp lies between the club and the quiver. All are in the National Museum at Copenhagen.

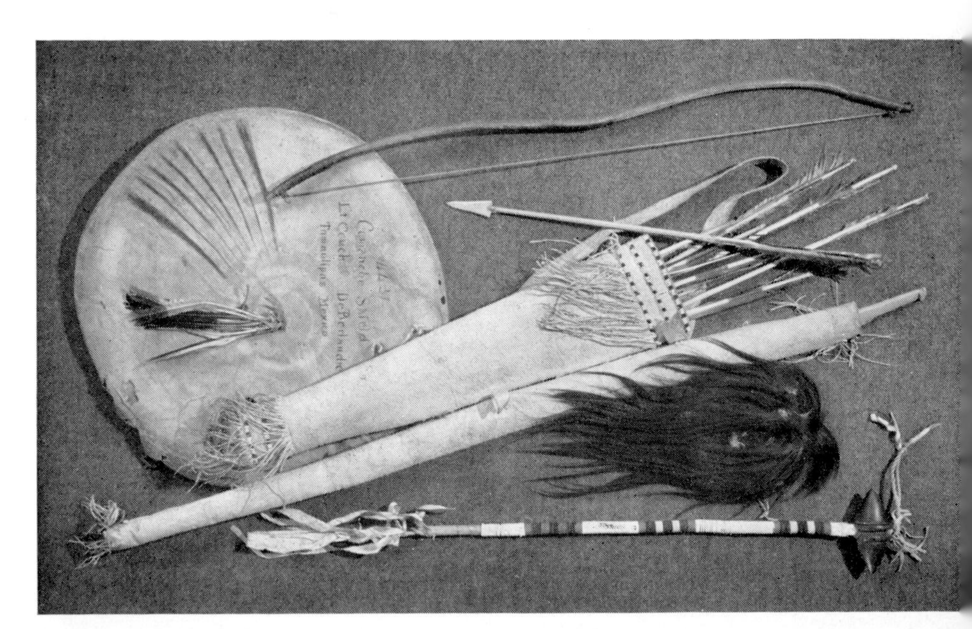

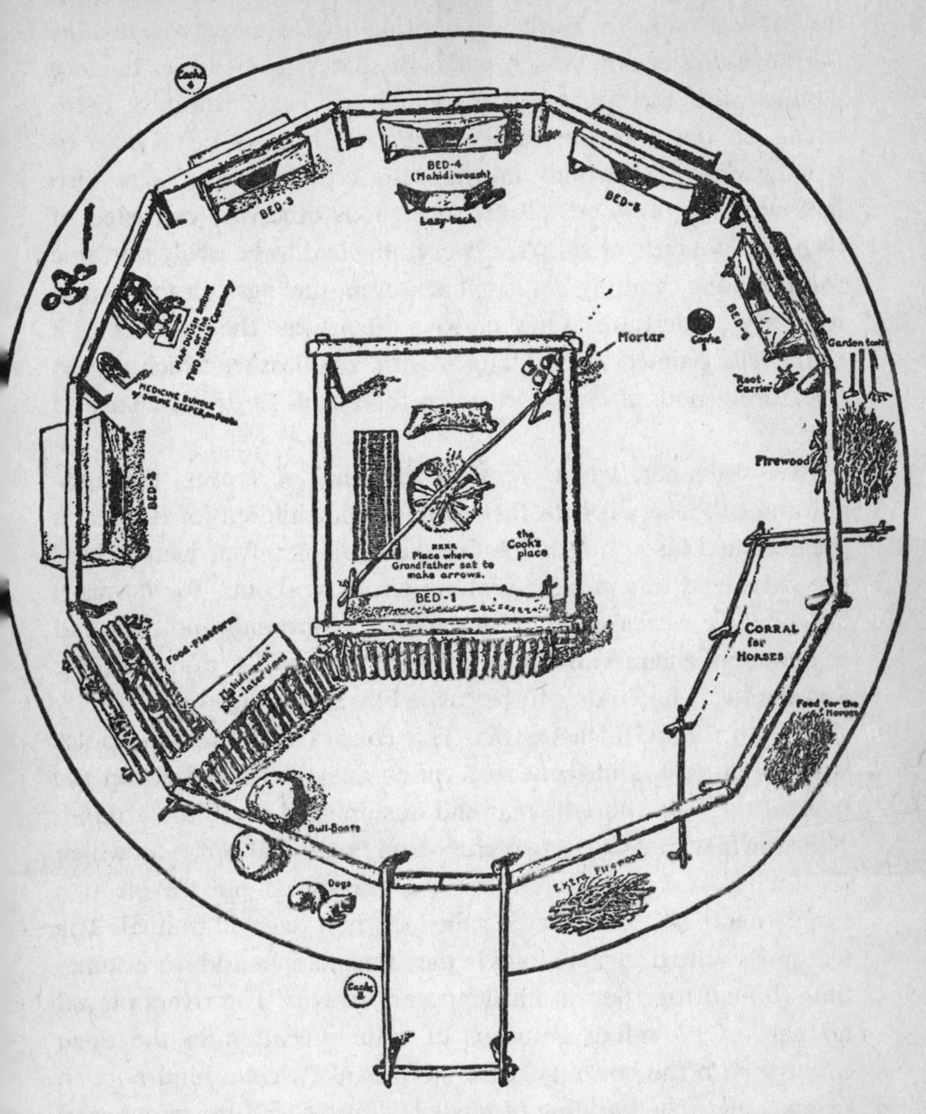

Diagram of a Hidatsa earth lodge (after Lowie). The hearth in the middle is screened against the draught from the entrance by logs. Near the screen are two round skin boats; behind it is a platform for food. To the right of the entrance is a pen for horses. Around the sides and at the back are beds and a shrine.

Eskimos, goes right back to Siberian prototypes. Fire was produced by a simple fire drill. The hunting tribes appear to have done their cooking in skin vessels with hot stones. Some tribes in close contact with the western plateau culture, baked roots in earth ovens. Spoons and soup ladles were carved out of bison horn or wood, while dishes and mortars for crushing corn were also hollowed out of wood. Household goods otherwise consisted of bags and pouches of skin, for everything had to be easily portable for the long hunting trips which even the agricultural tribes regularly undertook. One curious item was the parfleche, a beautifully painted folding bag of stiff, raw leather which served for storing both cooking gear and food such as dried meat and suet.

Every summer, when work in the fields was over, the agricultural tribes set off with their women and children for the year's great annual bison hunt. The Omaha appointed four men to lead the party and others were sent on ahead as scouts, for it was a two or three weeks' journey to the hunting grounds and they had to beware of enemies. In olden times the journey was done on foot, and the loads had either to be carried by the women or drawn by dogs with the aid of a travois. This consisted of two long poles which were joined in front to form an angle which rested on the back of the dog while the rear end was dragged along the ground. Near the rear there were two cross-bars or an oval frame on which the load rested. When horses were introduced the travois was simply made larger so that it suited the new draught animal. The tent poles were dragged along in the same manner and were sometimes bound together into a temporary travois. The rivers played no part in providing a means of communication in the open country—on the contrary, their steep banks were a hindrance to free passage. The building of boats had not, therefore, progressed beyond the making of clumsy circular bull boats consisting of an osier framework covered with bison skins. Sledges—the conventional Canadian toboggan—are mentioned in connexion with the Mandan and the eastern Dakota, but they were in all probability introduced by white traders.

Throughout the hunting season the Indians lived in tents. Pitching camp was carried out with military precision. First the leaders marked out the entrance to the camp, which had to face east. Then group after group of the picturesque tents sprang up clockwise until they all formed a large circle round the open place where in lonely state the tall council tent stood. When the order was given to strike camp, the women had the tents down in the matter of a moment, rolled them up and loaded them, together with the household goods, on to the animals. The typical plains tent or tipi, as the Dakota word has it, was conical in shape and consisted of a large number of poles and a tent cloth of tanned bison skins which were sewn together. The sticks were often very long and stuck out of the top of the tent cover; to support them three, or more usually four, poles were first tied together and then stood up. A unique feature of the tipi in comparison with other conical tents in North America were the two "wings" at the top, one on either side of the smoke hole, and they could be regulated according to the direction of the wind.

In the summer, when there was plenty of grazing, the bison collected in enormous herds, and whether they belonged to wandering or settled tribes, all plains Indians regarded the great summer bison hunts as one of the most important events of the year. Every grown man took part in the hunt and, as on every other important occasion, the strictest discipline was observed so that no one in his eagerness spoiled his comrade's chances. Certain warriors were appointed police during the hunt, and anyone who dared flout their orders received such a thorough thrashing that he was lucky if he were not crippled for life.

Latterly bison hunting was performed on horseback. Some of the animals were specially trained for hunting, which was dangerous and demanded a high degree of horsemanship. As soon as a herd of bison was sighted, the huntsmen cast off everything that could in the slightest degree hinder them and got as near to the bison as they could, using as cover the inequalities of the ground and keeping, of course, on the lee side of the herd. Even when they had been spotted, the bison often let them approach to within a few hundred yards. Next at a given signal they galloped towards them. Then, while they rode round the herd in circles, each huntsman picked off one victim after another. His hands had to be free to manage the bow, so he guided the horse with his knees. But the horse knew what was wanted and made its own way to the bison's right side so that the huntsman could send his fatal arrow deep into the vulnerable spot behind the foreleg.

Out of consideration for supernatural forces the bison had to be treated with respect. Though it was hunted there was no enmity between bison and man, for in the same way as it was part of man's nature to hunt, so it was part of the bison's nature to allow itself to be killed for man's benefit. Indeed the bison offered itself for slaughter. Among the Omaha, after the first four hunts of the season, the chiefs had to hold a feast at which they ate nothing but the tongue and heart of bison. This they had to do by putting them on the flaps of their robes and not using the usual dishes; they ate them to the accompaniment of sacred chants, without using a knife. Towards the end of summer before they went back to their villages, there were other ceremonies. Outside a tent consecrated for the purpose the bison clan erected a sacred pole, which was decorated at the top with a scalp and at the middle with a sacred bundle. The pole was also smeared with bison fat and in front of it dried meat was laid. The festival ended with a sham fight at which all the young warriors performed.

The agricultural tribes now returned to their villages to start on the harvest, but the others continued with their hunting existence the year round. Often, however, smaller hunting parties would also leave the villages during the winter and enjoy the delights of the open life. At this time of the year, when at least the northern plains are covered in snow, encircling the bison on horseback was impossible. Then occasionally the hunt was carried out on snow-shoes. Another method was to drive the herd between two lines of converging fences or stones a mile or so long. At the end of the fences there was either a sudden drop, down which the frightened animals fell, or there was an enclosure of tree-trunks and branches in which they could be shot easily. When there was no snow, the animals could be driven together by setting light to the dry grass. Alternatively a couple of hunters dressed as coyotes could creep up close to the herd and drive it towards the rest of the hunters. These are long established methods and probably go back long before the introduction of the horse.

When there were bison to be had, all other animals were left in peace. Otherwise, of course, no deer or antelope, nor even the dreaded grizzly bear of the mountains, was despised. But there was a general feeling among the tribes that they were above fishing. Meat not eaten immediately was cut into strips and dried in the sun. Sometimes the dried meat was pulverized, mixed with melted fat and seasoned with crushed wild cherries. The result was a tasty and nourishing food known as pemmican which, properly looked after, would keep for years.

A year in the life of a typical hunting tribe such as the Blackfoot, followed this pattern: in the beginning of November they pitched winter camp in a river valley, sheltered from blizzards and with easy access to water, fuel and fodder for the horses. They remained until the snow melted and the wild geese migrated north, i.e. about 1 April. Spring was often a difficult time, for not many bison were about and people hunted them in small groups. Otherwise the tribe had to make do with wild roots. At the beginning of June the various bands gathered for the big collective summer hunt, and notice went round about the celebration of the great Sun Dance (see page 93) which took place during August. After that the bands dispersed once more until the autumn hunts which provided the fattest meat for drying and making into pemmican for the winter.

Meat was by no means all that the bison provided. The skins were used for tents, robes and riding gear; the sinews for thread and bowstrings; the bones and horns for tools; offal for feeding the dogs; and the brain and the liver for tanning the skin after it had been scraped with a hoe-like implement of antler.

Everywhere, except, perhaps, in the extreme south, the bison robe was amongst the most indispensable items in a man's clothing. Otherwise bison skin was too thick and heavy for clothing which was usually made of deer skin. In the summer the men went about practically naked. A breech cloth drawn between the legs and tucked into the belt front and back, and a pair of shoes were often all that they wore. The soles of the shoes usually were of thick leather. The soft moccasins of the woodland Indians, made by folding a piece of skin up round the foot, were used only in the north and east. In the winter leggings were worn.

The poncho, a single skin with a slit in the middle through which the head passed so that it hung down loosely in front and at the back, and the loose shirt, which was actually a poncho sewn together at the sides, were less usual in olden times than they were later. We do in fact know that even in olden times it was worn by the Blackfoot, Assiniboine, Dakota, Crow, and one or two other tribes, whereas it was lacking among many others such as the Mandan, Pawnee, Osage, Arapaho and Comanche. Magnificent and fantastic they looked with their extravagant decorations of leather fringes, tufts of hair, strips of fur, ermine skins, painted designs and porcupine-quill embroidery. And, of course, to add to the warrior's impressive appearance, there were ornaments in his ears and hair and a large necklace of the fearsome grizzly bear's claws, which endowed him with the bear's strength.

An equally useful ornament on his breast consisted of rows of deer bones tied together to form miniature armour. Nose ornaments and tattooing were, on the other hand, fairly rare, whereas painting the face and body was essential at all festivals and other solemn occasions. Long hair was considered so becoming that even the men were not above improving on nature by sticking false hair on to their own so that it reached nearly to the ground. Usually the hair was either worn flowing or in two plaits. Some tribes allowed a lock in front to fall down over the nose, whilst others brushed the hair up. The Pawnee and some of the Siouan tribes had it cut off so that only a well-groomed scalp lock on the crown of the head remained as a defiant challenge to the enemy.

But the most distinctive and most picturesque adornment and the one which bore testimony to its bearer's standing as well as to his worth as a warrior, was the headdress. The popular idea that every Indian went about bristling with feathers is as false as to imagine every soldier nowadays a general and every civilian a knight. The tall crown of eagle's feathers with a tail of feathers hanging down behind, which was truly characteristic only of the Dakota, was a rare distinction reserved to a chosen few; and only the bravest would venture to wear a pair of bison horns, the symbol of strength, on their headdresses.

The women's dress, like that of the men, was of tanned deer skin and consisted of shoes, leggings reaching no farther than the knee and a long coat gathered at the waist by a belt. The coat was sewn of two hart skins, the form of which is easily recognizable in the scalloped lower edge and the open sleeves. Like the men's, it was richly fringed and embroidered, if possible, with the milk teeth of the deer, which were highly prized. In certain tribes (the Osage, Cheyenne and Pawnee) the oldest female dress is said to have consisted of two garments, a skirt and a kind of jacket, and this is of some significance for precisely this costume occurs among the Indians east of the Mississippi as far north as Labrador.

Costumes, bags and the like provided the only opportunities the Indians had of developing their artistic talents, and in consequence their art was confined to painting and sewing. One searches almost in vain for anything approximating to sculpture, either in wood, stone or clay. Their art was nearly always geometrical. Some designs were named after animals or real life objects, but this did not mean that they were stylized versions of what were once realistic pictures, for the same design occurred in different tribes under widely differing names. The designs on the curious parfleches were elegantly painted by some tribes such as the Arapaho, more massively and crudely by others such as the Crow. It is possible to differentiate between two styles, one based on triangles, the other on rectangles. The embroidery which decorated the costumes by emphasizing the seams and outline edges included several other figures: stepped pyramids, crosses, forked designs, etc. Latterly they were usually carried out in glass beads; formerly in split and coloured porcupine quills. There is, however, evidence that this latter form of decoration was not indigenous to the plains in the fact that porcupines do not live on the steppes proper.

In addition to their æsthetic effect many, if not all, the geometrical designs had a magical significance which was at least equally important to the Indians. The cross, for example, signified the thunder bird, a powerful protector. A white stripe through a green zigzag line on the sole of a child's shoe was there because a zigzag line signified a rattlesnake and thus the child was protected from the fatal sting of the snakes. As for the purely realistic reproductions on shields, tents and cloaks, the idea of any æsthetic effect was purely secondary—if it existed at all. What the Indian painted on his shield were his visions, the mighty helpers of his hour of need, and what he depicted on his cloak were all his meritorious deeds. Thus there was no attempt at composition. In bold and clear pictures to anyone comprehending he boasted of his courage as a warrior and horse rover. These pictures thus approximated to picture writing and in certain cases this is what they actually became. In their "Winter Counts" the Dakota had gone the whole way; here we find records, the principal events of the year being portrayed on a bison skin.

* * *

Confidence in supernatural forces permeated the whole life of the plains Indians. They had an intense religious conviction that by prayer, fasting and even self-torture they could get into communication with the divinities whose aid and protection they needed. But a comparison between the religious life of these tribes and that of the north-west coast Indians reveals differences as profound as those which appear in their social and material life.

Among the North Pacific Indians the ceremonies re-enacted episodes in the clan myths, and the participants appeared wearing the masks of supernatural beings of all kinds. The plains Indians, on the other hand, never dared to put on the outward garb of the divinities, and masks—beyond those used in the bison dance—were practically unknown. On the north-west coast the complicated ceremonies were primarily for the pleasure and profit of the individual and his kindred, especially by raising his social status. On the plains their object was to benefit the welfare of the whole tribe, and they were primarily religious.

It is widely believed that the Indians worshipped a supreme deity well known from innumerable adventure stories as the Great Spirit. There is some truth in this. Even after allowing for the influence of missionaries on this point, there remains an original core of belief in a Supreme Being. It is as well, however, to beware of assuming that the Indians have the customary conceptions of a personal god with well-defined characteristics and a prescribed field of activity. Their ideas seem to be not only vague and nebulous, but to be based on assumptions quite different from ours. The key to this, as to much else relating to the North American aborigines, lies in their idea of an exalted and sacred power, an all pervading vital force. The Dakota called it *Wakan Tanka*, the Omaha *Wakonda*, the Pawnee *Kawaharu*. Life as such and all else that could not be explained was, to the Dakota, sacred or *wakan*.

The two possessions of the white man which made the deepest impression on the Indians were the horse and the rifle, and they called them dog and iron respectively, each with the addition *wakan*. Thus, *wakan* had actually no existence of its own but was a kind of quality in something already existing. Nevertheless, it is not a big step from the idea of this power to the belief in a personal god which we find expressed in the idea of the Great Spirit. The Omaha and Ponca identified the deity with thunder, the Dakotas with the sun. The divine power permeated all existence and was in greater or less degree to be found everywhere, thus the religion of the Indians might be called nature worship. As an old Dakota put it:

> "Everything that moves comes to rest sometimes. The bird that flies stops in one place to build its nest and in another to rest. The wanderer stops walking when he feels so inclined. And the deity comes to rest too. The sun, which shines so brightly and clearly, is one of the places where he has rested. The moon, stars and wind are others, and so are the trees and animals. The Indians think of these places and pray to those where the deity has stayed in order to obtain help and blessing."

The Dakota have a fixed order of precedence for the deities of Nature. The sun comes first and alongside it the sky, the earth, and solid rock. Then come various spirits in groups of four: the moon, the winds, the bison, etc. The thunder birds, whose beating wings made the air tremble, were thought to live on a mountain far out west. They were war gods and had at one time provided the Dakota with the spear and tomahawk. The water bisons—enormous creatures whose horns reached to the heavens—had given them their sacred bundles and initiated one of their sacred dances.

To the Pawnees the Supreme Being was Tirawa and he differed to some extent from the Dakota deity. He was the gods' chieftain rather than a personification of sacred power, and was related to the heavens in the same way as the four wind gods were related to the four corners of the earth, and Atira, the Maize Mother to the earth itself. To the Pawnee the universe was an indivisible whole, and phenomena on earth were a reflection of those in the sky. There is a great deal in this, as in many other of their religious ideas, to suggest a Mexican origin.

Among the plains Indians there was also a widespread belief in a powerful culture hero who created, or rather, transformed, the world, though the morals of his deeds were often rather doubtful. To some of the western tribes he appeared in the shape of a coyote; to the eastern tribes he was more in the nature of a spider. To other tribes he was quite human and was linked to the ideas of daybreak and the east.

By fasting and visions even human beings could share in the sacred power. This applied primarily to the medicine men, who among the Dakota and Pawnee constituted a well-defined group, distinct from the laity. Among the Pawnee they were divided into two classes. Those in the higher class had even more influence than the tribal chieftains. They obtained their power from the stars, whereas those in the lower class had to be content with authority deriving from animal deities. But the medicine men were not a class apart in every tribe. Among the Arapaho and Assiniboine there were actually none at all for the simple reason that every single man strove to get into contact with the supernatural. And this could be done provided one went about it in the right way.

Removed from the bustle of daily life, fasting and praying, one awaited the revelation which proclaimed that one's prayers had been heard. But fasting and solitude were not always enough. The Dakota, among others, practised self-tortures of the most horrible kind, similar to those enacted during the Sun Dance (see page 93). The revelation appeared in the shape of an animal or of the sun, or manifested itself as a voice sounding in space—these were all forces which could take pity on an individual in his helplessness. "I have taken pity on you" was a standing formula used by these powers. The Crow Indians regarded the connexion between the protective spirit and man as one of adoption.

The outward signs of the connexion were the sacred bundles which contained the relevant "medicine"—a skin, for example, a feather, or other parts of the animal which had appeared to him. They were in a sense charms, though they worked not magically but by the force of the power contacted in the revelation. The owner of the bundle was required to observe certain taboos and to know the peculiar rites and songs connected with the use of the bundles. The curious thing is that among the Blackfoot, for example, the bundles —and thus the sacred power in them—were the subject of widespread trading, so that practically all the medicine bundles would have belonged at some time or other to one of the more important members of the tribe. But this was not the general custom. The Mandan, who also traded their bundles, thought that this increased their power, while if they took part in a warlike expedition their power decreased. After the fourth such expedition their power had practically disappeared and the owner then lived in peace.

In addition to the more personal bundles there were others which served the welfare of the tribe as a whole and were in a sense objects of common veneration: such things as the sacred pipe of the Arapahos together with an ear of maize and a crude stone figure representing a tortoise which had been preserved since the beginning of the world. Other examples are the four medicine arrows of the Cheyenne and the *taime* of the Kiowa, a little stone figure with the sun and moon painted on its breast. Among the Pawnee, in whose religion star worship was a prominent feature, each village had its own "star map" painted on bison skin.

Generally speaking the medicine bundles and the rites concerning them were more highly developed in the Pawnee than in any other tribe. A curious thing is that they all contained an ear of maize and were the centre of a number of fertility rites which started with the first spring thunder, reached their climax at the summer solstice, when there was a human sacrifice, and did not end before the autumn. An entirely new plains cult which started at the beginning of the nineteenth century, was linked to the horse, which was thought to have supernatural powers. Organized under a special leader, its object was to heal the sick and bring herds of bison within range.

Contact with divine powers manifested itself in other ways besides the experience of revelations and the receipt of "medicine". Their influence on people's lives was boundless and their help was required on all occasions of any importance.

Aid was invoked by prayer and sacrifice while tobacco smoke was solemnly blown to the four corners of the earth, to the heavens and to the soil. More energetic steps might also be taken. When the evening star appeared to a Pawnee in a dream or a vision, it was a sign that this powerful deity, to whom the most sacred of the tribe's bundles was dedicated, demanded a sacrifice. A young girl captured from another tribe was then lashed to a scaffold and shot with arrows—a custom strongly reminiscent of certain Mexican rites connected with Xipe, "Our Lord, the Flayed One", the Aztec god of planting. But human sacrifice was for the most part extremely rare on the plains, unless the offering of scalps, which to some extent turned the killing of an enemy into a sacred action, is included. Blackfoot warriors used to cut out bits of their own flesh and sacrifice them to the sun.

This brings us to self-torture. It was not enough to try and make contact with the supernatural powers by means of dreams and revelation on a single occasion. Whenever some important event was imminent, it was necessary to find out the will of the divine power and in doing this self-torture was a powerful aid. In some tribes it was so customary to chop off a finger joint that not one of the older men had all of them left. The Dakota, Assiniboine and certain others went even further. Of their own free will they had holes cut through the muscles of their chest and back. Sticks were then pushed into the wounds and the unhappy victim was hoisted to the ceiling by thongs fastened to the sticks. The more fanatical also had sticks pushed through the muscles of their legs, and to increase their pain heavy bison skulls were then hung from them. Thus they hung without food or drink for two, three or even four days in succession, staring at the sun or out into space, until their sufferings and delirium had their effect and brought them the vision they sought.

Closely related forms of torture were the annual *okipa* ceremony of the Mandan—a dramatic representation of the creation of the earth and all living things, which ensured the welfare of the tribe and the fertility of the bison—and the far more widespread Sun Dance. The name is something of a misnomer, for it was not exclusively connected with the sun. It took place among a great number of plains Indians including all the typical hunting tribes except the Comanches. There were also closely related ceremonies in other tribes. The various forms of Sun Dance quite obviously have a common origin, for certain basic elements are common to them all. It is evidently a combination of many widely differing features, some of which disappeared as it spread, others of which were added. Since there are some eighty different features in all, fourteen of which may be described as basic, there can be an infinite number of variations in the dance as performed. The Sun Dance was performed in its most highly developed form by the Atsina. Tribes nearer the border of the plains area were satisfied with much poorer forms.

With all its preparations, the dance extended over a whole week, and was always held in the summer, when the tribe had gathered for the great bison hunt. It took place in fulfilment of a promise by a person whose life had been in danger, or had met with some violent accident, but it was the concern of the whole tribe and the members of the various brotherhoods took part in the ceremony in turns.

Preparations started in a tent erected near the middle of the camp circle. Here the originator of the festival and his comrades came together to learn the dance, to receive instruction in how to paint the body (which varied according to the ceremonies) and to be rehearsed in the sacred songs. While this was proceeding, others collected sufficient bison tongues for the feast, and the hunters set off to obtain the skin of a bull bison. In the centre of the camp circle a dancing arena was erected. This can best be described as the open framework of posts and spars for a round house with a conical roof. But the most important was still to come—the centre post. A scout was sent off to find a suitable tree. This was an honourable task, and the Cheyenne would entrust it only to a man who, as a scout on the warpath, had killed an enemy in his own tent. The tree was felled and the warriors in full array counted their "coups" on it as if it were a real enemy. A bunch of twigs, often described as the thunder-bird's nest, was tied to the top; lower down the bull skin and various sacrificial offerings were fastened. A shrine surrounded by green branches was set up in the enclosure, a bison skull at its centre. An important feature of the shrine was the "earth painting" produced by sprinkling dried coloured powder in symbolic patterns.

Now at last the actual dance could begin. After having undergone a ritual cleansing consisting of a sweat bath and several days of fasting, the man whose promise had instigated the dance assembled with his companions round the ceremonial pole. Then, with their naked trunks painted in bright colours, wearing the fantastic headdress of warriors, and blowing whistles of eagle bone they began to dance. Dancing chiefly consisted of staying in one spot, raising themselves on their toes and staring at the sun. In this way they manifested their desire that the earth might be blessed and every living thing flourish—this in fact was the thought behind the whole complicated and protracted ceremony.

The Dakota and other tribes added self-torture to the pattern, and as a special sign of piety they pushed sticks through their skin—in the same way as they did at the vision quest—and fastened thongs from them to the ceremonial pole; then they continued to dance until the sticks were torn out of their bleeding flesh.

This description of the Sun Dance of course gives only the barest outline of the ceremony. It lacks, as it were, both colour and atmosphere. But with a little imagination one can picture the scene, the enthusiasm of the participants and of the swarm of spectators under the burning sun, the shouting and singing, the picturesque processions, the solemn symbolism which imbued each separate colour and movement with an inner meaning, the deafening music of the drums and whistles, the pious devotion and wild excitement . . . in short everything which touched the innermost being of the Indians and transformed what to us was a strange and barbaric rite into a deeply religious ceremony.

Nor must we forget the significance these annual gatherings had in providing a link between all the members of the tribe and an occasion for them to come together and demonstrate the tribal strength. Many an important decision has been made by elders gathered round the council fire, many a daring campaign planned by impatient and ambitious youngsters, many a romance started under the influence of the mysteries of the Sun Dance.

The deep inner craving for religion which so affects the behaviour of the plains Indians has manifested itself right down to the present day. An example of this is the Grass Dance or Omaha Dance as it is also—somewhat unfortunately—known, for it originated with the Pawnee and not with the Omaha. Not before the end of the last century did it spread to the Dakota, Arapaho and others, and it is now to be found not only over most of the northern plains but also among the neighbouring plateau tribes west of the Rocky Mountains. The participants, who wear a curious crest-shaped headgear of stiff animal hair, dance by night in special buildings, feast on dog meat and make gifts to the poor.

None of the religious movements of modern times has had such a fateful influence as the great revival, which, under the name of the Ghost Dance, spread across the plains like wildfire in the last decades of the nineteenth century. It actually originated in the plateau area, where in a delirium a young Paiute imagined he had experienced the revelation of a new doctrine. An Indian Messiah would appear on the earth, all palefaces would be banished, bison would again be plentiful in the hunting grounds and the golden age would return. A vital factor in hastening the new millennium was the dance, and during its performances many of the participants dropped in ecstasy. The certainty of victory felt by the revivalists was certainly not lessened by the painted shirts which they were given and which were said to make the wearers invulnerable.

Throughout the territory minds became inflamed. Among the Dakota, with the memory of their expulsion from Black Hills fresh in their minds (see page 77), it led to serious disturbances. Their leader was the renowned Sitting Bull, an outstanding warrior with all the fervour of a fresh convert. Finally, the United States' authorities intervened, Sitting Bull was shot by native police during an attempt to arrest him, and soon after the whole movement was dealt a mortal blow in the frightful massacre of Wounded Knee.

Another revival which has gained many supporters in fairly recent times is what is known as the Peyote Cult. Peyote is the name of a small cactus (*Lophophora Williamsii*) which is found in the region bordering the Rio Grande and in Mexico. It is mentioned as early as the sixteenth century by the old Spanish author Sahagún, who refers to its narcotic effect, and it is still the focus of extensive ceremonies practised by certain Mexican tribes. In the United States it has long been known to the Comanches, Kiowas and certain other tribes in the south-west. About 1890 it gave rise to a number of ceremonies towards which the partaking of peyote, visions and Christian rites all contributed.

In the course of a few years they spread across the whole of the plains area, except for the far north, and they also found acceptance among several tribes in the woodland region of the Great Lakes. Both the Ghost Dance and the Peyote Cult are outstanding examples of culture diffusion, for in both cases the movements can be traced historically. But they also point a timely warning against the widely held belief that a widespread culture element must necessarily be old.

It was widely believed by the plains Indians that a person had one or more souls which left his body at death. Sometimes it was believed that one of the souls died. As soon as death occurred,

In the Mandan tribe descent was traced in the female line although almost every male belonged to one of a system of brotherhoods in which a spirit of militarism was dominant. Even horse-stealing was organized as a military operation and, as this drawing of the interior of a dwelling shows, the tribe's most valuable animals as well as the human beings were accommodated therein.

An encampment of the Dakota Indians. This was the tribe that, driven to desperation by having the land which had been allotted to it by the government overrun by prospectors seeking gold and despite the realized inevitability of military defeat, went on the warpath and at the Little Bighorn River annihilated a force commanded by General Custer. Eventually the tribe was deprived of a third of its territory. On the right is shown a platform burial.

everyone broke into the most frightful wailing and demonstrated their anguish by cutting off their hair and making deep gashes in their arms and breast. The corpse was painted and ornamented as though it were still living. As Schiller puts it:

Farben auch, den Leib zu malen,
Steckt ihm in die Hand,
Dass er röthlich möge strahlen
In der Seelen Land.

In certain cases, among the Comanches for example, the corpse was then tied up and buried in a chasm west of the camp. Usually, however, it was first wrapped at full length in skins and then placed on a platform in a suitable tree or on tall posts. On rare occasions cremation was practised. The soul was believed to remain in the vicinity of the grave for four days, after which it started on its long journey to the Land of the Dead. This was situated either in the sky or in a distant country. There it lived a shadow existence, chasing shadow bison on the happy hunting grounds—a pale reflection of the life once existing on the plains and now long since disappeared.

* * *

The foregoing description has considered equally the semi-agricultural tribes to the east and in the Missouri Valley as well as the bison hunters in the more limited sense on the high plains. But as we have seen, it was among the latter that plains culture achieved its most highly developed form, and this was a direct result of the introduction of the horse: a clear example of the way a historical event and geographical adaptation can work hand in hand.

As already mentioned, the Indians took over several elements connected with the horse: the saddle, stirrups, the lasso and castration. Furthermore, several established features of their culture were transformed and some entirely new ones were added. The travois, originally for dogs, became larger. In consequence tent-poles and tent-sheets—and thus the whole tent—became bigger.

On the other hand the bow was shortened so that it suited the new conditions. And whereas the operation of driving bison into enclosures had previously been carried out on foot, this was now carried out on horseback.

Encircling the bison on horseback had its counterpart in the fire encirclement of earlier times. But the training of horses for the purpose was something new. So, of course, was the horse cult. Finally, let us not forget that the coming of the horse undoubtedly eased the women's burden; formerly they had to participate to a much greater extent in the constant struggle for food, apart from the fact that quite literally they had to carry a greater share of the burden in moving camp. The actual ownership of horses sowed the seeds of a kind of capitalism which was really completely foreign to the spirit of Indian society.

These are positive features of adjustment. But there were also negative features which led to a number of cultural losses. The first tribes to suffer were those coming from the east. They were forced to abandon agriculture—not because it was incompatible with bison hunting (for on the low prairie the two flourished side by side) but simply because the high plains, except for the river valleys, were unsuited to it. And when agriculture disappeared the permanent villages disappeared as well. Life on horseback seems to have been responsible for the disappearance of pottery, perhaps too for the almost complete disintegration of the clan systems and for the marked emphasis in the kinship systems on the generations as opposed to the kindred.

At first sight it seems astonishing that an area which acquired a large part of its population as late as the high plains did can display such a remarkable impression of cultural uniformity. The explanation is not far to seek and again would seem to have a geographical basis. With no interior boundaries and with much the same conditions prevailing both north and south, the country is one vast melting pot, where the most widely differing peoples—Athapaskans from the north, Algonkian and Siouan tribes from the east, Uto-Aztecans from the west and Caddoans from the south—came together and had their mode of life forced into similar channels, while at the same time there was an interaction of influences between them. Nothing gives clearer proof of this than the Sun Dance, in which elements of widely differing origin have been welded together into one of the most characteristic features of plains culture.

But the culture was not to exist for very long. Scarcely a century after it had developed into full flower it wilted under the impact of foreign immigrants who had in fact been partly responsible for causing it to blossom—and who had given a solemn promise that the country west of the Mississippi would remain for all time in the possession of its rightful owners.

BIBLIOGRAPHY

A general survey of culture in the plains is given by ROBERT H. LOWIE: *Indians of the Plains*, New York, 1954. Cf. also A. L. KRŒBER: "Cultural and Natural Areas of Native North America" (*Univ. Calif. Public. Amer. Anthrop. Ethnol.*, xxxviii, Berkeley, 1939). For prehistoric times, see W. DUNCAN STRONG: "From History to Prehistory in the Northern Great Plains" (*Smithson Miscell. Coll., c.*, Washington, 1940). WALDO R. WEDEL: "Culture Sequence in the Central Great Plains" (*Smithson Miscell. Coll., c.*, Washington, 1940). WALDO R. WEDEL: "Environment and Native Subsistence Economies in the Central Great Plains" (*Smithson Miscell. Coll., c.*, 3, Washington, 1941). WALDO R. WEDEL: "Culture Chronology in the Central Great Plains" (*Amer. Antiquity*, xii, Menasha, 1946-7). See too various treatises in JAMES B. GRIFFIN (ed.): *Archæology of Eastern United States*, Chicago, 1952.

Descriptions of the golden age of culture in the plains occur in numerous older works, i.a.—G. CATLIN: *Illustrations of the Manners, Customs, and Condition of the North American Indians*, i-ii, 7th ed., London, 1848. EDWIN THOMPSON DENIG: "Indian Tribes of the Upper Missouri", ed. J. N. B. Hewitt (*46th Ann. Rep. Bur. Ethnol.*, Washington, 1930). LEWIS AND CLARKE: *Travels to the Source of the Missouri River and across the American Continent*, London, 1814. WALTER MCCLINTOCK: *The Old North Trail*, London, 1919. MAXIMILIAN, PRINZ ZU WIED: *Reise in das innere Nord-America*, i-ii, Coblenz, 1839-41. An interesting picture seen from the point of view of the Indians is provided by CHIEF BUFFALO CHILD LONG LANCE: *The Autobiography of a Blackfoot Indian Chief*.

For works on the individual tribes, see ALFRED W. BOWERS: *Mandan Social and Ceremonial Organization*, Chicago, 1950. RICHARD DANGEL: "Tirawa, der höchste Gott der Pawnee" (*Arch. f. Religionswissensch.*, xxviii, Leipzig u. Berlin, 1929). J. OWEN DORSEY: "Omaha Sociology" (*3rd Ann. Rep. Bur. Ethnol.*, Washington, 1884). J. OWEN DORSEY: "A Study of Siouan Cults" (*11th Ann. Rep. Bur. Ethnol.*, Washington, 1894). J. OWEN DORSEY: "Omaha Dwellings, Furniture and Implements" (*13th Ann. Rep. Bur. Ethnol.*, Washington, 1896). J. OWEN DORSEY: "Siouan Sociology" (*14th Ann. Rep. Bur. Ethnol.*, Washington, 1897). GEORGE A. DORSEY: "The Cheyenne, I-II" (*Field Columb. Mus. Publ. Anthrop. Ser.*, ix, Chicago, 1905). JOHN C. EWERS: "The Horse in Blackfoot Indian Culture" (*Bur. Amer. Ethnol. Bull. 159*, Washington, 1955). ALICE C. FLETCHER: "The Hako, a Pawnee Ceremony" (*22nd Ann. Rep. Bur. Ethnol.*, Washington, 1903). ALICE C. FLETCHER AND FRANCIS LA FLESCHE: "The Omaha Tribe" (*27th Ann. Rep. Bur. Ethnol.*, Washington, 1911). FRANCIS LA FLESCHE: "The Osage Tribe" (*36th, 39th,*

43rd, 45th Ann. Rep. Bur. Ethnol., Washington, 1921, 1925, 1928, 1930). MALVIN R. GILMORE: "Notes on Arikara Tribal Organization" (*Ind. Notes*, iv, New York, 1927). GEORGE BIRD GRINNELL: *The Cheyenne Indians*, i-ii, New Haven, 1923. DIAMOND JENNESS: "The Sarcee Indians of Alberta" (*Nat. Mus. Canada Anthrop. Ser. 23*, Ottawa, 1938). A. L. KRŒBER: "The Arapaho" (*Bull. Amer. Mus. Natur. Hist.*, xviii, New York, 1902-7). A. L. KRŒBER: "Ethnology of the Gros Ventre" (*Amer. Mus. Natur. Hist. Anthrop. Pap. I*, 4, New York, 1908). STEPHEN H. LONG: *Account of an Expedition from Pittsburgh to the Rocky Mountains*, i-ii, Philadelphia, 1823. ROBERT H. LOWIE: "The Assiniboine" (*Amer. Mus. Natur. Hist. Anthrop. Pap. IV*, 1, New York, 1909). ROBERT H. LOWIE: "The Northern Shoshone" (*Amer. Mus. Natur. Hist. Anthrop. Pap. II*, 2, New York, 1909). ROBERT H. LOWIE: "Societies of the Arikara Indians" (*Amer. Mus. Natur. Hist. Anthrop. Pap. XI*, New York, 1915). ROBERT H. LOWIE: "Societies of the Crow, Hidatsa and Mandan Indians" (*Amer. Mus. Natur. Hist*, xi, New York, 1916). ROBERT H. LOWIE: "Social Life of the Crow Indians" (*Amer. Mus. Natur. Hist. Anthrop. Pap. IX*, 2, New York, 1912). ROBERT H. LOWIE: "Social Life of the Crow Indians" (*Amer. Mus. Natur. Hist. Anthrop. Pap. IX*, 2, New York, 1912). ROBERT H. LOWIE: "The Religion of the Crow Indians" (*Amer. Mus. Natur. Hist. Anthrop. Pap. XXV*, 2, New York, 1922). ROBERT H. LOWIE: "The Material Culture of the Crow Indians" (*Amer. Mus. Natur. Hist. Anthrop. Pap. XXI*, 3, New York, 1922). ROBERT H. LOWIE: *The Crow Indians*, New York, 1935. DAVID G. MANDELBAUM: "The Plains Cree" (*Amer. Mus. Natur. Hist. Anthrop. Pap. XXXVII*, 2, New York, 1940). JAMES MOONEY: "The Cheyenne Indians" (*Mem. Amer. Anthrop. Assoc.*, i, 6, Lancaster, 1907). JAMES MOONEY: "Calendar History of the Kiowa Indians" (*17th Ann. Rep. Bur. Ethnol.*, Washington, 1900). J. R. MURIE: "Pawnee Indian Societies" (*Amer. Mus. Natur. Hist. Anthrop. Pap. XI*, 7, New York, 1914). ALANSON SKINNER: "Ethnology of the Ioway Indians" (*Bull. Publ. Mus. Milwaukee*, v, 4, Milwaukee, 1926). A. SKINNER: "Political Organization, Cults, and Ceremonies of the Plains-Ojibway and Plains-Cree Indians" (*Amer. Mus. Natur. Hist. Anthrop. Pap. XI*, New York, 1914). ERNEST WALLACE AND E. ADAMSON HŒBEL: *The Comanche*, Norman, 1952. WILSON D. WALLIS: "The Canadian Dakota" (*Amer. Mus. Natur. Hist. Anthrop. Pap. XLI*, 1, New York, 1947). W. WHITMAN: "The Oto" (*Columbia Univ. Contrib. Anthrop.*, xxviii, New York, 1937). G. F. WILL AND HERBERT SPINDEN: "The Mandans" (*Pap. Peabody Mus. Amer. Archæol. Ethnol.*, iii, 4, Cambridge, Mass., 1906). GILBERT L. WILSON: "Agriculture of the Hidatsa Indians" (*Univ. Minn. Stud. Soc. Sci.*, ix, Minneapolis, 1917). GILBERT L. WILSON: "Agriculture of the Hidatsa Indians" (*Univ. Minn. Stud. Soc. Sci.*, ix, Minneapolis, 1917). GILBERT L. WILSON: "The Horse and the Dog in Hidatsa Culture" (*Amer. Mus. Natur. Hist. Anthrop. Pap. XV*, 2, New York, 1924). GILBERT L. WILSON: "The Hidatsa Earth Lodge" (*Amer. Mus. Natur. Hist. Anthrop. Pap. XXXIII*, 5, New York, 1934). CLARK WISSLER: "Material Culture of the Blackfoot Indians" (*Amer. Mus. Natur. Hist. Anthrop. Pap. V*, 1, New York, 1910). JOHN M. COOPER: The Gros ventres of Montana.

Religion and Ritual." (*Cathol. Univ. Amer. Anthrop. Ser.* 16, Washington, 1956). REGINA FLANNERY: "The Gros Ventres of Montana. 1, Social Life." (*Cathol. Univ. Amer. Authrop. Ser.*, 15, Washington, 1953).

For particular aspects of the plains culture in general see KAJ BIRKET-SMITH: "A Geographic Study of the Early History of the Algonquian Indians" (*Internat. Arch. f. Ethnogr.*, xxiv, Leiden, 1918). DAVID I. BUSHNELL: "Villages of the Algonquian, Siouan, and Caddoan Tribes West of the Mississippi" (*Bur. Amer. Ethno. Bull. 77*, Washington, 1922). JOSEF HÆCKEL: "Totemismus und Zweiklassensystem bei den Sioux-Indianern" (*Anthropos*, xxxii, Mödling, 1937). RALPH LINTON: "The Origin of the Plains Earth Lodge" (*Amer. Anthrop. N. s.*, xxvi, Lancaster, 1924). ROBERT H. LOWIE: "Plains Indian Age Societies" (*Amer. Mus. Natur. Hist. Anthrop. Pap. XI*, 13, New York, 1916). ROBERT H. LOWIE: "Reflections on the Plains Indians" (*Anthrop. Quarterly*, xxviii, 2, Washington, 1955). B. MISHKIN: "Rank and Warfare among the Plains Indians" (*Monogr. Amer. Ethnol. Soc.*, iii, New York, 1940). JAMES MOONEY: "The Ghost Dance Religion and the Sioux Outbreak of 1890" (*14th Ann. Rep. Bur. Ethnol.*, Washington, 1899). FRANK GILBERT ROE: *The Indian and the Horse*, Norman, 1955 (the section on hereditary biology should be read with great reserve!). HALFDAN SIIGER: "Indianerne og Bisonen" (*Geogr. Tidsskr.*, xlvii, Copenhagen, 1944-5). LESLIE SPIER: "The Sun Dance of the Plains Indians" (*Amer. Mus. Natur. Hist. Anthrop. Pap. XVI*, 7, New York, 1921). CLARK WISSLER: "The Influence of the Horse in the Development of Plains Culture" (*Amer. Anthrop. N. s.*, xvi, Lancaster, 1914). CLARK WISSLER: "Riding Gear of the North American Indians" (*Amer. Mus. Natur. Hist. Anthrop. Pap. XVII*, 1, New York, 1915). CLARK WISSLER: "Costumes of the Plains Indians" (*Amer. Mus. Natur. Hist. Anthrop. Pap. XVII*, 2, New York, 1916).

REGINA FLANNERY: "The Gros Ventres of Montana. I—Social Life" (*Cath. Univ. Amer. Anthrop. Ser.*, 15, Washington, 1953). JOHN M. COOPER: "The Gros Ventres. Religion and Ritual" (*Cath. Univ. Amer. Anthrop. Ser.*, 16, Washington, 1956).

THE LAPPS

Hunters and Nomads

Reindeer

MOST travellers to the north of Scandinavia remember their encounter with the Lapps as a colourful experience of something far off and strange. To the local peasants the Lapps, as they pass by with their enormous herds of reindeer, are something of a thorn in the flesh. To jurists and statesmen their seasonal wanderings and their long-standing contempt of state boundaries and international problems have proved a trial of professional skill and diplomacy. To scientists they are a mystery—the only purely European Arctic people and the first of any Arctic peoples to be known. Their way of life is as completely adjusted to Arctic conditions as that of the Eskimo—though in a completely different way. And in many respects they and their origins remain a mystery to this day.

The first reference to the Lapps, then described as Finns (*Fenni*), is in the year A.D. 98, when Trajan became Roman Emperor. The reference is in Tacitus, who writes:

> "They live like savages in a state of frightful poverty. They have no weapons, no horses, no houses even. For food they have wild herbs, for clothes animal skins, for a bed the earth. They put all their faith in their arrows which, in the absence of iron, are tipped with bone."

Later, in the middle of the sixth century, the Lapps reappear in the works of the Byzantine historian, Procopius, under the name of "Stride-Finns" (*skrithiphinoi*). The first part of the word is obviously a derivation of an old Norse word meaning to stride, and refers to their use of skis. Two centuries later there is a description of skis, the learned Paulus Diaconus, author of the history of the Lombards, writing:

> "Their name derives from the word in their barbaric tongue meaning to run, because they chase wild animals by running on a board bent artificially like a bow. They have an animal not unlike the hart. And from its skin, hairy as it is, I have seen a garment like that said to be worn by these *scritobini*. It was made like a tunic and reached down to the knees."

Finns is the old Norse name for the Lapps and has been preserved in Norway down to our own times. The word Lapps, or rather Lapland, does not occur before about A.D. 1200, when Saxo Grammaticus writes of *utraque Lappia*, i.e. the regions on either side of the Gulf of Bothnia. This is doubtless derived from Lappi, the Finnish name for Lapmark, though according to Wiklund it was originally no more perhaps than a name for an out-of-the-way deserted region. The Lapps describe themselves as *sameh* (sing. *sabme*) and are anxious for this term to be adopted in Norway and Sweden.

The popular impression of the Lapps as a largely nomadic people will not stand close examination. Of the 32,600 odd souls nowadays reckoned as Lapps, by far the majority—about 20,000—live in Norway, and of them only a small minority are nomadic reindeer herdsmen. By far the greater number are settled fishermen and sealers on the Arctic coast. In Sweden the Lapps are far fewer, in all scarcely 9,000, and again less than a third of them are nomads. In Finland the Lapps are fewer still—about 2,500—and in the Soviet Union 1,800.

Few in numbers though the population is, it is scattered over an enormous area, from North Cape as far south as the Røràs district in Norway and down to northern Dalecarlia in Sweden, and from the Atlantic coast to the eastern point of the Kola Peninsula. The Lapps are in a majority only in the northern districts, i.e. in the counties of Finmark and Troms in Norway, in Norrbotten and Västerbotten in Sweden, and in Utsjoki and Enontekiö, the narrow arm of Finland which stretches in between Norway and Sweden. In the south they keep mostly to the mountain districts.

Reindeer in their pen, a photograph taken at Lycksele by E. Manker. Fences of this type, sometimes miles in length and built on converging lines, were employed in the autumn and early winter, when the big collective hunts were organized, to drive entire herds towards a lake, in the waters of which the huntsmen could easily overtake their swimming prey, or over a precipice where the animals not killed by the fall were killed by waiting hunters.

Above: Kautokeino Lapps with reindeer and sledges: though used as draught animals, the reindeer are not ridden. Lapp clothing is more or less the same for both men and women, the basic garment being the simple poncho. To this day a poncho of bear-cub skin is worn above normal clothing by herdsmen.

Left: Milk utensils of the Swedish Lapps: at the top is a cheese-mould of coiled basketry; the other utensils (cheese-mould, milking cup, milk funnel and basin) are of wood. All are in the National Museum, Copenhagen.

Right: A woman of the Vittangi Lapps scraping a reindeer hide.

Below: A woman of the Karesuando Lapps milking a reindeer. Though the yield is small, reindeer milk has the fat content of cream.

Dwellings of the Lapps: (*above*) an old earth lodge in Finnmark; here, in a region of fjords and low mountains, precipitation is high and the winters are cold, so that substantial shelter is essential.

Below: An arched-post tent of the Kautokeino Lapps. In the foreground are sledges.

But as late as the eighteenth century they were to be found in the forests of Ångermanland.

As early as the seventeenth century, however, Swedes had begun to settle in the regions near to the principal rivers and lakes, and ever since then the forest Lapps have been steadily retreating. East of the Torne River Lapps are no longer found south of the 67° latitude. In former times they lived scattered over most of Finland. There are Lapp place names right down to the Gulf of Finland, and at the beginning of the Christian era there seem to have been Lapps still farther south in Ingria. Their gradual disappearance from southern Finland is closely connected with the reduced numbers of wild reindeer for, as we shall see later, they were chiefly huntsmen.

As early as the thirteenth century Swedes began to settle on the coast of Österbotten and ousted the Lapps. Farther inland things developed more slowly. So long as penetration northward by Finnish peasants was scattered and thin, the Lapps could get by on the plenitude of game in the forests; but as the scale of settlement increased and the settlers practised burning the forests for agriculture on a large scale, things became more difficult for the Lapps and they had either to withdraw northwards or were absorbed by the settlers. In Tavastland and southern Carelia they disappeared during the course of the Middle Ages; in Savolaks they held on until about the year 1600 and in the interior of Österbotten and northern Carelia they survived still longer.

Who precisely are the Lapps? To which race do they in fact belong? The old idea that they are purely and simply "Mongols" is no longer acceptable. But where these small, lean people with their swarthy, wrinkled skin, curious screwed-up faces and pointed chins really belong is still one of the unsolved mysteries of physical anthropology. In some respects they do not even constitute a racial unit. In spite of all their similarities and the inevitable admixture of Scandinavian and Finnish blood which has taken place down the centuries, there remains a not inconsiderable difference between the eastern and western Lapps, a difference which is reflected in their language and also to an extent in their culture.

True, they are all brachycephalic—but in the former the skull is low and the distribution of blood groups corresponds to that found in eastern Europe. In the Scandinavian Lapps we find a high cranium, and the distribution of blood groups corresponds to that usual in western Europe. There is no doubt that in the eastern Lapps there is a racial strain which is also found in the Samoyeds east of the White Sea. But some anthropologists believe them to be also akin to remote European racial elements. In the Valdai Hills south of Lake Ladoga bones of a Stone Age people have been found which are reminiscent of the Lapps, and even in Poland traces of Lapp-like elements are said to occur.

The language provides fewer difficulties—seemingly. No one has any doubt that it is related to Finnish and thus belongs to the big Finno-Ugrian group which, with Samoyed, constitutes the Uralian linguistic stock. Even though present day Lappish and Finnish appear to differ widely, they are not so far apart that they could not have sounded almost identical 2,000 years ago.

But the Finns are so different physically from the Lapps that the difference in the two races cannot possibly have been brought about in such a brief space of time. The only reasonable explanation seems to be that one of the two races must have changed its language. Two contrasting views are held on this. According to one, advanced by Professor K. B. Wiklund, the Lapps at some time borrowed their present language from their Finnish neighbours. There are stray words in Lappish which are possible survivals of a pre-Finnish original language. There are a few place names too—such well-known names as Luleå, Sulitelma and Abisko are examples. According to others—and foremost among them are the Finnish linguist Eliel Lagercrantz and Wiklund's successor, Björn Collinder—the situation is precisely the reverse. They believe that the Lapps originally spoke a Uralian language, possibly akin to Samoyed, and that it is the west Finnish peoples (the true Finns, Esthonians, Livonians, etc.) who have exchanged their former mother-tongue for Finno-Ugrian.

If this is so, it would provide an explanation of the racial similarity between the eastern Lapps, the Samoyeds and the Ugrian tribes of Siberia. But it provides no explanation of the more European appearance of the western Lapps. Perhaps the answer must be sought in archæology.

Romantic archæological researches of a hundred years ago saw the Lapps as the aboriginal population of Scandinavia. Curiously enough, this idea has been revived by modern science, though in a different way. In 1925 the Norwegian archæologist, Anders Nummedal, began a series of excavations which lasted many years and which completely upset all the beliefs which had hitherto been held about the oldest human settlements on the Arctic coast. One site after another was found on the coast of Finnmark, containing curious crude stone artefacts which were in many ways reminiscent of the primitive tools left behind by Ice Age people farther south.

We now have a pretty fair knowledge of the old Finnmark or Komsa culture, the area of which stretches from Alta Fjord to the north coast of Kola. At one time the region must have been inhabited by a hunting people who scraped a living together by fishing and hunting on land and sea in much the same way as the people of Greenland do. The similarity with the Greenlanders goes further, for at the time when the Komsa culture was at its height, the mountains of the interior were largely buried under the remains of the great Ice Age glaciers and an icy sea lapped the bare coasts. Though it cannot be proved, it is possible that the Komsa people are the distant ancestors of the western Lapps.

Opinions as to the origin of this culture are still divided. Some seek its links eastwards across the Kola Peninsula—either right the way across to Siberia, or failing that to Russia and Poland. One archæologist considers the related and largely contemporaneous Fosna culture between Trondheim and Bergen to be an offshoot of the Komsa culture.

In contrast to this, Johannes Brøndsted maintains that it is the Komsa culture which is derived from the Fosna culture, and that its roots are to be found in the Holstein and Danish Ahrensburg and Lyngby culture from about 10,000 B.C.*

* The idea, advanced by Wiklund, that the Komsa culture goes back to the last interglacial period has, however, never gained acceptance among archæologists.

This would, perhaps, explain the peculiar racial characteristics of the western Lapps, provided, of course, that at some time they acquired their present Uralian language from the eastern Lapps. But it must be emphasized that this is only a possibility, not a fact. The western Lapp type may perhaps be merely the result of an admixture of Nordic blood which has been going on at least since the time of the Vikings.

Later Stone Age and Bronze Age finds on the Arctic coast are few and not very informative. Not until the Iron Age do any clear lines emerge. The question as to who were the bearers of the oldest cultures is still open. What is certain, however, is that the graves from Nesseby in Varanger and Olennii Ostrov on the Kola Peninsula—where stone was still being used—as well as the finds belonging to a later period at Kjelmøy in Varanger, are all Lappish. The date of the excavations at Kjelmøy is put at A.D. 400-500, thus corresponding to the beginning of the late Danish Iron Age. They provide evidence of a typical fishing and sealing culture with implements of bone, antler and iron together with comb pottery which has some affinities to Russian and Siberian types.

So much for habitation on the coast. Things look different when we inquire into the distribution of Lapps inland. The later Stone Age in Finland and northern Scandinavia, which so far as northern Norway is concerned starts about 2,300 B.C., is characterized by slate tools, and pottery similar to that found at Kjelmøy. These are in fact the westernmost evidence of a circumpolar hunting culture. In Norway it extends as far south as Romsdal, and traces of it can be followed right across to north-eastern North America. To what extent its presence in Scandinavia is due wholly or in part to the Lapps cannot be determined with absolute certainty. But the idea is not impossible.

It is perhaps worth mentioning in this connexion that some of the place names on the Møre coast between Trondheim and Molde are said to be survivals of an old Lapp settlement, and that a peculiar form of heavy, edge-ground stone implement, the Rovaniemi axe of northern Scandinavia, and certain bronze axes in Finland, are attributed to the Lapps. Evidence that bronze was known in early times appears from the fact that, in contrast to the names of other metals, the term for bronze is pure Lappish. Finds of skis from *circa* 2000 B.C. are also regarded as evidence that the Lapps must have been present in northern Sweden as early as the late Stone Age.

Gustaf Hallström, on the other hand, and Wiklund too, maintain that the Lapps did not make their push from the Arctic coast before the middle of the last millennium prior to the Christian era. And why just then? Because, it is said, of the climate. In the milder climate which prevailed all over Scandinavia throughout the later Stone and Bronze Ages, the southern type of deciduous forest extended to the far north of Finland and the Scandinavian Peninsula, and wild reindeer would hardly have flourished in such conditions. And so long as reindeer breeding was unknown, only wild reindeer could have formed the basis of the Lapps' existence.

Then at the beginning of the Iron Age a deterioration of the climate took place. The summers became colder and damper. The spruce made its way across Finland and Sweden from the east, and in its wake came the reindeer. The "Fimbul winter" descended on the country.

It was a heavy blow to the agricultural Bronze Age inhabitants of the region. Extreme poverty characterizes Finnish finds of the period. But to the ancestors of the Lapps the change meant that they moved south into the interior of the country where reindeer hunting attracted them. If, on the other hand, the later Stone Age finds are Lappish, of which there is much evidence, then the deterioration of the climate must at most have caused a renewed push southwards.

However that may be, sometime during the Iron Age reindeer breeding must have been introduced, and it certainly came from the east. So far, the earliest traces of domesticated reindeer are in the form of a pair of small wooden figures which were the result of archæological excavations in the Minusinsk region in southern Siberia some years ago. This find dates from the first or second century A.D. Some centuries later, *circa* 500, tame reindeer are mentioned in a Chinese source. Moreover, it is certain that reindeer breeding was known in Scandinavia in the second half of the ninth century, for at that time Ottar, "who of all Norsemen lived farthest north", owned many reindeer which were presumably tended by Lapp herdsmen. But the southern or woodland Lapps in particular remained essentially huntsmen and fishermen right to the close of the Middle Ages, and even after then their reindeer herds were always small in comparison with those of the mountain Lapps.

We shall not delve into the subject of reindeer domestication here. Suffice to say that it seems to have proceeded at two tempi. The older form was certainly the direct result of the method of hunting, individual reindeer being used as decoys. Gradually they were also used as draught animals for sledges, in the same way as dogs had long been used. But it was not until much later, under the influence of horse and cattle breeding from the south, that reindeer came to be used as riding and milking animals. This last development evidently came about independently in two widely separated areas—eastern Siberia and Scandinavia. It is significant that Lapp words for such things as milking, etc., evince a long standing connexion with the Scandinavians and that—in contrast to the Siberian Soyot and Tungus—the Lapps never ride on reindeer. Even today there is a considerable difference in the way the reindeer is used by different groups of Lapps. Right down to our own time neither the Russian nor the Finnish Lapps milk their reindeer.

* * *

The common basis of reindeer breeding is thus an ancient hunting and fishing culture, and a description of the economic life of the Lapps might most suitably begin by elaborating that.

The Lapps were sustained by hunting wild reindeer, and the methods used were broadly those found throughout the northern coniferous zone, both in Siberia and North America. Right up to the fateful decline in the stock of wild reindeer during the last centuries, hunting survived as a living Stone Age relic, even though iron had come into use for arrow- and spear-heads and, later, firearms had been adopted.

The autumn and early winter, when the reindeer were still fat from their plentiful summer food and their skins were most suitable for clothes, was the time of the big collective hunts.

Lines of converging fences, miles in length, still bear witness to the way in which entire herds were driven towards a lake, where the huntsmen lay waiting in boats to turn the lake into a veritable blood bath as the poor beasts tried to swim away. Sometimes the fences ended in a precipice which the animals fell over—sometimes in an enclosure where they became easy prey. Or there were large systems of pitfalls, sometimes with a sharp stone or a spear in the bottom. In the forests snares were hung from trees round the enclosure, or a kind of cross-bow was set up which would shoot an arrow into an animal which moved it.

In the rutting season decoy animals were employed—a reindeer cow was tethered in the forest and decoyed wild bulls into close shooting distance. Or a snare was attached to the antlers of a tame reindeer bull so that a wild bull became hopelessly entangled if it engaged in a fight with its rival. In the winter and spring, when the country was covered in deep snow and the reindeer, in spite of their broad hooves, sank through its frozen top surface, the Lapps followed them on skis and shot them with bows and arrows.

One single Lapp bow has been preserved for us. It is slightly longer than a man and, like the Siberian bows, is made of two strips of birch and spruce glued together. The arrows had heads of reindeer antler or iron and were carried in a skin quiver on the back.

In the forests, elk were also much prized game. They live in herds only in the winter, and even then never in such numbers as the reindeer. Great collective hunts were thus an impossibility. Many kinds of furry animals were also hunted: beaver, otter, fox, marten, etc. But there are grounds for thinking that this developed to any degree only after fur traders and tax collectors had begun to make an impact on Lapp economy. Evidence that the Lapps knew how to exploit their resources is, however, provided by the big sixth- or seventh-century horde discovered at Laksefjord, which contained gold and silver objects worth some £2,500.

As far back as Viking times the Norwegians levied Lapp tax. In the Middle Ages the "Birkarlians" came upon the scene. Originally they were Finns from the parish of Pirkkala, near Tammerfors. They settled in the Torne River Valley, bought furs and levied taxes until, in 1554, Gustav Vasa deprived them of their rights—though this by no means meant the end of taxes. About this same time English commercial expeditions to the White Sea began, and they further encouraged fur trading.

Beaver and otter were taken in traps with trap-doors or by nets. Foxes were caught in a curious manner found as far as eastern Siberia—a forked stick was stuck into the ground, and when the fox jumped up to get the meat placed on the top, it was liable to get its foot caught in the fork.

Lynx and wolverine were caught in traps made of logs with a beam which fell on to the animal. Wolves were chased on skis and killed with spears. The spear was usually provided with a sheath of reindeer brow antler so that it also served as a snow shovel, while at the bottom of its shaft there was a ring so that it could also be used as a ski-stick.

There were also more refined methods of trapping wolves. Bait was poisoned with a particular kind of lichen. And there was a devilish device which was hidden in bait and consisted of a springy juniper stick which had been sharpened at both ends, bent into a bow and tied together with sinews. When the sinews dissolved in the animal's stomach the stick sprang open and lacerated its entrails. A similar method is still practised by the Eskimo.

More recently the larger beasts of prey were hunted mainly to protect the reindeer herds from them. The only exception was the bear. This provides another example of an ancient circumpolar culture link. From Lapland to Labrador the bear was considered as being in a class apart. It possessed sacred powers and had to be treated with respect. So the Lapps never spoke of it in ordinary terms. Instead they used words of Norse origin to describe the parts of its body: *fuotte* for foot, *nasek* for nose. Evidently bears could not understand foreign languages! Even the normal term for bear, *bierdna*, was a taboo word (primitive Norse: *bernu*).

But the bear had itself made it clear that it had no objection to

Ancient bowl-shaped drums and drum hammers of the Norwegian Lapps. Paintings on the lower drum depict, among other things, the sun and stars, reindeer and Norse gods. The drums are in the National Museum, Copenhagen.

Left: A Kautokeino Lapp on ski. In winter and spring, when reindeer sink into deep snow despite their broad hooves, the Lapps on ski can catch them.

Below: A Lule Lapp at Satisjaure with his boat.

being killed provided the proper ritual was observed. The principal method of bear hunting practised by the Lapps was to drive it out of its lair at the onset of winter. Having received due notice of the hunt, the men of the camp made off in solemn procession with their heavy bear spears, the man who discovered the lair going first. He carried a staff fitted with a brass ring—brass possessed magical powers.

When the bear had been killed they struck it with twigs and sang the first part of a hymn in its praise. At one time the meat was cooked and eaten on the spot, but later the carcass was carried back to the camp. But for a whole year afterwards no woman was allowed to ride behind the reindeer which had brought it home.

The huntsmen sang all the way back to camp, and as soon as they were within earshot the women made ready to receive it. Dressed in their best clothes they stood in the tents with their backs to the entrance, for the carcass was never allowed to pass through it. In their hands they held a brass ring, and when the men crept in under the tent cover at the back of the tent the women greeted them with songs, peered at them through the brass rings and sprinkled them with the blood-red juice of chewed alder bark, thereby neutralizing the dangerous power of the bear which had been transferred to the huntsmen.

The meat had to be eaten up in a single day with special ceremony. But only certain parts were permitted to the women who, not even daring to touch it with their hands, raised it to their mouths with a stick. During the meal all those present gave expression to their joy by antiphonal singing and by smearing themselves and the tent poles with blood. The bones of the bear had on no account to be broken. They were carefully collected, and to the accompaniment of an incantation, were buried with the snout and tail, a bark vessel of alder juice being placed in front of the snout. The skin was stretched between two trees and then, with eyes blindfolded, the women shot arrows at it, for the husband of the woman who first hit it would kill the next bear. Many other ritual details could be mentioned. Let it merely be added that for three days and nights the hunters had to keep away from their wives. After that they had to run round the fire three times while the women threw ashes on them and sang the concluding verses of the bear song. It was only then that they were sufficiently cleansed to resume normal life.

To the coast Lapps the wealth of sea mammals—the smaller whales, walruses, seals of various kinds, particularly the spotted seal, the gray seal and the saddleback—was of great importance. Among the Kjelmøy treasure are several harpoon heads of reindeer antler, some of them barbed for getting a secure hold on the quarry, others had toggle heads that turned in the wound once the animal had been hit. Seals were also caught in nets or they were killed on shore with a club. Another method of catching is mentioned in Finnmark and the Gulf of Bothnia: when the tide was out a log with strong hooks attached to it was buried in a sand bank where seals had a habit of gathering at high water. Thus they got caught on the hooks.

Other items of food which it is hardly necessary to mention were birds and eggs. Ptarmigan were caught in snares, and to catch gulls there was a kind of hook consisting of a splinter of bone sharpened at both ends and fastened to a line—an ancient culture element widespread in Siberia and North America. Similar hooks were also used for fishing, and it was fishing, coupled with reindeer hunting inland and the catching of sea mammals round the shores which provided most of the food. The commonest method of fishing—in more recent times at least—was to use nets laid out in the open water and also under the ice. Hooks and leisters were also employed. From Kjelmøy there are both hooks and leister prongs of reindeer antler. Hooks were also made of hard juniper wood. The use of fish traps made of willow is somewhat doubtful, even though they seem to have been employed at an earlier time in connexion with weirs in the rivers.

As already mentioned, reindeer breeding started as an adjunct to the hunting of wild reindeer and several features in the care of domesticated reindeer today still survive from that time, while other less widespread features resulted from the influence of neighbouring people. A feature common to all reindeer breeders, both nomadic and semi-nomadic, is the lassoing of animals—a practice which in fact is nothing but throwing a snare. There is indeed a Lapp tradition that wild reindeer also were caught in this way. The practice of luring reindeer with urine which they like to lick on account of its salt content also probably derives from hunting, and so does enticing them with a smoke fire which keeps the mosquitoes and gadflies at bay. The round pens into which the mountain Lapps drive the reindeer herds in order to sort them out according to their different owners also had their origin with the Lapp hunters. They are made of horizontal untrimmed tree boles and have long converging arms like the enclosures used for deer hunting.

So much for the heritage of hunting. Other old and common features of reindeer breeding proper are ear-marking and the castration of draught animals and those intended for slaughter. The usual method of castration, which was preferably carried out just before the rutting season, was for one man to seize the reindeer by the antlers and turn it over on its left side, whereupon another bit its spermatic cords with his teeth and then crushed its sexual glands with his fingers. Castration by knife is probably a more recent method and belongs to the so-called "extensive" method of reindeer breeding practised by the mountain Lapps—of which more later—and has spread southward with it during the course of the last hundred years.

Slaughtering is carried out by plunging a knife into the beast's heart or neck. This is evidently an old method of slaughtering and has been superseded among some Siberian peoples by strangling.

Reindeer traction, as already mentioned, followed the pattern of dog traction. Evidence of this is the fact that in its original form the harness is clearly derived from the dog harness, and is quite different from horse and oxen harnesses. It consists of no more than a loop of skin which is put round the reindeer's neck and then goes down between its front legs where the trace is fastened so that it continues between the hind legs. A broad back girth more or less richly decorated, kept the harness in place. It is only recently that this primitive type has been supplanted in many places by a pair of hames. The reins consist of either a single thong or of several strips twisted together and fastened to a noose round the reindeer's forehead.

Various features of the Lapps' reindeer breeding cannot have formed part of their original nomadic life, however, but must be Scandinavian loans. Among these are the use of herd dogs, the pack saddle and—above all—milking and the making of milk products. A pack saddle similar to the one used by the Lapps still occurs on Norse ground in the Faroes. It consists of two thin, curved boards connected above by an ingenious joint ending in a pair of short horns on which the load could be hung and tied together beneath the reindeer's body. Household goods are packed in a kind of oval pannier with sides of wooden chip bent and tied together and a bottom of osier. Round the upper edge of the sides are eyes through which the contents can be lashed.

Milking, which as already mentioned, is not practised by Finnish and Russian Lapps, is carried out once or twice a day during the summer. A reindeer cow yields less than a quarter of a pint of milk daily—but it has the fat content of cream. To prevent the calves from drinking the milk, the cows' udders are smeared with reindeer manure, or the calves are fitted with a kind of bit to prevent them from sucking. Milking is usually done by women. In the left hand they hold a round, scoop-shaped milk cup hollowed out of birch. Milk that is not drunk immediately, or used for porridge or gruel, is employed in various ways: it is turned sour with the aid of the leaves of common or mountain sorrel; or it is made into dried milk by being poured into a bladder which has fine holes at the bottom so that the whey runs out; or it is churned into butter or made into cheese with the help of rennet. For this, round forms of wood or coiled basketry are used, many of them ornamented so that the finished cheese is attractively decorated in relief. Then it is dried on a slatted shelf in the tent, and afterwards the cheeses are drawn in pairs by string to dry them still more. Sometimes they are smoked over the fire.

* * *

The methods of reindeer breeding employed by the Lapps varied, of course, according to local conditions and the historical background. This will be sufficiently obvious from the following description of their life during the course of a year.

From the flat and monotonous coast of the Kola Peninsula the country rises westwards to the low, fjord-indented mountains of Finnmark. Although the entire country is well inside the Arctic Circle, the climate only borders on the arctic, thanks to the warming effect of the Gulf Stream, which keeps the sea free of ice throughout the winter. Poor drainage and a minimum degree of evaporation in the cool summers result in the northern part of Kola being covered with tundra, bog moss and cotton grass, and it is some way into the interior before woods of low birches and stunted conifers begin to appear. Along the fjords of Finnmark the birch area stretches right down to the sea, but only a few hundred feet up it disappears, and in consequence of the heavy precipitation the snow line is much lower here than farther inland, although the winter in the interior is considerably colder. Seal, walrus, whale, and quantities of such fish as cod, haddock, halibut, herring and blenny—the last mentioned being mainly caught during the winter—make the sea a veritable source of wealth. In the summer there are large shoals of smelt-like fish—capelin. Salmon make their way up the rivers to spawn, and in former times herds of wild reindeer wandered across the mountains. It is no wonder, therefore, that the coast Lapps were as much fishermen and hunters as breeders of reindeer, and that settlement goes back to the earliest times.

Many of the present-day coast Lapps, particularly those in Nordland and southern Troms, are descended from former mountain nomads who have lost their reindeer herds, but the nucleus is certainly descended from ancient stock. This particularly applies to the so-called Skolt Lapps in parts of South Varanger and what was once Finnish Petsamo.*

The Skolt Lapps are best described as semi-nomads. Hunting

* When Petsamo became Russian in 1944 after the war between Finland and the Soviet Union, the Skolt Lapps were moved to the Lake Enare district.

and fishing have always been their principal means of existence. Their reindeer are few in number, and only in more recent times have they begun to keep a few sheep. The hunting ground, the *sijt*, is therefore still the basis of their society. The important thing about the *sijt* is not the geographical concept, not the earth as such, but the right to exploit its stock of game and fish. A number of families are connected with each area, and nowadays the families are not necessarily related. Originally the *sijt* seems to have been exogamous and the kinship system regulated mutual relationships between its members. The heads of the separate households constituted a council which had supreme authority. It was responsible for the distribution of fishing and hunting rights and the return they yielded. The *sijt* members had collective rights in the common fishing grounds in the sea and in the large rivers, and all of them took part in the collective wild reindeer hunts and shared the spoils. Rights in salmon fishing in the lakes were, however, distributed among the families, although with the approval of the council they usually descended from father to son. The same applied to the bear and beaver hunting grounds.

When the lair of a bear was found, the heads of all the different households had to be invited to take part in the hunt. The domesticated reindeer were the common property of the *sijt*. In the summer they were allowed to graze anywhere, even on alien ground. In the autumn and winter, however, they could graze only on the *sijt*'s ground.

If a member of another *sijt* violated the hunting rights, the matter was not dealt with by the council of the *sijt* whose rights had been violated. Instead, the council complained to the lawbreaker's own council, which then took the matter in hand.

These are the conditions under which the Skolt Lapps' year runs through a constantly recurring cycle, with their habitation shifting according to the season. In the summer, when the sun remains above the horizon for two months on end, they stay by the open sea and fish. Meanwhile the reindeer herds are left to wander at will over the coastal mountains. When the autumn storms make the coast uncomfortable and the night dew softens the reindeer moss in the forests of the hinterland, they move on to the fish spawning grounds in the lakes and rivers. This being the rutting season, the reindeer tend to collect in large herds, and watching over them is therefore comparatively easy. This is also the time when the big collective hunts of wild reindeer take place—or rather, used to take place.

At the end of November the long winter night begins, and the time has come to make for the winter camps, where the deep snow forces the inhabitants to stay quietly indoors and work, while their reindeer remain nearby. Only when the light gradually starts to return once more and the snow is still firm, do they start serious hunting once more. Then, before the snow has melted and the ice on the rivers has broken up, they make for their spring grounds up the fjord, where the reindeer calve and there are plenty of opportunities for profitable salmon fishing. And so the year ends by their making once more for the summer ground by the sea.

It is difficult to give a reliable picture of how the Norwegian coastal Lapps lived in far off times, for they have lived for a very long period just like the Norwegian fishermen and farmers of Finnmark. Presumably it was a life not very different from that of the Skolt Lapps. Certainly reindeer breeding has never played a very large part in it—which has made the catching of sea mammals all the more important. Those who now keep reindeer leave the herding to the Skolt and mountain Lapps.

As already mentioned, the Lapps have disappeared from Finland except in the far north, and of those remaining on Finnish soil a number are descended from Norwegian Lapps who immigrated in the eighteenth century, while others, of Swedish descent, were incorporated into Finland by the Peace Treaty of 1809. Even at that time the original Finnish Lapps, apart from the Skolts, were confined to the region of Lake Enare, whereas formerly they had been distributed over practically the whole of the country. The surface, an old peneplain of pre-Cambrian rocks, gradually falls in level from the north and east down towards the Gulf of Finland and the Gulf of Bothnia. It was furrowed by the ice of bygone ages and later partially covered by moraine gravel, sand eskers, and deposits from the sea. There are thousands of lakes, rivers, and an abundance of pine and spruce forest. On the hills the forests give way to heath and barren land, while stagnant water has turned extensive tracts of the highlands into moorland; no less than a third of the country is bog and marsh.

Like the coast Lapps, the Finnish forest Lapps lead a semi-nomadic existence, with the emphasis on hunting and fishing. Not much is known about the southern groups, which have long since disappeared. But it is possible to piece together a more or less satisfactory picture of the early existence of the northern Finnish Lapps.

They were peculiar in using domesticated reindeer exclusively as draught animals, beasts of burden and decoys, so that they never became numerous, and in leaving them to themselves for much of the year. As with the Skolts, the *sijt* was the basis of society. In the summer, i.e. from the middle of June to the end of July, the reindeer were allowed to roam the forests or the islands in the lakes while their owners fished. Then some of them were brought back for use at the big autumn hunts which lasted until some time in November. During the course of November the rest of the reindeer were caught so that they could take part in the journey to the winter camp where the old people, the women and children, remained until it was time for everyone to move off to the summer fishing grounds. In December and January the men were employed in catching beaver, etc., and in February some of them went to market while others hunted. In the spring the collective wild reindeer hunts took place, and at the end of April the domesticated deer were let loose once more, after which thoughts turned again to the summer move.

The life of the Swedish and Norwegian inland Lapps is considerably different from that of the Finnish Lapps, partly because reindeer milking leads to far more intensive reindeer breeding by the forest Lapps and partly because the mountain Lapps own such enormous herds that they are almost completely dependent on them and must therefore be regarded as true nomads—in the more restricted sense of the term. Like Finland, northern Sweden is an ancient peneplain of pre-Cambrian rock, well provided with foaming rivers, and rising gradually from the Gulf of Bothnia. Up towards the Norwegian border, and in Norway itself, the pre-Cambrian rock gives way to palæozoic sediments which were once raised into a mighty folding range of mountains, later to be worn away again and then once more to be raised into the plateau of Kjølen. The varying characteristics of the rocks play a significant rôle in the development of reindeer breeding, for the high mountains, in contrast to the lower-lying regions of granite and gneiss, provide soil for luxurious herb mats. Lower down in the foothills, a belt of open birch forest with an undergrowth of heather and crowberries is to be found, and a further 300-450 feet lower down the first signs of pine forest appear, to continue in an unbroken mass right down to the coast.

The pine forests provide the forest Lapps with a home throughout the year. The same old system of division into hunting grounds and hunting fellowships exists with them—as it also does with the mountain Lapps—under the name of *siida*. The *siida* comprises a group of families who move within the same area. The herds belonging to the forest Lapps seldom contain more than a few hundred beasts—often fewer—and their wanderings are much more restricted than those of the mountain Lapps. They remain, in fact, in the same area from the spring until the autumn, though they seldom occupy the same camp for more than weeks at a time.

At the end of April or beginning of May, just before calving occurs, they like to go to the marshlands near the lakes on the upper reaches of the rivers, and there they let their reindeer loose until shortly before midsummer. The lichen then becomes dry and uneatable and the animals prefer young willow and birch shoots in addition to grass and such plants as horsetail, buck bean, and so on. In June they are gathered again for milking. Since it is impossible in the forest to hunt them up as the mountain Lapps do, the tamest are first summoned by a bell, then bells are tied on to them and they summon the others until gradually the entire herd is collected. This done, they are driven out on to a bog or headland where they are sorted according to their various owners and the newborn calves are marked. Nowadays they are put into pens while being sorted. It can be demonstrated, however, that the pens used are different in origin from those used by the mountain Lapps. The latter derive from the old type of hunting enclosure, the former from more recent milking pens, milking not being carried out on the same scale as once was the case now that other cattle are kept—the reindeer in consequence being less tame.

After the reindeer have been sorted, the milking season starts, and it lasts until the end of August. All this time the herds are tended, smoke fires being lit to protect them from mosquitoes and gadflies. Then they are again allowed to wander at large for some months, apart from a short period when they are rounded up for the autumn slaughter. Fishing is not of course neglected at the summer grounds, for there is plenty of trout, char, houting, pike and perch. When the snow starts and stray animals can easily be traced, they are once more rounded up, and after renewed sorting the families and their herds trek back to the winter camps nearer the coast, where the windswept mountain ranges are more likely to provide the reindeer with food than the deep forest snow.

In short, reindeer breeding as practised here is much more intensive than it is among the Finnish forest Lapps.The herds are tended for much more of the year, and milking means that they are also turned to better account. But this method of reindeer breeding has in any case largely disappeared. Many forest Lapps have gone over to farming to some extent and keep a few sheep and goats which are left for the peasants to tend during the winter. In addition there has been a shift southwards in the mountain Lapps' reindeer breeding. From time immemorial they were accustomed to roam about at will regardless of territorial boundaries. But in 1852 the Finnish frontier was closed to Norwegian Lapps, and some of them who formerly belonged to Kautokeino settled on Swedish territory in Karesuando. In 1888 the frontier was also closed to Swedish Lapps, which resulted in some of the former inhabitants of Kautokeino returning to Norway, while others moved still farther south to Jukkasjärvi, Gällivare and Jokkmokk. After 1900, particularly after the Swedish-Norwegian treaty of 1919 had further restricted the freedom of movement of the Karesuando and Jukkasjärvi Lapps, still more families moved southward, some even penetrating as far south as the Ångerman River. Northern methods naturally followed in their wake, among them the modern extensive method of reindeer breeding, shortly to be described.

The mountain Lapps have aimed at self-sufficiency in their economy to a far greater extent or at any rate for far longer than the forest Lapps have done. As an eighteenth-century Swedish author, writing of the mountain Lapps' reindeer, put it:

> "To the Lapps they are their fields and meadows, their horses and cows. From their reindeer they get all that we get from the land and the sea, from India and the Levant."

The herds can number many thousand. But the remarkable thing is that this form of life, so generally regarded as typical, scarcely goes back further than the sixteenth century, and came into existence only after the introduction of firearms had more or less exterminated wild reindeer. It is thus an intensified form of the original Lapp culture, brought about by the pressure of Scandinavian civilization, and thus in a way a counterpart of what happened to the plains Indians. In a similar way a change in their basic activity radically changed the social organization. The old idea of joint ownership in the reindeer herds by the *siida* gave way to ownership by individual families, and this in turn led to revised ideas on the concept on reindeer stealing. Furthermore, fully developed nomadism led to a big Lapp advance southward across the uninhabited mountain plateaux, a movement corresponding to that which has taken place in our times (see page 122). Incidentally, the principal way in which the habits of the mountain Lapps differ from those of the Scandinavian forest Lapps are in the long treks of the former and in the difference between their spring and autumn grounds on the one hand and the summer grounds on the other.

Shortly before the calving season a move is made to the birch forests of the foothills. At this season trekking has to be done by night, when the surface of the snow is frozen, while resting is done by day. About a month and a half is spent at the spring grounds until calving is over and before the plagues of insects and the sun have begun to get too overpowering. Then a move is made to the summer grounds. The most northerly mountain Lapps, in Karesuando and Jukkasjärvi, who have no mountain plateaux available, make their way right down to the Norwegian coast, where during the summer the reindeer herds can roam the islands and the shut-in valleys in comparative freedom. The more southerly Lapps, on the other hand, make for the mountains and for the pastures above the timber line, where they mark their calves and start milking. Milking is carried out daily in a special pen or in a natural enclosure. So long as the herds are tended in the high mountains there is no need for animals belonging to different owners to be kept apart. In the autumn, after the move down into the birch forests where there are plenty of fungi for them to eat, the reindeer are let loose for the rutting season, which starts at the end of September. A few weeks later, when this is over, the herds are rounded up once more and the big autumn sorting takes place. Meanwhile milking continues and slaughtering is carried out to provide for the following spring. Finally there is the trek into the pine forests, where reindeer moss and beard lichen provide the herds with winter food. Here they stay until it is once more spring.

The mountain Lapps have had to change their habits during the last half century no less than the forest Lapps. Outside one or two places in Jokkmokk, nomadism as once practised no longer exists. Instead progressive transition to a cash economy and the development of means of communication have resulted in what is known as the extensive method of reindeer breeding, with large herds and the emphasis on the production of meat for sale, while regular milking has ceased. In consequence the herds of the different *siidas* are no longer kept apart during the summer; instead they are tended collectively, and women and children who do not take part in tending them remain in settled camps where they have time to look after cows and goats. Thus adapted to modern conditions, nomadic life would still appear to have a future.

* * *

Means of transport are obviously of prime importance to a people who move about as much as the Lapps do. In the deep winter snow skis are indispensable both to men and women. Discoveries of skis are even considered to be evidence that the Lapps were present in Sweden in the Stone Age. The shape of the oldest example, found in Kalvträsk in Västerbotten and dated *circa* 2000 B.C., clearly suggests Siberia. It is comparatively short and broad and has perpendicular holes for the foot binding. On later skis these are replaced by horizontal holes, and the final development is a ski with a groove running the length of the underside. Nowadays a Lapp ski is 2½-3 yards long, narrow, and springy under the foot. But it occurs in various forms according to local conditions and purpose. The right ski, which is used for pushing off, is sometimes a little shorter than the left. On rough ground the Lapps are probably unsurpassed as skiers. To help them they have a single stave, with a ring at the bottom to prevent it from sinking into the snow and a narrow shovel at the top which the reindeer herdsman uses to discover what sort of grazing exists beneath the snow. Sometimes he throws a lasso round a reindeer's neck and gets pulled along at a breakneck speed.

In snow reindeer are otherwise mostly used for hauling sledges. The Lapp name for sledge, *keris* or *gieris* (the word *pulka* which is often found in books and pamphlets is not Lappish but Finnish) is the same as the Scandinavian *kœrre*, which has caused some linguists to suppose that it was borrowed from the Norsemen. But there is no ground whatever for this view, since a similar sledge not only exists in Carelia and among the Volga Cheremiss, but also in Siberia among the Samoyed and Kamass. It most closely resembles a boat cut off at the stern, and is made of narrow boards with ribs and a keel. Like the skis, there are several sub-types. The huntsman hauls his bag home on a low, open sledge—if he is not satisfied with stuffing the meat into the beast's own skin. A larger and broader type of sledge is employed for carrying loads, another with a cover in front is used for conveying people and yet another, entirely closed in, is used for carrying food and valuables. Never more than one reindeer is harnessed to a sledge—no matter whether it is carrying people or goods. This contrasts with the Samoyeds who harness several together.

Incidentally, the Samoyed sledge has been adopted by the Kola Lapps and is slowly spreading to Varanger. It has a body propped up on two runners and is thus best suited to waterlogged, flat tundra, while the Lapp sledge is unsurpassed in forests and on mountains. It glides easily over the snow without cutting its way into it, slips between trees and rocks and is easily righted if it turns over. On a trek, the sledges are arranged in files (*raito*) of up to ten. The leading reindeer is either driven or led, and the rest follow on behind, the harness of one deer being fastened to the sledge immediately in front. The last sledge has no tail board and is used to carry the tent poles.

In snowless terrain the reindeer serve as beasts of burden with the pack saddles already mentioned. An infant having to make the journey is entrusted to a specially reliable animal. It is carefully wrapped in skins and lies in a sort of cradle which is hung on to the saddle. The last reindeer in the procession hauls the tent posts which are tied into two bundles, one on each side of the animal.

To cross waterways the Lapps sometimes make shift with a raft of dry spruce or pine logs. But the Lapps are in fact no mean boat builders, especially at the coast or near fast flowing rivers. Their oldest craft were quite certainly of skin, of a type which seems to have been widespread throughout the Arctic. Not only are there quite credible traditions about them, but from Trondheim to the White Sea there are numerous rock engravings which can hardly be construed as anything but pictures of skin boats. And the way the Kola Lapps still sew their plank boats together with sinews is certainly a last survival from them. Remains of craft similarly sewn with sinews or with root fibres have been found a long way south in Sweden. A similar method also was employed in the Hjortspring Iron Age boat on the island of Als. Some Lapp boats were so small that they could be carried across watersheds or round falls on a man's back.

Everything that the mountain Lapps possessed gradually came to be adapted to facilitate removal, the habitation (*kåhte*, *goatte*) in-

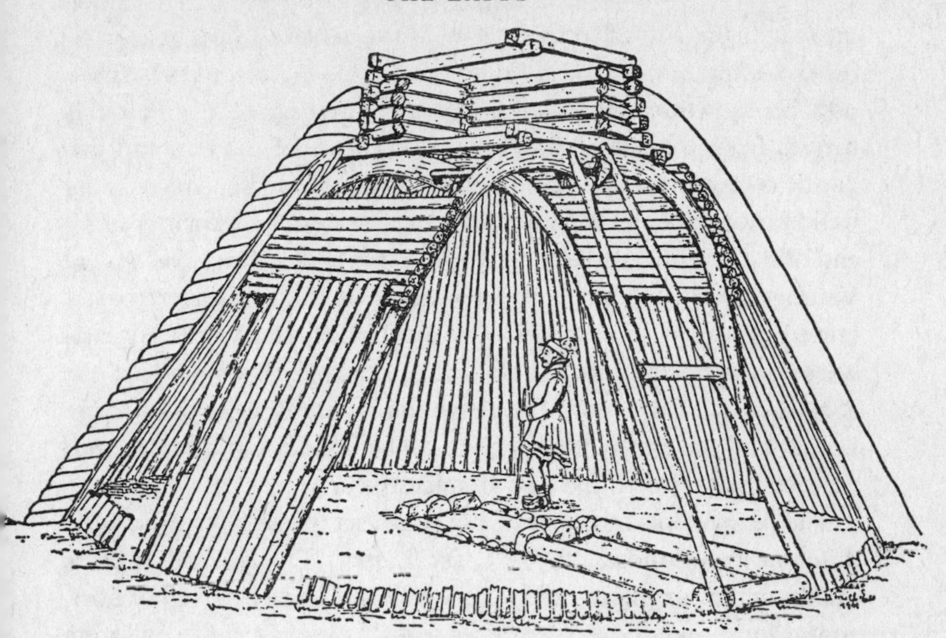

Diagram of a Lapp earth lodge (after Manker).

cluded. The semi-nomadic coast and forest Lapps on the other hand spent part of the year in permanent houses. In Finnmark as late as close on the year 1900 it was possible to come across old-fashioned earth lodges which were the original winter habitation of the coast Lapps. The frame consisted of four curved posts facing each other in pairs so that they formed arches. These arches were connected at the top by a ridge pole and farther down the sides by a pair of braces. The lower part of the walls consisted of logs placed close together, which leaned against the braces. The upper part was either of similar construction or consisted of logs placed horizontally. Outside, the whole building was clad first with birch bark and then with sods. In the middle of the house was an open hearth and in the roof above was a smoke hole, which could be closed by means of either a wooden shutter or a pane of bladder skin. No other window existed.

How old this type of house is cannot be said with any certainty. But it is worth mentioning that on Træna, a small island off the Norwegian coast near the Arctic Circle, Gutorm Gjessing has excavated the site of a Stone Age house which he has reason to believe is the remains of an earth lodge. As to the curious arched post construction, he advances the not unlikely theory that this derives from the use of whale bones, the use of the ribs and jaw bones of large whales for building material in the Arctic being well known, having been mentioned in Finnmark as recently as the end of the seventeenth century. From Finnmark—from Nesseby in Varanger, for example—we also know of the remains of partly buried houses with passages of a type which can be traced eastwards across Kola into Siberia, but nothing is known about the construction of the roof—or about the relationship between these houses and the earth lodge. There can be little doubt, though, that the sites belonged to the Lapps' ancestors.

The permanent dwellings of the southern forest Lapps are quite different from those of the coast Lapps. The ground plan is quadrangular or (more rarely) hexagonal. It has a low wall of horizontal logs, and above them rises a high pyramid roof consisting of two layers of upright boards with birch bark between them. In former times they were possibly covered with sods.

There are also various basic types of tent. One of them is exceedingly simple and of a type which is found all over the Arctic, i.e. a conical tent with a frame consisting of three posts forked at the top which are interlocked and which support a number of loosely stacked poles. Over these the tent cover is spread. This was originally of birch bark in the summer and of reindeer skin in the winter; nowadays these have been replaced by ordinary canvas and heavy homespun respectively. This conical tent requires long and comparatively straight posts, so its real home is in the forests and well-wooded valleys, though it does in fact occur all over Lapland, at least as a temporary habitation for reindeer herdsmen and hunters.

A more distinctive type occurs in the high mountains and generally amongst the mountain Lapps proper. The framework is similar to that of the earth lodge, i.e. two pairs of arched posts connected by braces and a ridge pole, this framework serving to support a number of sloping tent poles. Gjessing sees in this

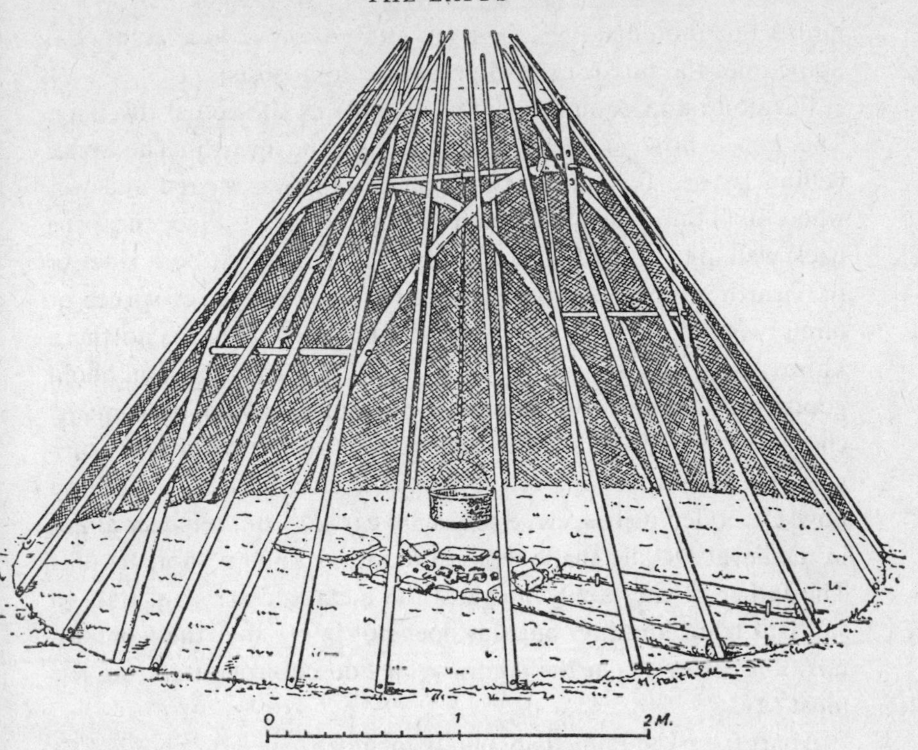

Diagram of a Lapp arched post tent (after Manker).

construction a combination of the earth lodge and the conical tent, whereas Ruong believes that the arches were directly derived from the crooked timber of the high mountains. Suffice to say that it is a type peculiar to the Lapps and furthermore unknown on the Kola Peninsula, though its lightness and rigidity make it excellently suited to the free nomadic life of the windswept open spaces. The fact that both conical and arched post tents are now to be found with sod walls is probably a secondary phenomenon connected with the increasing extent to which fixed dwellings are now used.

Store houses of various kinds are erected on regularly frequented camping grounds. Things not required for immediate use are put on staging at man's height out of reach of the dogs, whereas supplies of meat are hidden away from wolverines and other animals in a timber box mounted on a single smooth pole as is done in Siberia. Sometimes the box is erected on two or four posts.

Furniture and equipment are as simple as the actual dwelling. The pots—now of metal—hang above the hearth. The space behind is used for eating. In olden times it was sacred and was where such things as the shaman's drum were kept. Places near the back wall are still reckoned the most important. On both sides of the hearth are places for sleeping, with a thick layer of spruce or birch twigs below and a reindeer skin above. At night the northern Lapps hang a mosquito net of cotton over the bunk. Household goods are few, as befits a nomadic people, and apart from the cheese forms, cheese shelves and cradle already mentioned comprise no more than one or more oval wooden chests, some food bowls, wooden dishes, etc. Spoons are carved from reindeer antler in medieval Nordic shape with a broad bowl and a short handle. The father of the family prepares the meat and serves it out—a survival from hunting, but this does not imply that the woman's position is lowly. On the contrary, in household matters she has most say.

Apart from the immediate family members, the household often includes a married daughter and son-in-law, it being customary for a newly-married couple to live with the bride's parents. It is no doubt a consequence of this that in matters of inheritance the youngest son takes priority over his elder brothers, for they will usually be married and out of the home before the father's death. Marriage between cross cousins, i.e. between the children of a brother and sister, are common; and as mentioned before it is possible that originally the *siida* was exogamous.

In olden times clothes were always of skin, preferably of reindeer skin, which is both light and warm—necessary virtues in a blizzard or 90°F. of frost. Winter clothes are still made of the same material, though for summer wear they have been replaced long ago by woven cloth. Furs are dried and softened by being rubbed with fat made of boiled reindeer hoofs, bones or fish roe, whereas a dehaired skin needs more elaborate treatment. First it is soaked in water until the hairs loosen. Then it is scraped with an S-shaped iron scraper fastened to the middle of a wooden handle which is held in both hands—a common Siberian type incidentally. After being scraped it is put in a decoction of bark—birch, willow or alder—alder if the skin is to be dyed red. After renewed drying it is rubbed with fat and finally made pliable by being drawn backwards and forwards over an iron hoop which is fastened to a tree or to a tent post. Sinews twined on the knee or cheek are used for sewing. Weaving is a Scandinavian or more probably a Finnish loan. The coastal Lapps used to have a real old-fashioned upright loom. Ribbon weaving is widespread. For this a grid-like implement of reindeer antler or bone is used, and the women make such things as belts and shoe laces on it in the most attractive designs.

Clothing is more or less the same for both men and women and in spite of Nordic influences displays an obvious connexion with ancient arctic types of clothing. The basic garment is the simple poncho, consisting of a loosely draped skin with a hole for the head. To this day a poncho made out of bear-cub skin is worn above the normal clothing by reindeer herdsmen who have to be out in the extreme cold. Nowadays it is also made of cloth with a collar or hood for the head. The poncho cut can be clearly discerned in the jacket, the body of which is formed of two pieces sewn together at the sides but fitted, in imitation of the medieval dress, with gussets to give it greater width. The man's jacket, and formerly the woman's too, also had an upright collar which was quite certainly adopted from the Scandinavians. The neck is covered with a short breast cloth and those worn by women, and especially those worn by the southern Lapps, are decorated in various ways. The neck, wrist-bands and collar are edged with strips of cloth in gay colours, usually yellow and red. There are differences in the jackets worn by the northern and southern Lapps. The former are wider and shorter than the southern type which is also open in front. A similar cut has also been known to the Finnish Lapps. The jacket is gathered by a leather or cloth belt, or, in the case of the women, a woollen belt, lavishly decorated with silver mountings, or embroidered with pewter thread, the latter made by a technique originating in Nordic gold and silver drawing and transferred to the baser material. From the belt hangs the inevitable and indispensable knife with its characteristically curved and beautifully decorated sheath of reindeer antler, and from the women's hangs a needlecase and other odds and ends.

In the summer the outer jacket was originally of unhaired skin, or perhaps a much worn fur, but at least since the seventeenth century it has also been customary to have a dress of similar cut made of cloth or homespun, usually blue or grey, though in some districts it might be white or more rarely red. White was usual in Karasjokk, for example, while among the Skolts the man's dress is grey and the woman's white.

Trousers, which are similar for both sexes, are so short in the body that they do not reach above the hips and are so narrow that slits are necessary at the bottom. But while there is only one basic type of jacket, there are two distinct types of cut in the trousers. Those worn by the southern Lapps seem to have developed from a long pair of gaiters like Indian leggings which are sewn together with a median seam. Those worn by the northern Lapps, on the other hand, have side seams and must be derived from what was once a breech cloth. The northern type is widespread in northern Asia and is presumably of more recent origin than the southern. Among the Lapps it often has a pair of leggings sewn on below. The technical term for the footwear would be a moccasin with a turned-up sole sewn together by a seam at the heel. Joined to this are the instep and leg pieces. The turned-up toe makes any ski fastening beyond a simple strap unnecessary. For winter use the soles are preferably made of skin from the reindeer's forehead and the legs from its leg skin, both of which are particularly strong. Socks are not worn, but the shoes are lined with the hay from a kind of sedge grass.

No item of Lapp dress displays so many variations as the head-dress. The basic type in Sweden for men is a pixie cap. This is decorated with brightly coloured edging—in Jokkmokk with a discreet button in the top, in Karesuando with an enormous tuft of red wool. From Finnmark and Kola there is a man's cap which derives from one borrowed from the Russians (though it was originally Polish). This has a square crown, and is popularly known as "the four corners of the earth". Some women's caps are reminiscent of the men's pixie cap, but without the tuft, and sometimes with the point brought forward and fastened in front; others are bonnets with ear-flaps. The most striking of them all was the old headdress worn by women in Finnmark. This had a curved horn on the top like a crest. It probably goes back to the Gothic Middle Ages and is still preserved in the Icelandic women's festival dress. Among the Lapps it disappeared during the Læstadian revival of the last century because fanatics believed that "the devil sat in the horn". Oddly enough, the colourful decoration of the clothing has increased during the course of the last few centuries because, perhaps—as Gutorm Gjessing has suggested—metal ornaments have become rarer. The most impressive dress of all is that worn by the northern Lapps—"a final burst of flame," Manker calls it, "analagous to the tints of autumn before the fall of the leaves".

* * *

Nowadays all the Lapps are Christian—the Scandinavians Lutheran, the Skolts and Kola Lapps Greek-Catholic. Missions started up in a small way in the Middle Ages, but they only really got going in Scandinavia in the seventeenth and, especially, in the eighteenth centuries. In the beginning the most successful was the Orthodox church, for the Russian popes were considerably more liberal than the zealous Lutherans, and quite a number of Scandinavian Lapps crossed the border in consequence. What most interests us, however, is their original religion—ancient shamanism with its tinge of Asia. Among the Scandinavian Lapps it also contained a well-defined strain of old Norse mythology and to a certain extent even in heathen times included some Christian ideas. Curiously enough it is obviously deeply rooted in hunting life, whereas nomadism has had little influence.

According to ancient Lapp ideas, nature was alive just as man was, and contained forces with which it was essential to be on good terms but over which it was also possible to gain power.

Danger from bears could be counterbalanced by the careful observance of the hunting rites (see page 113) and a hunter could make certain of a good bag by magical means by engraving pictures of his quarry on rocks situated in places favourable to hunting. Any number of such Stone Age pictures exist right from the Atlantic coast through Russia to Siberia. Trees too contained a soul. It is said that when the Finnish Lapps prepared to fell a tree, they would first knock on the trunk to waken this soul; then they chopped off the lowest branch to provide a place of refuge for it. Certain lakes, curiously shaped rocks, or a stone in the apparent likeness of an animal or a man—all such *seides* contained sacred power, and sacrifices were made to them so that the reindeer would multiply and other good fortune ensue. Hundreds of such cult sites have been found, together with piles of antlers from sacrificed reindeer and occasionally a roughly carved wooden figure.

Under the earth there was another world of its own—the *saivo* land—and this was an exact counterpart of our world, where the departed lived a life of bliss together with their reindeer herds, for death did not mean an end of existence. There are also references to a kind of Land of the Dead, *Jabmi-Aimo*. What the connexion was between this and the *saivo* land is not quite clear, and it was not perhaps entirely clear to the Lapps either. Sufficient to say that the dead were dangerous, and sometimes they inflicted sickness on the living by stealing their souls. Everything to do with the dead had therefore to be dealt with extremely carefully. When a corpse was buried it was enclosed in birch bark or laid in a sledge or in a simple coffin of a hollowed-out tree trunk. Three days later the reindeer which had hauled the sledge was sacrificed at the grave, where its meat was eaten by the deceased's kin and its bones buried. Each year for three years afterwards a reindeer was sacrificed at the grave.

In addition to the semi-impersonal beings and forces there were others which had the character of deities proper. Some of them are also to be found among other Finno-Ugrian tribes and among the Samoyeds. Others have been adopted from old Norse mythology and have partly merged with the older deities. Jubmal, corresponding to the Finnish Jumala, was considered supreme among the gods by Finnish Lapps, just as Radien was by the Swedish Lapps. Possibly there is at bottom some ancient element in this conception of him, but obviously there has been some Christian influence too. Beneath him were other deities who controlled the winds, game, fish, and so on. The most important was Tirmes or Dierbmes, the God of Thunder. In Scandinavia he was identified with Thor, was in fact called Horagalles, derived from Thor-Karlen, i.e. the "Thor-Man", and was represented carrying a hammer in his hand.

Another old Norse god was Väralden-olmai, the "World's Man", corresponding to Veraldar-god, which was a surname for Frey, the god of fertility. He caused reindeer to multiply, and the genitals of reindeer were sacrificed to him. Lower down the scale and therefore closer to everyday life were the Akkas: Sar-akka, who dwelt beneath the hearth and assisted in the birth of children and reindeer calves; Uks-akka, who guarded the entrance to the tent, and Juks-akka, the special protector of boys, whose sacred symbol was the bow. They were all daughters of Mader-akka, "the Primeval Mother", who received children's souls from the hands of Radien before their birth.

Confronted with all these powers, man was small and feeble, and when dangers threatened it was essential to know their will. The father of each family had his drum, which he used in order to find out from which deity he should seek help on each separate occasion. These drums, of which quite a large number are still preserved, occur in two forms. One of them, belonging to the southern Lapps, has a ring-shaped frame like the usual circumpolar type, the other, which is northern, has a bowl-shaped bottom. Pictures of gods, sacrificial animals and the like, were painted in the sacred juice of the alder on the drum skin. Normally the drum was kept in the sacred space behind the hearth, and on journeys it was carried in the last sledge, for no woman was allowed to cross its path. It was played by a small hammer of bone and this caused a ring or some other small brass object which was laid on the skin to move about among the figures, and from the path it took the will of the gods was deduced. If this did not suffice, reference was made to the *noaidde*, the counterpart of the Siberian shaman. The monotonous sound of the drum so worked on the *noaidde*'s nerves that finally he was lost in ecstasy. While he lay unconscious his soul travelled among the *saivo* people with his spirit helpers, who had either come to him of their own free will or had been inherited from former colleagues. In the *saivo*-country there were also a number of animals at his disposal. With his magic reindeer he could fight an adversary's reindeer and nullify unfriendly intentions. The Scandinavian peoples greatly feared the Lapps for their witchcraft, and as early as the thirteenth century in *Historia Norvegiæ* there is a description of one of their shamanistic seances. Evidence that shamanistic ideas were at the heart of their religion appears from the fact that they have persisted under a veneer of Christianity right down to quite recent times.

* * *

Thus a clear picture of Lapp culture emerges—a culture influenced by local conditions on an ancient circumpolar foundation. This same foundation is recognizable in the Eskimo culture, but whereas the path of development there is towards increasing dependence on the sea, with the Lapps it has gone in the opposite direction—towards the forests and from there up into the mountains. If the Komsa culture derives from the Lapps' ancestors, we find them first of all on the sea coast, where sealing and fishing could be supplemented by hunting in the ice-free interior in the autumn. But this is still uncertain. There are at any rate grounds for believing that the late Stone Age culture, the Slate Culture, is of Lappish origin. Possibly in the interior of the country, too, winters were at first spent on the shores of the lakes and rivers. If so, a culture then existed which in many respects must have been similar to the one preserved down to the present day by the inland Eskimos of the Canadian Barren Grounds west of the Hudson Bay. But the advent of skis brought new possibilities. The ski cannot have been a Lapp invention. It came from the east where, in Siberia, it still occurs in a primitive form. Without skis it is impossible to travel in the deep forest snow, and they were therefore a prerequisite for moving away from the lakes with their abundance of fish, and for hunting wild reindeer during the winter as well as in the summer. Equally well adapted to snow was the runnerless sledge. In short: a further adjustment to environment thereby took place, and development continued along the same lines with the coming of the knowledge of how to domesticate reindeer, thus laying the foundations of the subsequent nomadic life.

But now a new factor, also based on geography, comes into play—namely, the proximity of the Lapps to the Scandinavian agricultural and cattle-breeding culture. It was this factor alone which enabled the Lapps to take the final step from semi-nomadism—and continued dependence on hunting—to the fully developed nomadic life entirely dependent on the reindeer herd. The impulse to this came only with the disappearance of wild reindeer. From this followed the need to abandon all forms of permanent dwelling and the use of the tent as the only habitation. Other ways in which the Scandinavian peoples influenced the Lapps—in dress, for example, in religion and, by no means least, in language—have already been demonstrated. The language influence has been so strong that the extent of the Scandinavian component in the culture has often been exaggerated by linguists. From the form of the words it evidently goes back to Primitive Norse times, i.e. to A.D. 300-800. From that time onwards cultural influences have steadily continued through the Viking period and the Middle Ages right down to our own day, when, in spite of clinging stubbornly to their language and to some degree also to their peculiar way of life, the Lapps are gradually merging more and more into Scandinavian, and thus into European, society.

BIBLIOGRAPHY

An old, and therefore somewhat out-of-date, survey of Lapp culture, still worth reading, is given by GUSTAF VON DÜBEN: *Om Lappland och Lapparne*, Stockholm, 1873. Excellent modern works are BJÖRN COLLINDER: *The Lapps*, New York, 1949. ERNST MANKER: *De svenska fjällapparna*, Stockholm, 1947. For the culture development of the Norwegian Lapps, with the emphasis on more recent times, see GUTORM GJESSING: "Changing Lapps" (*Monogr. Social Anthrop.*, xiii, London, 1954). Excellent works of a more popular nature are EMILIE DEMANT HATT: *Med lapperne i højfjeldet*, Stockholm, 1913. OSSIAN ELGSTRÖM: *Karesuandolapparna*, Stockholm, 1922. ERNST MANKER: *Vägen går krokigt*, Stockholm, 1936. ERNST MANKER: *Markens människor*, Stockholm, 1944. An interesting description of Lapp life seen through Lapp eyes is provided by JOHAN TURI: *Muittalus samid birra*, publ. E. Demant Hatt, Copenhagen, 1910.

Problems of pre-history are dealt with i.A. by JOHS. BRØNDSTED: "Nordens første bebyggelse" (*Fra Nationalmus. Arbejdsmark*, Copenhagen, 1950). GUTORM GJESSING: "Fra steinalder til jernalder i Finmark" (*Inst. f. Sammenlign. Kulturforskn. Ser. C*, iii, 3, Oslo, 1935). GUTORM GJESSING: *Norges steinalder*, Oslo, 1945. GUSTAF HALLSTRÖM: "Kan lapparnas invandringstid fixeras?" (*Norrlands försvar*, Stockholm, 1929). O. SOLBERG: "Eisenzeitfunde aus Ostfinmarken" (*Vidensk.-Selsk. Skr. Hist.-filos. Kl.*, Christiania, 1910). On the question of the Lapps' race, see BERTIL LUNDMAN: "Ergebnisse der anthropologischen Lappenforschung" (*Anthropos.*, xlvii, Posieux-Froideville, 1952).

The most important works on the domestication of the reindeer are GUDMUND HATT: "Notes on Reindeer Nomadism" (*Mem. Amer. Anthrop. Ass., VI. Washington, 1919*). KARL JETTMAR: "Zu den Anfängen der Rentierzucht" (*Anthropos.*, xlvii-xlviii, Posieux-Froideville, 1952-3). B. LAUFER: "The Reindeer and its Domestication" (*Mem. Amer. Anthrop. Assoc.*, iv, Lancaster, 1917). N. T. MIROV: "Notes on the Domestication of Reindeer" (*Amer. Anthrop. N. s.*, xlvii, Menasha, 1945). U. T. SIRELIUS: "Über die Art und Zeit der Zähmung des Renntieres" (*Journ. Soc. Finno-Ougr.*, xxxiii, Helsinki, 1916). G. M. VASILEVICH AND M. G. LEVIN: "Tipy olenevodstva i ikh proiskhozhdenie" (*Sovetsk. Etnogr. 1951*, 1, Moskva-Leningrad, 1951).

Among older sources are JOHANNES SCHEFFERUS: *Lapponia*, Francofurti, 1673 (is based not on original observations but on the accounts mentioned below by Niurenius, Rheen, Graan, Tornæus and others). OLAUS GRAAN: "Relation, eller En Fulkomblig Beskrifning om Lapparnas Ursprung, etc." (*Bidr. svenska landsmål.*, xvii, Uppsala, 1899). KNUD LEEM: *Beskrivelse over Finmarkens Lapper*, Copenhagen, 1767. OLAUS PETRI NIURENIUS: "Lappland eller beskrivning över den nordiska trakt, som lapparna bebo" (*Bidr. svenska landsmål*, xvii, Uppsala, 1905). SAMUEL RHEEN: "En kortt Relation om Lapparnes Lefwarne och Sedher, etc." (*Bidr. svenska landsmål*, xvii, Uppsala, 1897). JOHANNES TORNÆUS: "Berättelse om Lapmarckerna och deras tilstånd" (*Bidr. svenska landsmål*, xviii, Uppsala, 1900). GABRIEL TUDERUS: "En kort underrättelse om The Österbothniske Lappar, som under Kiemi Gebiet lyda" (*Bidr. svenska landsmal*, xvii, Uppsala, 1905). Valuable information on the Finnish and Norwegian Lapps is also to be found in the following later works: M. ALEXANDER CASTRÉN: *Reiseerinnerungen aus den Jahren 1838-1844*, St. Petersburg, 1853. JACOB FELLMAN: *Anteckningar under min vistelse i Lappmarken*, i-iv, Helsinki, 1906. FREDERIK RODE: *Optegnelser fra Finmarken*, Skien, 1842.

Of the vast amount of other material the following are noted: SIGRID DRAKE: *Västerbottens-lapparne under förre hälften av 1800-talet*, Uppsala, 1918. A. RUD EM: "Die Rentierzucht der Waldlappen" (*Zeitschr. f. Ethnol.*, lxix, Berlin, 1938). JOHS. FALKENBERG: "Bosætningen ved indre Laksefjord i Finmark" (*Nordnorske Saml.*, ii, 3, Oslo, 1941). GJERTRUD AND GUTORM GJESSING: "Lappedrakten" (*Instit. f. Sammenlign. Kulturforskn., Ser. C*, iv, 2, Oslo, 1940). GUTORM GJESSING: "Bæl'ljegammen" (*Norsk Geogr. Tidsskr.*, ix, Oslo, 1942). GUDMUND HATT: "Lappiske Slædeformer" (*Geogr. Tidsskr.*, xxii, Copenhagen, 1914). FILIP HULTBLAD: "Flyttlapparna i Gällivare socken" (*Geographica*, 1, Uppsala, 1936). FILIP HULTBLAD: "Några drag ur skogslapparnas äldre kulturgeografi" (*Geographica*, 15, Uppsala, 1944). T. I. ITKONEN: *Suomen lappalaiset*, i-ii, Porvoo-Helsinki, 1948. T. I. ITKONEN: "The Lapps of Finland" (*Southwest. Journ. Anthrop.*, vii, Albuquerque, 1951). NIKOLAI N. KHARUZIN: *Russkie lopari*, Moskva, 1890. RAFÆL KARSTEN: *Samefolkets religion*, Stockholm, 1952. OLUF KOLSRUD: "Finnefolket i Ofoten" (*Nordnorske Saml.*, viii, 3, Oslo, 1947). ANDERS LARSEN: "Om sjøsamene" (*Tromsø Mus. Årshefter. Human. Avdel.*, 13, Tromsø, 1950). ERNST MANKER: "Die lappische Zaubertrommel, I-II" (*Acta Lappon*, i, Stockholm, 1938, 1950). ERNST MANKER: "Lapsk kultur vid Stora Lule Älvs källsjöar" (*Acta Lappon*, iv, Stockholm, 1944). ERNST MANKER: "The Nomadism of the Swedish Mountain Lapps" (*Acta Lappon*, vii, Stockholm, 1953). ASBJØRN NESHEIM: "Finnish *hiisu* and Lappish *sii'dâ*" (*Finn.-ugr. Forsch.*, xxx, Helsinki, 1951). AXEL OLRIK: "Nordisk og lappisk gudsdyrkelse" (*Danske Stud.*, Copenhagen, 1905). STEN STURE PATERSON: "Anthropological Studies among the Jokkmokk Mountain Lapps" (*Göteborgs Kungl. Vetensk- och Vitterh.-Samh. Handl. 6, Följd. A*, vi, 2, Göteborg, 1956). JUST KNUD QVIGSTAD: "Kildeskrifter til den lappiske mythologi" (*Kg. Norske Vidensk. Selsk. Skr.*, 1903, i, 1910, 4, Trondhiem). EDGAR REUTERSKIÖLD: *De nordiska lapparnas religion*, Stockholm, 1912. ISRAEL RUONG: "Fjällapparna i Jakkasjärvi socken" (*Geographica*, 3, Uppsala, 1937). ISRAEL RUONG: "Studier i lapsk kultur i Pite lappmark och angränsande områden" (*Svenska landsmal*, lxvi-lxvii, Stockholm, 1943-4). ISRAEL RUONG: "Något om den gamla skogsren-skötseln i Arvidsjaurs socken" (*Geographica*, 15, Uppsala,

1944). CARLO RÖNNOW: "Renskötseln hos Arjeplogs fjällsamer" (*Sv. Geogr. Årsbok*, Lund, 1944). CARLO RØNNOW: "Om kastrering hos de renskötande folken med särskild hänsyn til rennomadismen i Sverige" (*Folk- Liv.*, Stockholm, 1948-9). P. L. SMITH: "Kautokeino og Kautokeinolapperne" (*Inst. f. Sammenlign. Kulturforskn., Ser. B*, xxxiv, Oslo, 1938). ERIK SOLEM: "Lappiske retsstudier" (*Inst. f. Sammenlign. Kulturforskn., Ser. B*, xxiv, Oslo, 1933). V. TANNER: "Antropogeografiska studier inom Petsamo-området. I, Skoltlapparna" (*Fennia*, xxxix, 4, Helsingfors, 1929). HELMER TEGENGREN: "En utdöd lappkultur i Kemi lappmark" (*Acta Acad. Åbœnsis. Human*, xix, 4, Abo, 1952). K. B. WIKLUND: *De svenska nomadlapparnas flyttningar till Norge i äldre och nyare tid*, Uppsala, 1908. K. B. WIKLUND: "Lapparnas forna utbredning i Finland och Ryssland, belyst av ortsnamnen" (*Le Monde Oriental*, v, Uppsala, 1911). K. B. WIKLUND: "Die Herkunft der Lappen" (*Folk-Liv.*, Stockholm, 1937). K. B. WIKLUND: "Untersuchungen uber die älteste Geschichte der Lappen und die Entstehung der Renntierzucht" (*Folk-Liv.*, Stockholm, 1938). ØRNULV VORREN: "Dyregraver og reingjerder i Varanger" (*Nordnorske Saml.*, vi, Oslo, 1944). ØRNULV VORREN: "Sjösamene" (*Heimen*, ix, Oslo, 1952-4). D. A. ZOLOTAREV: "Kolskie Lopari" (*Mater. Komiss. Ekspedit. Issledov. IX Ser. Severn*, Leningrad, 1928).

THE TUAREG

Desert and Oasis

The Camel

AFRICA, it has been said, begins south of the Pyrenees—and there are in fact many similarities between the Spanish plateau and large tracts of the Dark Continent. But it might be said with equal truth that the north-west corner of Africa, the Atlas region, belongs to Europe. Almost a complete ring of geologically young mountain ranges encircles the entire western Mediterranean. Summer droughts and winter rains produce on both sides of the Mediterranean the same kind of evergreen forest and scrub. When the Roman legions landed at Carthage, the landscape that met them was not unfamiliar. Beyond the mountains, however, things were different. There the steppes began. East of the Atlas Mountains they even reached right down to the sea, while farther inland the steppes merged into endless desert. Though the Roman aqueduct builders gradually transformed the South Tunisian plains into the Empire's granary, with a density of population considerably greater than that of present-day Wales, and even though the Empire's safety was ensured by pushing its borders out beyond the farthest oases, the deserts remained strange and mysterious.

Before the Romans, both Phœnicians and Greeks had founded colonies on the coast of North Africa, but they had penetrated even less far inland than their successors. Their cities were largely bases for sea trade and therefore faced out to sea. Their knowledge of the interior was limited, but they knew it to be mainly desert. Herodotus describes it as "desolate, without water, without animals, without rain, without plant life and devoid of all trace of humidity". What confronted the ancients was the world's mightiest stretch of desert, the Sahara.

Herodotus's graphic description was, of course, exaggerated, and he is probably equally unreliable when he writes of the North African people, the Atarants: "They curse the rising sun, reviling it with the most dreadful oaths, for it burns up the men and lays waste their land." Nevertheless, it is not difficult to appreciate the feelings aroused by the desert. Day after day a pitiless sun shines with a blinding glare out of a cloudless sky. In the summer the heat rises to the unbearable—a shade temperature of over 112°F. has been registered, far above blood temperature—and only the dryness of the atmosphere makes it possible to survive at all. The intense heat produces rising air currents, and at times the atmosphere is darkened with a mist of fine dust which has been lifted high above the surface of the earth. If equilibrium is further disturbed, dry sand and dust storms can ensue. On the other hand, powerful radiation produces violent fluctuations of temperature. One groans at the heat by day, only to shiver at the cold by night. In the winter, the chill wind in conjunction with the blazing sun can be extremely unpleasant, and night frost is by no means rare. But the desert is not completely devoid of rain. In the extreme north offshoots of the Mediterranean winter rains reach its fringes and provide a sparse rainfall, while during the summer what remains of the Sudan's moist monsoon air reaches its southern regions. But in the central area the drought is almost unbroken.

Even more characteristic than the paucity of the rainfall is its irregularity. A place which has only 0·2 in. of rain one year can have had more than 6 in. two years earlier. And when rain finally does come it falls in such torrents that streams of mud gush through the gorges and river beds, carrying everything along with it. There is some reason for saying that next to dying of thirst the greatest danger in the Sahara is death by drowning!

In other respects the Sahara is far from being as monotonous as is generally supposed. "But what about sand?" it will be asked. Sand dunes do cover vast areas, though in fact they form only a minor part of the whole. Far more extensive are pebble and stone plateaux, the remains of mountains destroyed during past ages. Lack of water reduces chemical disintegration to a minimum, but the violent changes in temperature break the rocks up into gravel. Sand storms wear away exposed rocks at the base and transform them into grotesque mushroom-like shapes. In the hollows there are often salt marshes which are of great importance to both people and cattle. Here and there is a lonely tamarisk, a thorny genista or a dusty acacia, but only where the roots can reach down to water which sometimes exists below dry river courses is there an unbroken strip of vegetation. Mile after mile often lies completely bare of all but an occasional stunted bush. And when, after an interval of some years, a torrential shower of rain does suddenly occur, clusters of annuals will suddenly shoot up, and in the space of a couple of weeks blossom, bear fruit and wither.

Even this is not the whole picture of the Sahara. In some places underground forces have raised masses of Arch-rock and sandstone into plateaux 6,000 feet or more high, which are furrowed by deep ravines and crowned with picturesque summits of lava. These areas, Tassili-n-Ajjer and Ahaggar* in central Sahara, for example, and Aïr and Adrar-n-Iforas in the south, have a more plentiful precipitation than the lower-lying districts, and are therefore natural places for the people of the desert to congregate. They are frequently described by Arab travellers as an earthly paradise, with an abundance of wells, rippling streams and luxuriant vegetation. This lyrical description must be seen against the barren desert background, for in fact the vegetation is poor enough. In some of the most favoured valleys there are stretches of something approaching open forest and savannah with grasses, doum palms and one or two species of acacia. But in the hills, vegetation is more scattered and only after the late summer rains are they also transformed for a few months into welcome pastures. In the mountains there is abundant animal life, including wild desert sheep and one or two species of gazelle; in the extreme south there are monkeys, and in the rainy season even lions find their way up from the Sudan.

* Ahaggar is the Tuareg name; Hoggar is its Arabic form.

The ostrich is also to be found and at one time could even occur much farther north.

A great deal has been said about the gradual and progressive drying up of the Sahara. In fact there is every indication that the climate has not materially changed since the days of the Romans. It is true that for periods of the Ice Age and afterwards conditions were considerably more favourable with an abundance of rain. The explanation for this is said to have been a shift in the prevailing winds each time Europe lay buried under the ice.* But the situation is scarcely so simple. Suffice to say, however, that in the most inhospitable regions of the Sahara there is clear evidence that for the enormous period of time which comprises the earlier part of the Old Stone Age, there were on at least two occasions large lakes and rivers in the desert. Regions through which camel caravans now make their way under the blazing sun and find only the most meagre supplies of food were once rich in animal life. Innumerable primitive stone implements provide evidence of contemporary hunting peoples, and no one need be in any doubt as to the manner of their existence, for on numerous rocks there are carvings of the game which provided their food. Buffalo, elephant, hippopotamus, rhinoceros and many other animals, which have since had to move to more favourable districts, then frequented the Sahara. The last period of humidity occurred during the transition to the Neolithic Age. Quantities of arrow heads and fragments of crude pottery, together with containers and beads of ostrich-egg shell, though only a few polished stone axes, date from that time. While the early finds come mainly from the desert itself, the more recent ones were largely concentrated round the old river beds and the shores of the lakes. Curiously enough, the finds in the mountain districts proper, on the other hand, are few and far between.

* * *

In those times, then, the desert did not form a sharp divide between black Africa in the south and the Mediterranean countries

* What is known as the Ice Age comprises four glaciations separated by warmer (inter-glacial) periods.

This photograph of a veiled Tuareg leading two riding camels was taken in the Ahaggar Mountains. Riding camels are precious and zealously cared for; in the exigency of a tribal raid a journey of sixty miles might be made in a single day.

Left: Even when riding an ox the Tuareg is veiled.

Below: Watering goats at Tassil-n-Ajjer. Hereabouts agriculture is practised, mainly by Negroes, and the vassal tribes are content to pay for a wife in goats—a practice regarded with contempt by the Ahaggars who pay seven camel mares. Yet goats and sheep are the basis of economic life; there being as many as forty to each human.

of the north. It has been suggested that the aboriginal population of the Sahara were Negroes. There can be no certainty about this. True, a Neolithic skeleton with negroid characteristics from Asselar in the southern desert, west of Adrar-n-Iforas, is known. But a single find does not reveal much. In the same connexion, attention has been drawn to some statements by Herodotus. In his description of the Garamants, a powerful people from the oasis of Fezzan, he relates how they literally hunted the "cave-dwelling Ethiopians". He goes on to say that these were the most nimble-footed of all peoples, that they existed entirely on snakes and lizards and spoke an incomprehensible language which sounded like the squeaking of a bat. There are certain indications that these "cave-dwelling Ethiopians" are the ancestors of the present-day Tubu of the eastern Sahara; racially the latter approach the Negro, and their language is related to the Kanuri language of the Sudan, but the distribution of their blood groups tallies with that of the Berbers in Atlas, and generally speaking their origin is somewhat obscure. From other quarters there is said to be no certain evidence of Negro peoples in the Sahara before the first centuries of the Christian era, except for the Aïr plateau which was peopled by Hausa from the Sudan right down to the Middle Ages. It is no proof, the argument runs, that the oasis dwellers of today chiefly belong to the black race, for trade in Sudanese slaves is deep rooted and in addition many Negroes have immigrated voluntarily during the course of the last hundred years. Who the Sahara's oldest inhabitants actually were must remain an open question until further discoveries have been made.

So much is certain, however: the central Sahara's ruling people, the Tuareg, in spite of a Negro strain among those living in the far south, belong to the light-skinned, Europid Mediterranean race, and speak a Berber language related to those which were once widespread over the greater part of North Africa and which, even today, centuries after the Arab immigration, still survive in out-of-the-way parts of the Atlas Mountains. And no one doubts that the Tuareg came from the north and gradually spilled over the borders of the Sudan. Though they are now generally regarded as desert people it is well to remember that this description really applies only to the two northern tribal groups in Tassili-n-Ajjer and Ahaggar. The populations of Aïr and Adrar-n-Iforas are already a transition towards the southern Tuareg who live in the Sudan as far south as the Niger.

Still more significant is the fact that though the area occupied by the two northern groups is no smaller than that occupied by the southern groups, the northern groups comprise no more than 7,000-8,000 or 2-3 per cent. of the total number of Tuareg, which amounts to about a quarter of a million. When one reads the impression that this promised land in the south made on the French ethnologist Henri Lhote after a difficult crossing of the desert, it is not surprising that the Tuareg turned their backs on it. He writes:

> "When I caught sight of the plains of the Sudan with grass at knee height and mimosa flowering, the contrast was so great that I felt overwhelmed. A sweet perfume intoxicated my parched nostrils, a warm vapour rose up from the fertile ground, antelopes and gazelles frisked about on all sides, birds flew from tree to tree and everywhere one had an impression of teeming life concealed in the abundant vegetation. . . . Some days later we reached the first camps of the Sudanese Tuareg, and they were surrounded by hordes of goats and sheep and oxen which, more than any words could do, bore witness to the country's wealth."

Though the northern ancestry of the Tuareg cannot be doubted, the details of their immigration are extremely vague. The Arabian author Ibn Khaldun, who died in 1406, and who wrote a history of North Africa and the Berbers, takes the view that they originally came from southern Arabia—which is in line with the desire of all Moslems to trace ancestry back to the Prophet's fatherland. But it has, of course, as little in common with fact as the fantastic idea that their ancestors were Crusaders who sought refuge in the desert. However, even the soberest attempts to clear the mystery up leave a number of gaps and are often more or less self-contradictory. Presumably the explanation is that several different Berber elements have merged at various times to make up the present tribes.

One point of certainty we have is the fact that excavations in Fezzan, which, according to Herodotus, is the native home of the ancient Garamants, have brought to light skeletons with Tuareg racial characteristics. Furthermore, a number of the folk names quoted by Ptolemy from the Sahara are interpreted as denoting Tuareg tribes. This had led to the view that Libya, and Fezzan in particular, is the original home of the Tuareg. But when did the move to the desert take place and what gave it its impulse?

The Garamants were farmers and cattle-breeders and travelled in ox carts and with pack-oxen. Armed with iron spears and round shields they drove their four-in-hand war-chariots against their enemies, until later in ancient times chariot fighting gave way to cavalry. Now it so happens that any number of the more recent rock pictures in the Sahara represent warriors armed in exactly this fashion. But while the pictures of war chariots are mostly confined to the northern parts of the desert, the pictures of cavalry are found as far south as the Sudan. From this Henri Lhote concludes that it was the horse, particularly as a riding animal, which as it were, opened up the Sahara to the Mediterranean peoples. One difficulty with this theory is the fact that the horse needs plenty of food and water. But it is not inconceivable that the humid periods of the Neolithic Age exerted an influence as late as about 1000 B.C. and the centuries immediately following, and that some of the poverty-stricken agriculture which is still carried on by certain Tuareg perhaps goes right back to the time of this first immigration.

Later, however, there seem to have been fresh impulses from the north. It is still impossible to decide yet when the camel came to be domesticated. There are indications that this might have taken place in central Arabia perhaps as early as about 3000 B.C., though the camel played no military rôle until much later when, at the beginning of the first millennium B.C., under the influence of the horse saddle, the camel saddle had achieved its final form. In any case, the camel did not become common in Egypt until Hellenistic times, and not until still later in the Atlas regions. True, when Julius Cæsar defeated King Juba and the Pompeians at Thapsus in 46 B.C. the booty did include twenty-two camels, but they seem to have been no more than something of a curiosity, and the camel became of vital significance to nomadic life only when the Berber Zenata tribes, after an uprising under Emperor Trajan, left their homes in Cyrenaica and trekked westward with their herds. The camel was conceivably responsible for a new folk movement in the Sahara.

Ibn Khaldun thinks that at least some of the Tuareg descended from the Berber group which he calls Botr and which are practically the same as the Zenatas. It is a well-known fact that the camel plays a vital part in the Tuareg's division into noble and vassal tribes and this will be enlarged upon later on. In this connexion mention should be made of the camel-breeding Sanhaja-Berbers who at the beginning of the eleventh century founded a powerful confederation in the western Sahara. The fact that they overthrew and Islamized the Negro kingdom of Ghana in the Sudan,* concerns us no more than the fact that they set themselves up as masters first in Morocco and then in Islamic Spain. What does matter to us, however, is that some Sanhaja tribes are counted among the Tuareg's ancestors.

Finally there is a possibility that the Arab invasion of North Africa also contributed to their immigration. The Arabian conquest of 641 or 642 was purely military in character. It was only in the eleventh century that the big stream of Bedouins followed. It was on this occasion that Fezzan fell into their hands and it is said that the Berbers, the late successors of the Garamants, who were driven from there, joined their tribal kinsmen in the desert.

Be that as it may, various aspects of the Tuareg's pre-history have still to be cleared up. Broadly speaking, however, the boundaries of their distribution east, west and north seem to have remained more or less unchanged since the beginning of the Middle Ages, apart from the loss of Fezzan, and the fact that the western Sanhaja tribes in present-day Mauretania have become Arabianized. To

* This medieval Ghana must not, of course, be confused with the newly-formed state of the same name, the former colony of the Gold Coast.

the south the boundary has been more fluid, for the desert never formed a complete obstacle. In the Sudan this led to the setting up of a number of medieval Negro states under Berber princes and Islamic religion. Ghana, mentioned above, was founded as early as the fourth century and was supplanted in the thirteenth century by the Mali kingdom; 200 years later this was in turn supplanted by Songhai, which was subverted by the Moroccans in 1591. While these states were at the height of their power they extended their domain—commercially, if not always politically—over large parts of the desert, where the salt fields were a constant source of dispute. These boundary adjustments hardly mattered to the Tuareg. They always managed to assert their real independence in the natural mountain fastnesses of the desert.

* * *

The history of the Tuareg immigration is clearly reflected in their remarkable political organization. Highest in the social scale are the nobles. These comprise not scattered families, however, but whole tribes and under them, as their subjects or vassals, are other tribes. The noble tribes, *Ihaggaren* or *Imachegh*, constitute only a small part of the total population, i.e. no more than one-fifth in the northern groups and one-eighth in the Sudan. They despise all physical work and, as Tacitus says of the ancient Germanic tribes, "consider it shameful to achieve by sweat what could be achieved by the sword".

Originally it was their special privilege to own camels. At the camps, however, they keep only such animals as are necessary for riding, plus as many goats as will keep them supplied with milk. The big herds are left to the care of the vassals. The vassals probably comprise an older population subjugated by the camel riders who immigrated later. Their name, *Imghad*, is probably derived direct from a word describing them as goat-keepers. In return for tending the herds of the nobles they are under their protection. On the other hand, at any rate in Aïr, they have to pay the nobles part of what they receive in bride price, and they also pay certain levies, while the nobles can fine them for offences. The sharp division between the two is disappearing, in that the vassals now have the right to a half-share in the issue of camels and thus to become camel owners themselves. They can also take part in the nobles' campaigns and raiding expeditions and even undertake such enterprises on their own account in return for handing over part of the booty to their overlords. One at least of the vassal tribes on the Niger has even managed to make itself completely independent. Under the present peaceful circumstances, the economic conditions of the nobles have, as might be expected, deteriorated while the prosperity of the vassals has increased.

Both noble and vassal tribes have their chieftains or "elders", but their influence is strictly circumscribed by the people's assembly, in which all adult men participate. The elders' badge of office is a bowl-shaped drum, which is used to call the subjects together. In the autumn they receive tax on the year's yield in the form of camel foals, sheep, dates, millet, etc. Each desert tribe owns its own pastures through which strangers have the right to travel, though they must not pitch camp without the approval of the relevant tribal chieftain, essential, for example, in the event of a period of devastating drought. In the Sudan, where vegetation is more luxuriant, the rights of the tribe do not go beyond the watering of their animals at certain wells, pasturage being open to all.

Individual tribes are again joined into federations, such as Kel Ahaggar and Kel Ajjer in the north, Kel Aïr and Kel Adrar farther south, and Kel Geres and the two Ioullemeden federations in the Sudan. At the head of the association is the head-chieftain or *Amenokal*. The office is hereditary and goes first to the eldest surviving brother, then to the eldest son of the deceased's mother's sister, and in the final instance to the eldest sister's eldest son—a curious order of succession which is directly contrary to Islamic custom. Only the Ioullemeden have adopted the Arabian hereditary succession of father to son. The *Amenokal* belongs, of course, to the nobility, but he has to be approved not only by the noble tribes, but also by the vassals, and it is the latter's representatives who speak first in the assembly.

In Ahaggar and Aïr the vassals even had the final word, and the Sultan of Agadez is chieftain more in name than in fact. When he leaves the city he is accompanied by an impressive cortège of all the inhabitants on horseback or on foot, with twelve drummers out in front. In actual fact, however, he has long been devoid of power, and one of the Air tribes, the Kel Oui, recognizes only its own chieftain, who is elected for three years at a time.

[According to the investigations of Mr. Nicolaisen, published after this chapter was written, the socio-political system of the Tuareg has to some extent been misunderstood by earlier authors. What formerly were called "tribes" are rather matrilineal and theoretically endogamous clans. Several vassal clans are attached to a single noble clan, thus constituting a "drum group", so called after the insignia of the chieftain of the noble clan. A federation consists of several "drum groups", of which one of the chieftains is *Amenokal*. The Sultan of Agadez is not at the same time head chief of a "drum group" and therefore has very little actual power. (Cf. Johs Nicolaisen, *Political Systems of Pastoral Tuareg in Aïr and Ahaggar*, Folk., i, Copenhagen, 1959.)]

A long way below the vassals come the *Iklan*, or slaves, who are mostly descended from Sudanese prisoners of war. They differ not only in race but to some extent also in dress, for originally they did not wear the characteristic veil. Even within the slave caste there are certain differences in rank. Those who tend the herds, who accompany their masters when camp is moved in order to load the camels, fill the water bags, and so on, consider themselves a cut above the oasis slaves who are employed in agriculture, etc. All in all the lot of the slaves is not too bad. They can own property, though at their death it passes to their masters. Children and old people who cannot support themselves must not be set free but be given their keep, while if a slave is ill-treated he can demand that he be sold to a less brutal master. A kind of fictive kinship exists between masters and slaves, so that they form an integrated part of society. This contributes in no small measure towards good personal relations between them. Most of the black oasis dwellers (*Izzegaghen*, though they are better known by the

Arabic name, *Haratin*) really cannot be considered slaves in the normal sense of the term, even if they are dependent on the nomads. They have more the character of copyholders. Many of them are the descendants of Negroes who immigrated late in history from the Tidikelt oases. In sum, the presence of Negroes in the Sahara is an extremely complicated problem and one that is by no means cleared up (see page 145).

Parallel with the strata of society just described are certain others which cannot be passed over without a mention. Some tribes with a strong admixture of Arabian blood, are more independent than the normal vassals, without however attaining the level of the nobility. Tribes occupying a special position are the "spiritual" tribes, *Inislimen*, who correspond to the Maraboutes (Arabic: *Murabit*) of the Atlas countries. Rightly or wrongly these are held to be the descendants of Islamic saints. They look after the children's religious education, though this does not mean a great deal, since their own knowledge is not developed to any noticeable degree. They also make amulets bearing inscriptions from the Koran and in laymen's eyes this is probably considered even more important. Some, moreover, claim descent from the Prophet himself—which further raises their prestige—and these are treated as the nobles' equals. Some of them even act the part of warriors with vassals under them, though strictly according to the Koran this is forbidden.

Different in character and economically rather more important is what is known as the smith caste. These constitute a closed section of society, despised and at the same time feared. Its members are of mixed origin, chiefly of unmistakably Negro descent, but obviously with a strain of Jewish blood in their veins. In addition to the actual work of smiths they occupy themselves with all manner of crafts such as wood carving and saddle making—tasks which no self-respecting Tuareg would undertake. Sometimes they also act as barber-surgeons and jugglers.

To describe the Tuareg as nomads, then, is only part of the story. Their society is in fact extremely complex and the actual herdsmen constitute only a single component of a rather complicated organism, the separate parts of which have been mutually adapted in order to function.

* * *

Though the Tuareg have never constituted a political unit, they are thought of as one nation both by the Arabs and by themselves. One of the ways in which this idea finds expression is in the words used to describe them: the Arabic *Muleththemin* and their own *Kel Tagoulemoust*. Both names have the same meaning: "People of the Veil". The designation refers to the curious custom by which all freeborn adult men, in contrast to the women, veil their faces so that only the eyes are uncovered. The reason for this is uncertain. They themselves can give no explanation beyond the fact that from time immemorial it has been the custom. It has been explained on the practical grounds of giving protection against sandstorms. If so, then why do young men wait for several years after puberty before adopting the veil? And why are they not worn by women? It could be argued that women are less subject to the discomforts of long desert journeys. Some magical basis has also been suggested, though little foundation for this exists at present. Whatever the original reason, it has now been forgotten and veiling is purely a matter of propriety.

It is considered indecent for men to uncover their mouths, even when they are eating—at any rate in the presence of certain relations. Curiously enough the custom seems to be comparatively recent, for it is extremely unlikely that Roman writers would have ignored such a curious custom if it had been practised in ancient times. The first reliable mention of the custom is by medieval Arab travellers, which suggests that it started sometime during the second half of the first millennium. The veil is a long, narrow piece of cloth consisting of between nine and eighteen strips of cotton sewn together, draped round the head and chin. The best kinds are bought in the Sudanese town of Kano and correspond in value to no less than something between three and five goats. Among northern tribes the noble's veil is black and the vassal's white, but this rule does not apply in Aïr. At one time on festive occasions the men also wore a tall cloth headdress with large tassels and silver decorations.

The rest of the dress is no more the result of an adaptation to desert conditions than is the veil. It is, rather, the consequence of historical influences. But it cannot be denied that, like the dress worn by the Bedouins, it is well suited to the climate, since it gives protection not only from the burning sun but also to a certain extent from the chilly night air. It is simple enough. The men's dress consists of a knee-length white shirt which is, in fact, no more than a large unsewn piece of cloth with a hole in it for the head, and fastened together at the corners. Sometimes it is nicely embroidered. Underneath are long, wide trousers. A belt is worn high round the waist which stiffens the body in riding. On the feet are large thick-soled leather sandals with a strap for the toes —and very necessary they are, seeing that on a summer day the sand can reach a temperature of nearly 160°F. Amulets with inscriptions from the Koran are, of course, indispensable, for though the Tuareg are by no means fervent devotees of Islam, they are extremely superstitious.

As soon as a young man reaches years of discretion he puts on the characteristic armring of polished serpentine and the weapons which from now on form part of his daily equipment: the long two-edged sword with its cruciform hilt, the long slender spear which is forged for combat entirely out of iron, the broad shield of sable antelope's skin and finally, and not to be forgotten, the curious dagger which is fastened to a broad leather strap and worn with the hilt downwards on the left forearm. Bows and arrows, however, are left to the Negroes to handle—only the Kel Oui tribesmen in Aïr constitute an exception in this respect—the result of Sudanese influence. The throwing knife, the despised weapon of the Tubu, they certainly would not condescend to use.

The women wear a head cloth and a long skirt wrapped round the loins. The northern tribeswomen also wear a shift of similar cut to the men's, but in Aïr they are content with a short jacket, and in the Sudan they even go about naked to the waist or, at the most, scantily covered by a shoulder cloth. Their ornaments are as simple as their dress, amounting to no more than simple bracelets, necklaces and ornaments of silver at the temples. Sensibly enough for a poor people, they consider gold unlucky. On the other hand both men and women care for their appearance in other ways. They frequently rub butter into the skin, which is, of course, a practical measure in the bone-dry atmosphere. Both sexes also rub the eye surrounds with black antimony-sulphide to protect them from the glare of the desert. The indigo colour of the clothes, also, tends to come off on to their skin. In addition, like so many of their sisters in the Middle East, the women colour their nails with henna and make themselves up with yellow ochre and white clay. Tattooing scarcely occurs at all, though women in the Sudan frequently prick small designs in the neighbourhood of the mouth.

Boys and young men shave their hair off except for a ridge along the crown of the head, whereas grown men and women wear the hair in small plaits, while old men shave their heads completely. Moustaches are never worn, probably on account of the veil. The continual application of butter and dye suggests that cleanliness is not the Tuaregs' greatest virtue, and, of course, this is hardly to be expected from their environment. It is unusual for anyone to come into voluntary contact with water, and even the obligatory washing before prayer prescribed by religion is performed symbolically—admittedly with the approval of Islamic law—by touching the sand with the hands. In one respect alone are there no grounds for complaint in the matter of cleanliness: rinsing the mouth and cleaning the teeth with a frayed stick is a daily performance.

The Tuareg no more concern themselves with weaving than with any other form of craft—all of them are beneath their dignity. The fabrics they use are bought in the Sudan and many of them are modern industrial products from Europe. In bygone days, when woven materials were less common, their clothes were made of fine tanned leather. In out of the way places it is still possible to see children running about with a leather breechcloth, and until quite recently even grown men sometimes wore one under their cotton trousers. The use of shirts and skirts of leather was continued by male and female slaves until comparatively recently. The only Tuareg dress of leather which has been preserved is now to be found in the *Musée de l'Homme* in Paris. It appears to be a knee-length poncho with fringed edges, shaped at the waist, which gives it a certain, scarcely chance, similarity to Libyan dress familiar from ancient Egyptian paintings.

As might be expected of a pastoral people, the tent is their favourite habitation. In the Sudan the tent cloth is of calf skin; in the desert, of goat skin rubbed with butter mixed with red ochre. A normal tent requires no fewer than thirty to forty goat skins which are cut and sewn together with thin strips of leather by means of a bone bodkin. The cloth is stretched over pairs of upright posts of tamarisk wood and pegged down. One pair of posts is in the middle and on either side of them are two pairs of shorter posts. Each pair of posts is usually connected at the top by a crossbar transverse to the length of the tent. There are, however, certain variations of this basic type. Instead of two middle posts one sometimes suffices, and the crossbar is tenoned to it so that they form a letter T. Alternatively arches of bent sticks can take the place of one, or both, of the centre posts.

Among the Kel Geres in the Sudan only the centre post has a crossbar, while the side posts are connected to each other and to the crossbar by means of lines. The T-shaped arrangement is a recent characteristic which is hardly likely to have originated with the Tuareg. More probably it has been borrowed from the black goat-hair tent of the Arabs, and according to Johannes Nicolaisen's researches was first introduced by the noble camel-breeding tribes. The arch construction, on the other hand, is old and certainly a survival from an original type, for the southern Tuareg also appear to have barrel-vault tents covered with hide or mats, and it can scarcely be doubted that the arch construction derives from them. This is all the more reason for considering the barrel-vault dwelling as the original one since a similar construction was found amongst the old Libyans and, under the name of *mapalia*, it was widespread in ancient North Africa.

All in all the Tuareg have a greater variety of dwellings than might be expected of a nomadic people—without including the natural caves, where they often seek shelter from the winter cold of the mountains, and the proper clay houses in such towns as Agadez. In the dry season, when it is too hot to stay in a tent, it is quite usual in the semi-permanent camps at wells and oases to build conical-roof houses of rush and straw; in Aïr the Kel Oui tribesmen, who have a strong admixture of Negro blood, use dome-shaped huts. This lack of uniformity is scarcely the result of adaptation to natural conditions, however different they may be in the desert and on the steppes of the Sudan; rather is it the result of the complex nature of the culture which again is a result of its complicated history—North African and Sudanese elements having merged into a confused mixture.

But to return to the tent—which in spite of all else is still the most important form of dwelling—the tent cloth usually functions as no more than a roof so that during the heat of the day the air can flow freely beneath it. In cold weather and during sand-storms mats are erected as walls, and in the winter walls of piled-up stones are often built. But not even such a tent is very effective against the night cold, so a fire is often lit outside the entrance. The fire for cooking, however, is situated some steps away from the tent. If there is difficulty in finding wood, dry manure is used as fuel. The ancient method of making fire, incidentally, was to run a stick backwards and forwards in a grooved wooden block.

The tent was erected so that its entrance faced south. The eastern side was the men's compartment, while the women kept to the western side. The floor was strewn with fine sand while along the back wall and at the sides the sparse equipment was stacked: saddles and saddle bags—the latter handsomely ornamented with colourful designs in leatherwork—leather bags for grain and dates, simple wooden dishes and bowls, etc. Hanging on a pair of posts were the skin sacks containing the precious drinking water, and elsewhere hung the horns of desert sheep which contained the butter churned during the course of the day; other butter was kept in leather bottles: churning was carried out simply by shaking the milk in a skin sack. There were milking vessels of wood, flour sieves of basket work, a flat quern stone for coarse grinding grain or perhaps a rotating mill (a later element) and finally a wooden mortar for pounding guinea corn and dates. The food was cooked in clay pots which were no more made by the Tuareg themselves than most of the other things. Evidence that they are not original appears from the fact that the Tuareg also knew how to cook with heated stones. From of old they sleep on blankets of sheepskin. Only the southern groups, which have a close link with the Negroes of the Sudan, have wooden beds of the same kind as those of the Hausa. Generally speaking their household goods are somewhat more plentiful than those of the desert tribes proper.

The poverty of the land prohibits big agglomerations of people. Five to six, or eight to twelve in the Sudan, is the average number of tents found in a camp, for the prime requisite is enough fodder for the herds, which are essential for the maintenance of life. Water, of course, is also a vital necessity. But partly from fear of attack, partly to avoid contamination, the camps are pitched some little distance from the wells. The animals are watered every second or third day. The group remains at one spot normally for a month at the most—often considerably less—after which they seek fresh pastures.

* * *

The most valued animal, it need hardly be mentioned, is the camel, or rather the dromedary. War, love and camels are the main subject of Tuareg poetry, and the significance of the camel in the class structure has already been mentioned. Nevertheless it is not the camel which provides the basis of economic life; this rôle is performed by more modest creatures: the goats and sheep. Of these, the goats are decidedly the more important. There are about ten times as many goats as sheep—altogether some thirty-five to forty per person—and the importance of the rôle they play can be judged from the simple fact that there are no less than twelve terms for describing them according to their sex and age, and at least seventeen for describing them according to their colour, etc.

And they are only too well aware of their importance. The kids roam at will in the tents and even the fully grown animals are incredibly tame. But it goes without saying that to have crowds of goats running about is not the best way of promoting the growth of trees—which is poor enough anyway without all the damage done by the goats. It is not at all unusual to see a couple of goats climbing about in the crowns of low trees and destroying the young shoots.

Goats are milked morning and evening. The kids are allowed to drink only half the milk. To prevent them from sucking they have a stick fastened in their mouths, either tied to their horns or, far more barbarous, stuck through their cheeks. Milk is drunk both fresh and sour or is churned to butter. If there is butter milk to spare, as happens in good pasturage years, it is made into cheese which is dried as hard as stone and then pounded into meal in the mortar and mixed with the food or drinking water. As a general rule only barren goats or castrated bucks are slaughtered. But the sheep, which are an old fur-coated, long-legged and long-tailed race, are kept mainly for slaughter or are bred for sale in the oases.

From Herodotus we know that the Garamants owned herds of horned cattle, and both rock engravings and rock paintings testify that, in antiquity, they were widespread in the Sahara. There are even grounds for believing that the oldest trade connexions through the desert were maintained by caravans of oxen. Under present conditions horned cattle occur in any number only among the southern Tuareg. They belong to the zebu and serve both for riding and as beasts of burden. The same applies to donkeys, which are much commoner in the desert than the more demanding oxen. The donkeys are insufficiently tended and are in consequence semi-wild—often completely wild. When this happens they are rounded up by camel riders or caught by wheel-traps—an old and wide-spread hunting implement consisting of a ring with numerous wooden spikes inside to prevent the animal from getting away once its foot is in it. The horse is used solely for riding. Like the oxen it was presumably commoner in earlier times and as already mentioned is even thought to have made it possible for the Tuareg to spread through the desert. Nowadays the only place where it occurs in any frequency is the Sudan.

If the horse was responsible for the earliest move from the north, it was certainly the camel which was chiefly responsible for the subsequent immigration. The Aïr-Tuareg differentiate between no less than sixteen different breeds and colours of camel, but all of them, with their capacity for existing on next to nothing, for managing for days without water and for enduring a long journey, are unsurpassed in the desert. They are employed principally for riding and as beasts of burden. Only at the very largest of festivals does the slaughter of a camel foal come into question and then it is roasted whole in ashes. The Ioullemeden tribe in the Sudan will not eat camel meat at all. Camels are also a sign of prosperity. Certain payments, such as bride price and blood money, have to be made in the form of camels. In theory the wergild for a free man is as much as 100 camel mares of ten different colours, but in practice it is much less. For a bride of noble birth the western tribes pay six camel mares, a Negro slave and a complete costume; the Ahaggar tribes pay seven camel mares and look down with contempt on the vassal tribes in Ajjer who are content to pay in goats. Among the desert tribes the camel is the only animal for a dignified man to ride, whether on a peaceful trading mission or out for war or plunder. And while sheep and goat watching is left to women, tending the camel herds is exclusively men's work. True, this is due not only to the respect which the camel enjoys, but is the simple consequence of the method employed in tending them. Small cattle are preferably kept in the vicinity of the camp, but the camel grazing grounds are often miles distant and only the necessary number of riding animals are kept near the tents. The Ahaggar Tuareg can have the greater part of their herds to grass in the Sudan 500 miles from their camps.

A camel mare gives five to nine pints of milk a day, but obviously the herdsmen get most of the benefit of this. Camel milk is unsuitable for cheese and is churned into butter for rubbing into the hair only if there is insufficient goat's-milk butter in the warm season. Significantly enough the churning is done by the men, who trot about

Camel riders in Aïr: the one nearest is too young to have begun to wear the veil. Among the desert tribes the camel is the only animal for a dignified man to ride. The veil probably had its origin as an essential protection for the face from wind-driven sand to which all raiding parties and other desert travellers are exposed; in a sandstorm exposed flesh can be seared to the bone.

The photographs on this page are of objects in the National Museum, Copenhagen; all are from the Ahaggar Tuareg. Because the creed of Islam forbids the use of the human figure in decoration, geometric patterns are commonly used and among the Tuareg the cross often is featured. In this picture *above* are shown a decorated leather bag, a sword, and a dagger which is carried on the arm. The objects in the picture on the *right* are a camel saddle and leather shield.

Right: A Tuareg woman from Ahaggar.

Below: Women from Ahaggar cooking. In summer women, children and slaves gather in the dry river courses the seeds of wild grasses which they bake into bread. Vegetable products and milk (a camel mare gives between five and nine pints a day) constitute the greater part of their regular daily diet.

Tents of the Tuareg: the favourite habitation of these pastoral people is found in numerous forms; *above* is a goatskin tent in Ahaggar with walls of matting. A normal tent of this kind requires 30-40 goatskins.

Below: Matting-covered, barrel-vaulted tents in Aïr. Tents of arch-construction probably derive from these barrel-vault dwellings, which type is widespread in North Africa and probably is the original form of Tuareg tent.

with a sackful of milk fastened to the saddle. Camels will let themselves be milked only when their foal is nearby. If the foal dies then its skin must be stuffed and put up beside the mother as the African and Asiatic pastoral tribes are accustomed to do with cows. The camel is chiefly important as a riding animal, and riding camels are reared and trained with the utmost care. As a rule the stallions are castrated at the age of five, a slit being made in the scrotum and the sexual glands removed. The Tuareg are extremely jealous of their precious animals; they seldom put them into a trot and usually do not allow them to travel more than twenty-five to thirty miles daily. But if need be, on a raiding expedition, for example, then a good riding animal can cover over sixty miles a day.

The saddle is unusual. A round seat rests upon a roof-shaped underframe. The pommel is often in the shape of a cross and at the back there is an ogive-shaped cantle as support for the back. It is covered with red and black, and sometimes also green, leather and may even be mounted with silver. The saddle is light and practical, and is laid on the animal's shoulders in front of the hump. The rider sits aloft with his bare feet resting on the camel's neck and steers by the aid of a single rein fastened to a nose ring, or more rarely by the aid of a bit. The chieftains' women have special saddles rather in the shape of rectangular low-legged stools mounted with copper and decorated with large tufts of goat hair. They are placed over the actual hump without touching it and are sometimes fitted with a canopy. The pack saddles are, of course, much simpler and consist of no more than a pair of arches, connected by side pieces, and with padding of straw or manure.

There is a characteristic difference between Arab and Tuareg caravans which can be ascribed to geographical adaptation. While the North African Bedouin allow their camels to spread themselves out over the open country, the Tuareg tether theirs into a file—a practical method in their mountainous country. At night the animals are put out to graze with a rope round their forelegs so that they shall not wander off too far. Loading in the morning has its moments of drama, not only on account of the heartrending cries which every single camel feels in duty bound to utter, but also because by the time fifty of them have been loaded, at least five will quite certainly have thrown off their loads and gone back to grazing.

One might have imagined that the Tuareg would never lack meat for a meal. But as will be seen from the foregoing, meat is far from being the daily diet, for only on very rare occasions will a nomad slaughter an animal unless it is worn out or sick. In the desert they eat meat scarcely more than once a week, and this they mostly obtain from hunting, which is a favourite form of sport. The importance of hunting is apparent from the fact that at least one tribe, the Dag Ghali, have rules for the preservation of game and well-defined hunting territories, which are inherited through the female line. Gazelles, antelopes and wild desert sheep are the most common game. The ostrich has pretty well disappeared from the desert proper but is still to be found in the Sudan; likewise the giraffe, which is considered the most delicious of all game. The animals are often caught in spiked wheel-traps, but in the mountains the hunter, accompanied by his dog, something like a greyhound, tries to creep close enough to them to spear them—while the most exclusive method of all is to hunt them on camel or horseback. This is a method used for hunting the ostrich, which is chased until it is tired, one rider taking over from another. Under Islamic law only animals which have bled to death may be eaten. So domestic animals are slaughtered by a slit in the throat or in the case of camels by a stab in the heart. But on the hunt the Tuareg know how to evade the law, and a prick in the animal's ear, so that a few drops of blood flow, will do well enough if need be.

Like so many other desert peoples, the Tuareg heartily dislike fish, and curiously enough the northern, though not the southern, tribes have a similar attitude to both birds and eggs—with the single exception of the ostrich. Only the Negro slaves do not let anything edible go by them, but will fish in water holes and set bird snares. They will also eat snakes and other reptiles, for instance the yard-long desert monitor, which the Tuareg themselves avoid since they regard it as a "mother's brother". Some ethnologists interpret this as a survival of ancient totemistic ideas

—which is somewhat dubious. On the other hand they have no scruple about eating locusts, plagues of which sometimes occur, and in this they are like the ancient Libyans of whom Herodotus tells a similar tale.

On the whole, food gathering is an essential part of Tuareg economy. In the summer, women, children and slaves are in the habit of gathering the seeds of wild grasses in the dry river courses which they bake into bread. In fact, vegetable products and milk constitute the greater part of their daily diet. But it is only exceptionally that they have been produced by the Tuareg themselves. Settled, field-cultivating Tuaregs live in the Ghat Oasis. Otherwise only a few nomads in Ajjer condescend to sow a little wheat in the river valleys after a shower of rain, returning later to harvest the crop. In earlier times, however, this also occurred in Ahaggar and Aïr.

Otherwise farming is left to the Negroes in the oases, and proof that they constitute no small part of the population is provided by the fact that a little over half the inhabitants of Ajjer and a good 40 per cent. in Ahaggar devote themselves to agriculture. It is significant, too, that the most popular grain cultivated is not Mediterranean wheat but guinea corn, the typical Negro cereal related to millet. In addition there are dates, figs and vegetables. The owner of the ground provides the seed and tools and in return he receives a large share of the yield—in former times four-fifths, nowadays two-thirds or even only a half. The small quantity of wheat and barley grown is largely disposed of in Tidikelt, whereas guinea corn is made into porridge.

The ground is worked in Negro fashion without a plough, solely with a mattock, harvesting is done with a sickle and threshing with a simple stick. Irrigation is, of course, essential. Where it is not possible to make use of a well, as in Ghat and Ajjer, then more laborious methods must be employed. There are wells with counterpoised sweeps and wells where the water is drawn up by an ox or an ass, but the commonest are variants in a primitive form of the peculiar irrigation system which under the name of *foggara*, *karez* or *khanat* is widespread in the arid zone from the Atlantic right into the interior of Central Asia. The genuine *foggara* consists of an underground pipe through which the water is drawn from higher-level districts many miles off into open channels in the ground and which, to facilitate digging and subsequent cleaning, is connected to the surface by a number of narrow shafts. This type, however, is not found south of the Tidikelt and Ghadames oases. In central Sahara, where the installation was introduced late in history from Tidikelt, it never reaches down to solid rock and is only underground for a short stretch, after which it forms an open canal ending with a reservoir from which smaller ditches branch out over the fields.

Apart from raiding expeditions, which were once a feature of the economy, all the most important aspects of the Tuaregs' activities have now been described. But no picture of a nomadic folk's existence would be complete without reference to their seasonal wanderings. This brings us to a circumstance which at first glance might seem strange: the journeys made for the benefit of the herds, even those made by the desert tribes proper, are quite restricted and in any case much shorter than the journeys undertaken for the benefit of trade. The wanderings of the Sudanese Tuareg are undertaken largely because the camels do not stand up to the humid monsoon at all well, and have to be taken to the salt steppes in the north. The Aïr tribes like to spend the dry season in the vicinity of wells and ponds and spread out again when the grazing grounds are once more green after the rain. Even in Ahaggar the journeys seldom extend over more than a couple of days at a time. Only in the event of drought are the camels driven really far away from the camps. Goats on the other hand are carefully kept in the vicinity.

Since rainfall and thus pasturage are so irregular, the wanderings of the desert nomads are generally less tied to the seasons than those of the steppe-dwellers. The Dag Ghali, one of the Ahaggar tribes, occupy an exceptional position and are best described as mountain nomads. From the end of the summer until the end of the winter they live in the high mountains, where the good grazing permits such a comparatively large number as fifteen tents to one camp, and they move to the lower-lying regions only for the spring and summer. The other Ahaggar tribes spend the entire year there, shifting from pasture to pasture within the tribal district and only occasionally sending their camels up into the mountains where they are tended by slaves.

By contrast the trading journeys are very much longer. From ancient times the caravans have made their way through the desert and brought Sudanese treasure—gold dust and ivory, ostrich feathers and slaves—to Mediterranean markets to be exchanged for silks, sugar, European sword blades, etc.—a large trade in which the Tuareg acted as caravan guides and middlemen. For a thousand years, from the eighth to the eighteenth centuries, the big Tafilelt group of oases in Morocco was a focus of this trade. The Tuareg themselves supplied the Negroes in the south with the indispensable salt from the desert salt fields. The Ahaggar Tuareg extract the salt at the end of the summer, when the worst of the heat is over, and about the beginning of October they make the long journey to Agadez and Zinder, a distance of no less than 750 miles as the crow flies. There they sell the salt at an average price of one load of salt for three to four loads of millet.

Soon after the New Year the caravans are back in Ahaggar, and, after a rest of no more than a couple of weeks, they are on their way northward again to Tidikelt or the other large groups of oases at Touat or, more rarely, to Ghat and Ghadamès. Here goods from the Sudan are disposed of together with dried mutton, butter and outworn camels for slaughter, while dates, sugar and tea are purchased. This done the long journey home can begin.

Big trading caravans also set out from Aïr for the Tubu in Tibesti and for the Sudan, though they are careful to be back again before the rainy season sets in. So far as the Ajjer Tuareg are concerned trade nowadays has decreased in volume and is carried on mainly with the northern oases, though the salt trade with the Sudan has not been entirely abandoned.

These journeys are continued in spite of their hardships and in spite of the dangers of losing valuable camels simply because they are essential. Without the profit and the foreign goods which they provide, the Tuareg could scarcely maintain existence in their frugal homeland. All things considered it is scarcely surprising or outrageous that before the French administration intervened they carried on their ancient profession of robbery as long as they could. This had developed into an almost recognized means of existence. Only by the payment of a considerable sum could a caravan feel safe from attack, and only then while it was in the tribal district where the payment had been made. A former Ahaggar head chieftain devised the following rules for the plundering of trade caravans under the protection of the Ajjer group: return in toto of all load-bearing camels; payment of one fully grown camel for each participant on his own steed in the raid and of one young camel for each participant on a borrowed or hired steed.

Not only trading caravans were subject to attack. Foreign Tuareg camps were also fair game. Raids took place in the summer for preference, when camps were small and scattered. They numbered anything from 10 to 100 camel riders who elected a leader and who took a solemn oath to stand by each other. Food depots were laid out in advance so that as little equipment as possible was carried. Apart from his weapons each participant took no more with him than a little water and a sack of dates. In this way they could cover long distances although they usually made the animals go at a walking pace so that they should not tire. Before the attack took place the band divided into two groups, one of which captured the beasts of the camp while the other plundered the tents. It was, however, an established rule that women should be respected while bloodshed, not to mention homicide, was as far as possible avoided. The booty was divided between participants of the raid, though if they were vassals a certain proportion had to be surrendered to their masters. It sometimes happened, however, that the plunderers voluntarily returned some of the booty to the plundered. But if the latter felt strong enough to take their property back again, they tried to reach a well which they knew the robbers would have to pass on their return journey before the latter arrived, and there a bloody battle could ensue. Large-scale fighting, however, was reserved for tribal feuds and there was a sharp dividing line between these and a raid. Such wars mainly took place in the winter when there was plenty of food for the families while the warriors were away. But even wars were waged with a certain degree of chivalry. The Tuareg carefully obeyed the Prophet's command not to poison wells or to fell the date palms at the oases. "Even hell detests infamy," runs a Tuareg proverb.

* * *

Chivalry is a feature of their whole social life, especially chivalry towards women, whose position is in sharp contrast to Islamic custom. The extraordinary rules for the succession of the chieftainship have already been mentioned, and generally speaking it is the female line which is dominant. Not only have sister's children certain priorities in the matter of inheritance, but a man's tribe is entirely determined by his mother's. This idea is so deep rooted that the nobility in Ahaggar trace their family tree back to a certain Queen, Ti-n-Hinan, and the vassals trace theirs back to her servant or sister, Takama. Obviously this is a survival of an ancient mother right which was once widespread in the Mediterranean area. The women, too, have most say in the choice of their intended, though they have to obtain their father's consent, and are determined not to tolerate the presence of any rival, whatever the laws of the Prophet may say. It is also somewhat misleading to speak of bridal purchase, even if the bridegroom in accordance with ancient custom does "pay" for his wife. The "price" is in fact only an expression of the new ties established between the two families, and the children inherit from the parents of both sides. In other ways, too, the marriage carries certain obligations between the connected families. A strict rule of avoidance exists between parents-in-law and son-in-law, whereas brothers and sisters in law may tease each other in the most intimate way. The object of both these customs is obviously to relieve any tension that might exist between the families. Like the preferential marriage between cross-cousins (see page 29) they probably have some connexion with the ancient matrilineal descent. Joking relationship also exists between members of a noble tribe and their own vassals, whereas otherwise avoidance prevails between the classes.

The kinship system is strictly classificatory, i.e. a man refers not only to his parents but also to his uncles (though not his mother's brothers) and aunts, and furthermore to his parents' cousins, as "father" and "mother". This extends the rule of avoidance to quite a large circle, and the fictive kinship between masters and slaves already mentioned makes it still greater. For example, a young slave may be regarded by his master as a "son", and the avoidance rule applies as between the master and the slave's wife. Parallel cousins are of the same standing as brothers and sisters and, if they are older than the person addressing them, they are entitled to the same respect as his parents. On the other hand, no kinship exists between cross-cousins and they can joke with each other in the same way as brothers-in-law and sisters-in-law can.

After marriage the young couple spend their first year in the wife's camp, after which a show is made of carrying her off to the husband's camp. She takes her own fortune with her and is on the whole free to look after her own affairs. The women are on a completely equal footing with the men. In this connexion it is of no significance that they go about unveiled; their sisters among the Arab Bedouins do the same. It is likewise worth noting that they are mainly responsible for having preserved knowledge of the old Libyan alphabet of twenty-four signs and it is they who keep the tribal traditions going, just as they learn from childhood to play the characteristic one-string violin. In the evenings young people of both sexes foregather to enjoy themselves playing, singing and flirting—even married women can, without arousing the jealousy of their husbands, continue a romantic affair with admirers reminiscent of the romances in the age of chivalry. "Man-friends and women-friends are for the eye and the heart, not for the couch," says the proverb. This, of course, has aroused the surprise and indignation of orthodox Arabs. Ibn Battuta, the great geographer who journeyed to the Sahara in the middle of the fourteenth century, tells the following story:

"One day I came into Abu Muhammed's house and found him

sitting on a mat. In the middle of the room was a bed and on it a man and a woman sat beside each other talking. I said to Abu Muhammed:

" 'Who is this woman?'

" 'She is my wife,' he replied.

" 'And who is the man who is sitting beside her?'

" 'He is her friend.'

" 'Can you really approve such behaviour, you who have been among us and know the teachings of divine Law?' I said.

"He replied,

" 'In this country men and women associate in a respectable manner, and no one need have any suspicions about them.'

"I marvelled at his foolishness and went my way, never to go there again, though he invited me many times."

Generally speaking it must be admitted that the Tuareg do not exert themselves unduly to keep the laws laid down in the Koran. The Arabs insist that they have deserted Islam no less than fourteen times and that their name derives from the word *terek*, meaning "to desert". Etymologically this is impossible. The term comes, rather, from the old tribal name, Targa. The generally recognized form of Islam is that practised by the orthodox Sunnites of the school—it can hardly be called a sect—for which Malik Ibn Anas is responsible, and which prevails over more or less the whole of Mohammedan Africa. But religious fervour is hardly to be expected for, as a former investigator quite properly observes, "Prayers and pilgrimages demand time; fasting and alms-giving presuppose plenty; and they have neither the one nor the other."

Some writers have thought that the Tuareg were Christian before they adopted the teachings of the Prophet. It is in fact beyond doubt that Christianity once was widespread in North Africa. According to Procopius, the inhabitants of Fezzan were converted under the Emperor Justinian in 566-7. Reference has been made to the frequent use which the Tuareg make of the cross in their trinkets and saddle-mountings. This, of course, is an abomination to orthodox Moslems. Reference is made also to words such as *mesi*, God (Messiah), and *anjelous*, Angel (Angelus). It is, however, extremely doubtful whether much weight should be attached to this. Symbols of the cross seem to have come not direct from North Africa, but to have been introduced as amulets in the eighth century by Coptic goldsmiths via the Sudan. And as for the conversion of the Fezzans, this was a political move which scarcely had any significant consequences. Prior to Islam the only religious influence worth mentioning is Judaism, which for a time had a grip on several North African Berber tribes.

It is impossible now to determine what the original form of the faith of the Tuareg might have been. Present-day customs and ideas are too few and unrevealing to form a picture, and it is not always easy to decide which features are original and which have been introduced as Islamic folklore. The idea that nature abounds in ill-disposed spirits living mostly in the desert and in certain trees is as much a matter of course as is the idea that protection against them can be obtained by amulets consisting not only of passages from the Koran but also of lion's claws, animal bones, and so on.

The prohibition already mentioned against eating certain animals has been interpreted by some writers as a totemistic survival, but the basis for this interpretation is slight. A custom of undoubted antiquity—similar to one said to have been practised by the ancient Libyans—is the way in which the women receive dream-omens by laying themselves down to sleep on the graves of their forefathers. In doing so they must not have a scrap of iron on them, not so much as a single pin.

One or two festivals held in Agadez possibly indicate a heathen past, but they may have been borrowed from the Hausa. At one, the men divide themselves into two parties. Then, dressed in their best clothes and carrying palm leaves in their hands, they run about pretending to be intoxicated, and finally enact a violent sham fight. At the other festival, the Sultan followed by a large procession makes his way to an ancient pile of ruins west of the town, and there too a sham fight between mounted men takes place. Finally, mention should be made of a pair of crude stone figures found in Ahaggar, one of them representing a bull's head. Whether they belonged to the ancestors of the Tuareg is a question which must remain unanswered. Here, as elsewhere, Islam has shown a remarkable capacity for erasing former religions, even though it is not inconceivable that an ancient deity or two remain concealed behind the figure of some Islamic saint.

* * *

The life of the Tuareg as we now find it has been clearly shaped by the forces of their environment. If they are described as nomads, it must be with the reservation that there is economic interdependence between the purely pastoral tribes of the desert and the agrarian inhabitants of the oases. The interplay between them is so intimate that it is very doubtful whether the Tuareg could manage to exist on their own. It is not improbable that their forefathers themselves originally cultivated the soil, and only after moving into the desert did they gradually lay the emphasis more and more on cattle breeding, leaving the more trivial farming to slaves and underlings. The most important domestic animals have always been the sheep and goats, and this is still the case with the vassal tribes.

The ideas put forward here are in line with the present state of knowledge on the subject of nomadism in North Africa and the Middle East, where from earliest times there has been a close interplay between wandering pastoral tribes and settled peasants. In this way it differs fundamentally from reindeer nomadism, which developed out of a hunting culture. So far as the Tuareg are concerned, the horse seems to have asserted itself in an exceptional way, if Lhote is right in ascribing most of the credit for the conquest of the desert to it. Later on, of course, the camel obviously contributed to a further intensification of nomadic life, and this is clearly reflected in the division of society into nobles and vassals. Increasing adaptation to pastoral life finds corresponding expression in the transformation of the dwelling, for though the tent is now the prevailing type, its construction clearly derives from a hut of primitive but none the less more permanent kind.

The reason that the Tuareg have managed to preserve various ancient features in their culture—of which the many matrilineal survivals are one example among many—and speak the purest Berber language, is of course to be found in the remoteness of their home in the heart of the Sahara. But it must not be forgotten that they have never been completely cut off. It is not even impossible that the very reason why they turned their backs on the Mediterranean countries is to be found in the intercourse which, from very early times, has connected the great culture regions of antiquity with the Sudan. Ancient caravan routes run from southern Morocco and Tidikelt to Timbuctoo, from Ghadamès to Aïr and Kano, and from Fezzan to Bornu. To modern European eyes accustomed to connexions overseas, it is not always sufficiently apparent that the Sudan originally turned its face towards the desert, just as China did both in prehistoric times and in the Middle Ages, and has done so again in our time. Both directly and indirectly the Tuareg have profited by trading across the Sahara and they have taken over the most important salt exports themselves. Thus fresh influences have steadily infiltrated—Islam first and foremost amongst them. But influences from the Sudan have not been insignificant either. The desert was a tough and dangerous adversary. But not invincible.

BIBLIOGRAPHY

For the prehistoric and geographical background to Tuareg culture, see H. ALIMEN: *Préhistoire de l'Afrique*, Paris, 1955. ORIC BATES: *The Eastern Libyans*, London, 1914. ROBERT CAPOT-REY: *Le Sahara Français*, Paris, 1953. E. F. GAUTIER: *L'islamisation de l'Afrique du Nord. Les siècles obscurs du Maghreb*, Paris, 1927.

Important works on nomadism and related problems are AUGUSTIN BERNARD and N. LACROIX: *L'evolution du nomadisme en Algérie*, Alger and Paris, 1906. E. W. BOVILL: *Caravans of the Old Sahara*, London, 1953. ROBERT H. DYSON: "Archeology and the Domestication of Animals in the Old World" (*Amer. Anthrop. N. s.*, lv, Menasha, 1953). C. G. FEILBERG: "La tente noire" (*Nationalmus. Skrift. Etnogr. Række.*, ii, Copenhagen, 1944). REINHARD WALZ: "Zum Problem der Domestikation der altweltlichen Cameliden" (*Zeitschr. d. Deutsch. Morgenländ. Gesellsch.*, ci, Wiesbaden, 1951). REINHARD WALZ: "Neue Untersuchungen zum Domestikationsproblem der altweltlichen Cameliden" (*Zeitschr. d. Deutsch. Morgenländ. Gesellsch.*, civ, Wiesbaden, 1954).

The first modern travel book with a detailed account of the Tuareg is HEINRICH BARTH: *Reisen und Entdeckungen in Nord und Central-Afrika*, i, Gotha, 1857. No account of the Tuareg *in toto* exists; the following works are useful: MAURICE BENHAZERA: *Six mois chez les Touareg du Ahaggar*, Alger, 1908. H. BISSUEL: *Les Touareg de l'Ouest*, Alger, 1888. HENRI DUVEYRIER: *Les Touareg du Nord*, Paris, 1864. F. FOUREAU: "Esquisse ethnographique" (*Documents scientifiques de la mission saharienne*, iii, Paris, 1905). C. JEAN: *Les Touareg du Sud-Est. L'Aïr*, Paris, 1909. ARTHUR KÖHLER: *Verfassung, soziale Gliederung, Recht und Wirtschaft der Tuareg*, Gotha, 1904. HENRI LHOTE: *Comment campent les Touareg*, Paris, 1947. HENRI LHOTE: "Quelques coutumes en usage chez les Kel Oui" (*Mém. de l'Inst. Franç. d'Afrique Noire*, x, Paris, 1950). HENRI LHOTE: *La chasse chez les Touaregs*, Paris, 1951. HENRI LHOTE: *Les Touaregs du Hoggar*, 2nd éd., Paris, 1955. JOHANNES NICOLAISEN: "Some Aspects of the Problem of Nomadic Cattle Breeding among the Tuareg of the Central Sahara" (*Geogr. Tidsskr.*, liii, Copenhagen, 1954). FRANCIS NICOLAS: "Les industries de protection chez les Twareg de l'Azawagh" (*Hespéris*, xxv, Paris, 1938). FRANCIS NICOLAS: *Tamesna. Les Ioullemmeden de l'Est ou Touâreg "Kel-Dinnik"*, Paris, 1950. FRANCIS RENNELL RODD: *People of the Veil*, London, 1926. FR. DE ZELTNER: "Les Touareg du Sud" (*Journ. R. Anthrop. Inst.*, xliv, London, 1914). LUDWIG G. A. ZÖHRER: "Studien über die Tuáreg (Imohag) der Sahara" (*Zeitschr. f. Ethnol.*, lxxii, Berlin, 1941). Cf. also L. CABOT BRIGGS: "L'anthropologie des Touareg du Sahara" (*Bull. Soc. d'Anthrop.*, 10 ser., vi, Paris, 1955). WALTER DOSTAL: "Zur Frage der Entwicklung des Beduinentums" (*Arch. f. Völkerk.*, xiii, Wien, 1958). AYMARD: *Les Touareg*, Paris, 1911. JEAN GABUS: *Au Sahara*, i-ii, Neuchâtel, 1955, 1958 (not finished). JOHANNES NICOLAISEN: "Slavery among the Tuareg in the Sahara" (*Kuml*, Aarhus, 1957). A. RICHER: *Les Touareg du Niger. Les Oulliminden*, Paris, 1924.

POWHATAN AND PAMLICO

Semi-Agriculturists

Maize

NONE of North America's many linguistic stocks, the Uto-Aztecan alone excluded, equals that of the Algonkians in extent. We have already encountered it on the plains (see page 64 *et seq.*) and right across in California there are two small tribes whose language also belongs to the family—incidentally the only known example of the same stock occurring on both sides of the High Plains. None the less, the Algonkians are mainly distributed over the north-east, from the region of Lake Winnipeg all the way round the south coast of the Hudson Bay to the mountain plateaux of Labrador, and at one time they lived in an unbroken stretch as far south as Tennessee and North Carolina.* In the south of this vast area, however, there were some Siouans, and with the Iroquoians they constituted an enormous wedge which peopled both the Appalachian Mountains and the country round Lakes Erie and Ontario and down through the St. Lawrence Valley.

The north is the original home of the Algonkians—of this there seems to be no doubt. From time immemorial they hunted the boundless coniferous woodlands for game, moose, caribou, beaver and bear, and fished in the countless lakes and rushing rivers; from there they spread to more southerly districts, where they learned to cultivate the soil and generally speaking to adapt their way of life to the new conditions. What reason there was for

* For a short time (ca. 1680-1731) a small isolated Algonkian group belonging to the Shawnee tribe lived by the Savannah River in South Carolina.

their wanderings we can only guess. These probably took place in several waves; at any rate we know that as late as the sixteenth century fresh Algonkian tribes pushed down from the north into the region of the Great Lakes. The most southerly Algonkians on the Atlantic coast were the Powhatan confederation in Virginia, plus the Pamlico and a couple of less important tribes in North Carolina, where the dangerous Cape Hatteras reaches out into the sea.

It was a curious, uniform and almost depressing country in which these Indians settled—a low-lying, infertile coastal plain of raised sea bed, bounded by lagoons, sand dunes and marsh. The plain is at the most 120 miles wide and gradually rises from the coast. But large tracts lie so low that they are bog. Here, on the borders of Virginia and North Carolina, is the enormous Dismal Swamp, in its original form some 700 square miles in area. In the middle of the swamp lies Lake Drummond, surrounded by swamp cypresses which manage to grow in the oxygen-deficient soil thanks to their aerial roots. The water of the lake is clear and pure but completely amber-coloured by dissolved plant debris. Hundreds of streams wind across the plain and end in great estuaries—in reality submerged river valleys, the largest of all being the Delaware and Chesapeake Bays. Inland, at a height of up to about 300 feet, the coastal plain passes into what is known as the Piedmont Plateau along the foot of the Appalachians. The boundary between the loose deposits of the coastal plain and the plateau, which is actually an old peneplain of crystalline rock, is marked by a number of falls in the rivers, and these put a stop to the navigation of ocean-going vessels, though they provide hydraulic power and have thus given birth to a number of towns: Raleigh and Richmond and, farther north, Washington, Baltimore and Philadelphia.

Here in Virginia and North Carolina the temperate climate approaches the sub-tropical. The Piedmont Plateau is covered by a deep, fertile weathering crust and was at one time an almost unbroken stretch of broad-leaf forest, punctuated only by the villages and fields of the eastern Siouans. But conditions on the coastal plain east of the Fall Line where the Algonkians lived were quite different. Only open forests of the hardy pine plus occasional deciduous trees would flourish in its sandy soil, while swamp cypresses and black gum grew in the acid soil of the marshes.

Inevitably one asks oneself how this agreement between topography and distribution of the people is to be explained: the Siouan tribes on fertile plateau and the Algonkians on frugal coastal plain. Did the Algonkians also inhabit the plateau once and were they driven down towards the coast by the Siouans, or did the reverse happen—the Algonkians keeping to the coast and pushing the original Siouan population up on to the plateau without being able to cross the Fall Line themselves? It is easy to put the question—but no conclusive answer to it can be given.*

At this point, unfortunately, archæology offers no help. The extensive excavations in the last decades which have revealed the broad outlines of the United States' prehistory have only to a limited extent taken place in Virginia. No imposing mounds, no finely painted pottery and fantastic copper ornaments have attracted the detailed investigation that they have done in the regions west of the Appalachians. Chipped or polished stone objects with no well-defined characteristics, and rough pointed-bottom pottery with primitive decoration imprinted by sticks, cords and fingers, constitute most of the finds.

Evidence that the Indians arrived at an early stage in North America's history would seem to be provided by certain stone points reminiscent of the Folsom point (see page 6). However, the cultural development is far from being clearly elucidated. All that one can say is that the pottery just mentioned shows a certain connexion with forms which are characteristic of what is known as the Burial-Mound or Woodland culture, i.e. an older stage of development present in the whole area east of the Mississippi, which in its essentials, however, has been preserved late in history

* Carl F. Miller has recently raised the question whether some of the supposed Siouans in Virginia and the two Carolinas were not actually Algonkians. The linguistic sources are too meagre to settle the problem.

The so-called "Powhatan Mantle" now in the Ashmolean Museum, Oxford.

Pomeioc, a stockaded village of one of the Algonkian tribes in North Carolina.

in places outside the path of the subsequent southerly culture waves, including the Atlantic coast itself. So far as can be determined at present, there is no break of any consequence in the development of Virginia which can be interpreted as evidence of the immigration of new folk elements; but there can be two different explanations of this: either that the Algonkian tribes have been living there for a very long period of time, and that the remains which the excavations have brought to light are theirs—or, on the contrary, that they arrived so recently that they have not managed to leave any impression on a culture which they mainly adopted from an older population. All that is certain is that at some time or other they must have immigrated from the north.

Not infrequently one comes across the erroneous impression that the Indians are entirely extinct in the eastern United States. Actually, of the Powhatan tribes alone, a couple of thousand members are still living—or at any rate less than a lifetime ago were still living—in Virginia. True, they are of more or less mixed blood, and, except for a few words, have given up the use of their original language in favour of English. But in their mode of life they remain faithful to their old habits. They still hunt deer and otter in the marshes, set their traps for racoons and musk-rats, make simple dug-outs and build fish weirs out of branches in the rivers. But the most remarkable feature of all is the fact that the most important tribe in the old confederation, the Pamunkey, still constitute a state within the state with certain laws of their own, and though they are under the supervision of the Virginian administration are nationally independent in respect of the privileges granted in 1677. How large the population of the south-eastern Algonkian tribes originally was it is impossible to determine with certainty. But it has been estimated at 13,000-14,000.

* * *

Anyone wanting an idea of the culture of these peoples should refer to contemporary sources, when it was still in its prime. Obviously the picture is bound to be incomplete. Even the best contemporary descriptions cannot satisfy the demands of modern science either in respect of detail or of profundity and understanding. The most important works date from the start of British colonization in the region. In 1584 the famous seafarer, Sir Walter Raleigh, received royal permission to explore and settle "such remote, heathen and barbarous lands, countries and territories which are not actually possessed by any Christian prince or inhabited by Christian people", and in the following years he made repeated and vain attempts to found colonies on that part of the American coast which, in honour of the Virgin Queen, he named Virginia, and which at that time also comprised the northern part of North Carolina.

From one of these unsuccessful settlements there exists almost the only source of knowledge of the most southerly tribes in the form of an account by Thomas Hariot, with superb illustrations by John White. Not before 1607 did what was known as the London Company succeed in setting up an enduring colony a little farther north where Jamestown now stands, thereby providing England with a foothold in North America.* The local Powhatan Indians in particular are described by William Strachey and by Captain John Smith, who by his energy and dash succeeded in getting the colony through its first troubled years.

John Smith's name is linked for all time with one of the most dramatic events in the continent's history. On a hunting expedition he had been taken prisoner by the Indians, and surrounded by 200 rough warriors he was taken to the chief who, clad in a fur robe—the time was January—had seated himself in his house in front of a large fire. On either side of him sat a young girl, and throughout the house stood men and women with faces and shoulders painted red, white feather headdresses and long chains of shell beads round their necks. Water was brought so that he could wash his hands and a bundle of feathers so that he could dry them. After a meal, a long and evidently heated discussion took place.

* It is significant that it should be the Powhatan Indians who have provided English and other European languages with such words as moccasin, tomahawk opossum, etc.

The result of it was that two large stones were brought in, and John Smith was dragged forward and made to put his head on one of them, whereupon the executioners made ready to batter in his head with their clubs. Suddenly the chief's young daughter ran forward at the last moment, threw her arms round his head and thus saved his life. The young girl in question, Matowaka, or to call her by her Indian pet name, as she is generally known, Pocahontas, became a faithful friend of the English, and was largely responsible for the fact that hostilities did not go too far between them. She became legally married to a young Englishman, but died of smallpox during a visit to her husband's homeland, when only twenty-two years old.

It might appear from this episode that the Powhatan were wild barbarians. But this was by no means the case. They knew how to cultivate the soil and lived in permanent villages of considerable size—consisting of up to fifty houses. The houses were the joint dwellings of several families. Often they were over fifty feet long and nearly half as wide. In appearance they were barrel-vaulted and covered with bark or rush mats over a framework of poles. In warm weather some of the mats could be removed to provide an entry for fresh air. Along the inside walls there were sleeping platforms covered with mats and blankets of skin. In the middle of the house was the hearth, the smoke from the fire finding its way out through a hole in the roof, though this did not prevent the whole room from being filled with smoke, which gradually left a thick layer of soot on everything. In the semi-darkness it was possible to discern the simple household equipment, consisting of large wooden mortars for crushing corn, basketry sieves for the flour, baskets, wooden dishes and bowls, gourd containers, earthenware pots, etc. One special kind of building which we shall return to later was referred to by the old-time writers as a "temple".

The villages were situated on rivers—which were important means of communication—and preferably in the vicinity of a spring with fresh drinking water. Sometimes the whole village, or at any rate the chieftain's dwelling plus the houses nearby, was surrounded by a high, though not particularly strong, stockade as a protection in time of war. But other villages were unfortified and the houses were scattered among the maize and tobacco fields. In the village of Secotan, as described by Hariot, there was an open square beside the "temple" where people gathered round a fire to say prayers, and immediately opposite it was a round festival place surrounded by a circle of stakes carved at the top in the shape of human faces. Here the natives made merry after their ceremonies. Yet another festival place existed right in the middle of the village street and nearby that was another row of stakes. These places were quite certainly used on special religious occasions, but unfortunately we are quite ignorant of their deeper significance.

At daybreak, the Indians bathed in the river, but neither undressing nor dressing can have caused them much trouble, though it is not easy to comprehend the dress in all its details from the bare descriptions that exist. The most important item in the man's clothing was a fringed breechcloth or perhaps a knee-length loincloth of tanned deer hide, while the women's was a corresponding skirt which sometimes at any rate left the buttocks uncovered. To this in chilly weather was added a robe which was worn over the left shoulder so that the right arm was free. Normally it reached to the knees, though priests wore it shorter, and it was sometimes perhaps sewn together at the side. In the summer it was of dehaired skin, in the winter of fur, and the most expensive were also painted in bright designs or decorated with shell beads and copper ornaments. Some robes were made of the feathers of wild turkeys or other birds, knotted in a fine net of plant fibres. Exceptionally, especially on hunting expeditions, etc., when they had to make their way through thick forest and undergrowth, they also wore a kind of legging and soft-soled moccasins.

In contrast to the dress, other aspects of the toilet required considerable preparation. The men of the North Carolina tribes let their hair grow long at the sides and tied it up in a knot at the ears, but over the crown of the head it was cut short and brushed up like a cockscomb. Distinguished persons stuck a long feather in the front of the crest and a shorter feather over either ear.

The hair style of the Powhatan was slightly different from that of the southern tribes: with the aid of a mussel shell or a knife of cane they shaved the right side of the head and on the left side wore the hair long and well oiled. But they, too, had the characteristic crest over the crown. In their hair they sometimes arranged a whole stuffed bird or a bird's wing from which hung the tail rattle of a rattlesnake or small ornaments of shell. Married women cut their hair off short. Tattooing of the face, breast, hands and legs was extremely common among women. But if this form of adornment was rare among the men, its absence was fully counterbalanced by the way in which they painted themselves with soot, ochre and vegetable dyes mixed with oil.

In other ways too the strong sex was not backward. Their ears were pierced in two or three places for strings of shell, beads, copper ornaments, birds' bones and animal claws—Strachey reports that some even put tiny live snakes in the holes! Round their necks hung breast-plates of large mussel shells and long strings of shell and copper beads; and the chiefs could also have armbands and frontlets of the same kind. All this obviously made a certain impression on the older writers. Our ignorance of the ideological background is thus all the more to be regretted. One must content oneself with saying that with their grotesque hair styles, fantastic ornamentation and barbaric paint these Indians must indeed have presented a spectacle quite out of the ordinary.

And yet their culture, as already stated, was by no means at a low level. Agriculture was the solid basis of their existence. The most important plant they cultivated was maize, of which there were at least three varieties. In addition there were beans, gourds and tobacco, possibly also sunflowers, even if they are not mentioned before about the year 1700. The quantities produced were by no means small. In 1610, for example, an English officer could buy nearly 400 bushels of maize and beans from the native chiefs.

Each village owned according to its size between 20 and 100 fields—though they were fairly small. It must be remembered that every single patch cultivated had to be won from the forest. First the ground was cleared by ringing the larger trees with stone axes; then the undergrowth was set on fire. The ashes were allowed to lie, but manuring was unknown, so that when in the course of a few years the ground was exhausted the only thing to do was to clear a new piece of ground—typical burn-beating in fact, which was still to be found in out-of-the-way parts of Scandinavia down to our own day. The following year, some days before sowing took place, which was usually in May, both the men and women went to the clearings and broke up the soil, the men using a kind of wooden mattock or bent digging stick, while the women, who worked sitting on their haunches, used a shorter tool. After the weeds and old stubble had been left to dry a day or so, they were set alight, and from then on the women had to take over, for it is characteristic of primitive semi-agriculture that the job of actually tilling the soil devolves on the women, while the man's part in food providing is mainly confined to hunting and fishing.

Thus it was the women who did the sowing. They dug small holes in the earth about a yard apart with a dibble, and in each hole they put four or five grains of maize together with a couple of beans, the stalks of which climbed up round the maize straw. A large part of the population met on an appointed day to sow the chieftain's land, and when the work was done the chieftain himself walked round the field whilst the participants walked backwards in front of him and gathered up the beads he threw to them. Presumably this was some form of fertility rite, the deeper meaning of which unfortunately remains unknown.

During the course of the summer the women and children hoed and weeded once or twice and some kept continual watch in small huts built out in the fields to scare off venturesome birds and other vermin. Harvesting took place in August or September. The cobs were picked one after another, laid in baskets and later dried on mats, being carefully covered up at night against the dew, and finally stored away in large storage baskets. The chieftain's fields were harvested collectively, just as they had been sown. While green cobs of late-planted maize were usually grilled, ripe maize was crushed to meal in a wooden mortar, then sieved and mixed with water into dough which was made into a loaf and baked in hot ashes. Maize and beans could also be boiled together or cooked with meat or fish. The months immediately following on the harvest, roughly to the middle of November, were the time when food was most plentiful, and for this reason the big festivals and religious ceremonies took place then.

During the rest of the year the Indians had largely to fall back on the results of food gathering, fishing and hunting. Food gathering took place mainly in the summer between sowing and harvesting, and yielded not only clams, crabs and other shellfish on the coast, but also berries, nuts and, as the summer advanced, the rootstock of an arum-like marsh plant called Tuckahoe—presumably either *Orontium aquaticum* or *Peltandra virginica.* The juice is poisonous, so the roots were either baked in an earth oven for twenty-four hours, or cut into slices and dried, after which they were crushed into meal and baked into bread.

Fishing took place mainly in the spring and summer, which were the seasons for catching sturgeon, chad and herring. The usual method of catching sturgeon was with great care to get a snare round its tail and then suddenly to tighten it. But it was not uncommon for the catcher to get pulled away by his prey, and he had to hold on tightly until the fish had tired itself out and, panting and half-drowned, he could get it ashore. At the high-water mark in the river estuaries plaited fish weirs of wickerwork were built out from the banks to a depth of some ten feet and the fish trapped were lifted out with a landing net. Near the Fall Line, where the water was shallow and the stream rapid, stone dams were built and traps were inserted into the gaps between the stones.

There were several other methods of fishing: with bone hooks and simple spears, tipped with the point of a swordtail, or by shooting the fish with a bow and arrow trailing a long string. Spearing and shooting often took place at night from a canoe by torch-light. Canoes were hollowed out of a thick tree-trunk by burning, the charred portions then being chopped or scraped away with clam shells. Canoes usually carried ten to twelve men, but the largest could accommodate double that number. Possibly the Virginia Indians knew how to fish by poisoning the water with certain plants; at any rate this was common practice among most tribes in the south-east of the United States. Still, this is less likely, since in most places the tide prevents the formation of quiet pools.

The winter was the principal hunting season, and it is curious to find two ancient customs connected with it which the Algonkian tribes evidently brought with them from their distant northern homeland where they are kept up to this day. One is the division of the hunting grounds into separate family territories, the other is the taboo against a young man's eating the first game he kills.

The ability of the Indians to follow a trail and to steal up close to their quarry is proverbial, but it was also vital to their existence. Wrapped in a complete deer skin, with one arm stuck through the skin's neck, or carrying a stuffed animal head on a stick, they managed to get close up to the deer at their watering places and shoot them with a bow and arrow. The bows were simple long-bows and the arrows had a shaft of cane into which was inserted a foreshaft of wood tipped either with a stone head shaped by a flint flaker or made of antler or the spur of a wild turkey. They were carried in a quiver made of skin or bark or of rushes.

Far more profitable than individual hunting were the big collective hunts in which a couple of hundred men or more took part. They took place inland near the Fall Line, several days' journey from the villages, and not only men took part—women joined in too, one of their jobs being to put up the conical huts which served as temporary dwellings. Sometimes it was possible to frighten the animals out into the rivers, where the hunters lay in hiding and made after them in canoes. At other times the hunters surrounded a section of forest several miles across and set the dried leaves and grass on fire. This could be done without much danger since the principal tree, a species of pine, was not very combustible. Gradually the hunters moved in towards the centre of the circle, lighting fresh fires until the circle became so small that they could see the animals which, senseless from fear and half choked with smoke, were rushing aimlessly to and fro. It was then possible to slay them without difficulty. Though the huntsmen were more or less hidden by the smoke it was said to be a very rare occurrence for any of them to get shot by accident. Black bears, which are considerably more timid than either their brown or grizzly cousins, were often chased up a tree and shot—but like the beaver and racoon they also were caught in traps. Wild turkey were decoyed by aping their cry with a whistle made out of cane or the bones of birds. The meat was either roasted on a spit, boiled or dried over the fire for later use.

The Virginia tribes, like other North American Indians, lived in a Stone Age. They did, it is true, know how to work copper, but only by hammering it cold, for both smelting and casting were unknown to them. Stone arrowheads and axes have already been mentioned; so, too, their wooden implements, pottery, baskets, mats, etc. Suffice to add here that knives, in addition to being made out of cane, were also made from polished stone shaped like a half moon—obviously an ancient type widespread throughout the north-east of North America and among the Eskimo. Fire was made by a simple fire drill. Thread and string were of plant fibre or deer sinews twined between the flat of the hand and the thigh. Unfortunately we have no knowledge of how these Indians prepared the skins they used for clothes and other purposes. But it can hardly be doubted that they knew how to treat them by scraping, by tanning with brain substance and by smoking—as practised by so many North American tribes.

* * *

The old-time writers have something to tell us about the social conditions, but what they have to say must be treated with some reserve, for it is only too evident that they were not able to put behind them their European prejudices, nor did they always understand what they saw. This applies for example to the curious custom which both Strachey and John Smith construed as child sacrifice but which Beverley, a bare century later, more correctly described as a trial of manhood, even if its real meaning was not completely apparent to him. It was in fact a typical form of youth initiation. The half-grown boys, painted white, sat at the foot of a tree, while nearby, their fathers and other men of the village arranged themselves in two rows with bundles of brushwood in their hands. Five young men were then ordered to fetch the boys, and as they passed between the two lines of men, blows were rained down on them. The boys' mothers sat a little way off, chanting dirges and wailing as though they were at a funeral. As soon as the boys had left the tree the men charged it furiously, had it down and stripped it of its twigs and leaves, which they stuck into their hair and then went about mourning, with eyes downcast. The boys were thrown into a pit as though they were dead, and a solemn ritual was performed beside it. During the night certain spirits were said to appear and suck blood from their left breasts so that some of them died. Those remaining had to spend several months segregated in the forest, where they lived in a cone-shaped hut under observation, and among the things they had to drink was the decoction of a certain plant (a species of periwinkle?) which deprived them of both memory and sense. When they were eventually allowed to return to their village, they were unable to remember what had happened to them.

In this description several features of a fertility rite (the thrashing and the decoration with green leaves) are clearly recognizable, and so is the widely held notion that boys at puberty die and are restored to life. It is, of course, altogether unlikely that they suffered lasting loss of memory. This was rather—as Beverley himself indicates—a way of expressing a conscious break with the past and the fear of revealing the secrets of initiation, for probably during their segregation they were instructed in the sacred rites of the tribe.

The old accounts make no mention of division into tribal moieties, totem clans and so on, even though this was quite common in the south-eastern United States. The reason for this was presumably neither neglect nor ignorance on the part of the authors, but rather the fact that it simply did not exist, which is the case to this very day among the most northerly Algonkian tribes. And so the description they give of the chieftaincy is all the more remarkable. If they are to be believed, at any rate the Powhatan tribes formed an autocratic kingdom. The despotic powers of its ruler, though not, of course, its geographical extent, interior organization or military strength, were as far reaching as those of the Inca Empire in Peru. This is, of course, quite foreign to North America as a whole, and to what extent the description is coloured by a European way of thinking cannot now be determined. But it cannot have been entirely imaginary.

We are told that the "king" or the head chief, called, like one of his subject tribes, Powhatan (though his personal name was Wahunsonacock), received tribute from his under-chieftains, that he owned great riches preserved in special store houses round the countryside, that he surrounded himself with a large harem and a life-guard of some forty to fifty picked warriors and generally wielded such power that everyone trembled and obeyed his slightest wish. All that can be said about this now is that probably such unbridled power was largely owing to the purely personal qualities of the said chieftain and was only to a smaller extent rooted in the hereditary principle. Wahunsonacock was obviously a powerful warrior and a ruthless dictator whose rule over a large number of tribes was the consequence of his own conquests. To this extent also it is somewhat misleading for the Powhatan tribes to be described as a confederation, for very likely their mutual connexion was far from voluntary. On the other hand in many places in the south-east of the United States there was to some extent a tendency to form a kind of monarchy—presumably a reflection of the more highly organized states in Mexico, and one may well come to the conclusion that something more than personality accounted for the situation in Virginia, for the chieftaincy passed through the female line, which is customary in the south-eastern culture area, whereas patrilineal descent is otherwise typical of the Algonkian tribes and, for example in Virginia, manifested itself by the bride moving over to the father-in-law's village.

As the history of the Powhatan tribes shows, war was nothing unusual. Most battles were purely in revenge of some earlier assault, but the desire to abduct foreign women was also one of the most frequent causes. In addition to bows and arrows, clubs were the traditional weapons. The old descriptions of the latter are not very clear; but it does appear from them that there were several different types. As far as can be judged, the usual kind was a flat, sickle-shaped weapon something like the Australian boomerang and was perhaps chiefly intended for throwing. Other clubs, possibly derived from this, had a curved shaft with a heavy ball-shaped head, and a third type had a point of antler or stone inserted into the wooden shaft. For defence there was a round bark shield which was carried over the left shoulder when the bow was being used, but it does not seem to have been particularly common. There is also a single mention of a kind of armour consisting of sticks bound together. In modern times some doubt has been cast on the authenticity of this; but since its existence is known for certain among the Iroquois these doubts seem to be somewhat unjustified.

As for the mode of warfare, there is not much to tell. As was the case with other peoples on the same cultural level, it seldom took the form of open battle but rather of ambuscade and assault, the warriors in their fantastic warpaint endeavouring to steal upon the enemy unawares. Before the campaign the higher powers were consulted through the medium of the priests, and the North Carolina tribes were said to take their idols with them to ensure success to the campaign. All the enemy dead were scalped—as Captain John Smith relates of Wahunsonacock's warriors when they attacked a foreign village in the year 1608:

> " Twenty-four men they slewe, the long haire of one side of their heades with the skinne cased off with (knives of) shell or reeds, they brought away. They surprised also the women and the children and the *Werowance* (the chieftain). . . . The *Werowance*, women and children became his (i.e. Wahunsonacock's) prisoners, and do him service. The lockes of haire with their skinnes he hanged on a line unto two trees. . . ."

Sometimes severed hands also were dried as a sign of victory.

A curious circumstance, which to some extent differentiates these southern Algonkians from their northern kinsmen is the fact that they maintained their position not only by waging war but also by means of their extensive trading activities. Probably the most active merchants in these tracts were the Siouan tribes on the Piedmont Plateau. One of their villages on the borders of Virginia and North Carolina was situated at the point where several paths traversing the country came together, and for that reason it became something of a focus for the exchange of goods. Furthermore the language spoken there was the *lingua franca* of a considerable area. There is, however, both direct and indirect evidence that the Algonkian tribes were not backward where trading was concerned and that this very circumstance helped to develop the power of the chieftaincy. At least it seems as if the chiefs and their families had a kind of monopoly in trade with the English settlers, in addition to acting as middlemen in the exchange of goods between the English and the Indians farther inland.

From the plateau tribes red dyes and copper, most of which came from places as far distant as the region round Lake Superior, were obtained. In return the coastal tribes had at their disposal something in such demand as the disc-shaped shell beads known as *roanoke*. These were obtained from the shell of a kind of sea-snail and were so highly prized that they were put on strings and used as money. Tubular shaped shell beads, *wampumpeak* (usually shortened to "*wampum*") chiefly belonged to a later time and were imported all the way from New York and Rhode Island until enterprising Englishmen and Dutchmen produced them in such enormous quantities that they completely lost their value.

It is interesting now to see how the approach towards a money economy which the shell beads signified had begun to affect social life not only as regards the power of the chieftain but also in the acceptance of wergild in place of blood revenge, professional prostitution, and so on. It is true that these matters are most plainly documented among the Siouans on the Piedmont Plateau. But they were certainly not unknown to the Algonkian tribes on the coastal plain. Knowledge of such mnemotechnical devices as knot records which, like the Peruvian *quipus*, could be used for simple calculations probably also has a certain connexion with the development of trade.

* * *

Most of the religion practised by these Algonkians will unfortunately always remain a closed book to us—at any rate so far as its innermost secrets are concerned. No more than a few outer, and not very informative traits have been preserved. We hear of demons or spirits which were called *oke*—when John Smith uses this term as the name of a single supreme being it is presumably the result of a misunderstanding—and likewise there is mention of veneration for the four winds or for the four corners of the earth, and of a mighty culture hero in the shape of the Great Hare which seems to be linked to the dawn. Recognizable in these figures are the old Algonkian notions which were presumably brought by the Indians from their distant homeland in the north. But alongside them are other features in the religion which have obviously been adopted from their southern neighbours. At any rate one searches in vain for anything similar in the original culture of the Algonkians. Among them are deities in human form, idols, special temples and a regular priesthood in addition to the normal medicine men, as well as fertility rites and harvest festivals connected with agriculture. Some of the names of the gods have been preserved; but of their nature nothing is known.

The idols were in many cases nothing but simple wooden posts, carved and painted at the top in the form of a human face. But they could also be more carefully made, clothed in skins and ornamented with chains of shell and copper beads. In appearance the temples were usually not very different from the usual barrel-vault houses, though from one of the villages in North Carolina there is mention of a round or oval temple building. "Som tymes they haue two of these idoles in theyr churches, and som tyme 3, but neuer aboue, which they place up in a darke corner wher they shew terrible," says one of the old writers.

In addition to serving as the home of the gods, the temples also served other purposes. They were partly the store-houses of the chieftains, where their wealth of corn, fur, beads, etc., was kept in safety out of the reach of any rapacious subjects, partly—and in particular—a sort of bone-houses where the chieftains were laid to rest. Whilst the common people were buried after death—a fact which has not only been reported but which has also been confirmed archæologically by the investigation of bone pits containing up to 500 skeletons—the earthly remains of the chieftains were treated with very much more respect. The body was carefully fleeced and all the flesh removed from the bones without harm being done to the sinews. The flesh was then dried in the sun and folded inside mats, while the complete skeleton together with beads and other treasures was put into the skin and sewn up. The resulting mummy together with the flesh and various burial gifts was laid beside its forefathers on a nine to twelve-foot-high platform inside the temple, where it was watched over by a priest who slept under the platform. At the funeral, the village echoed with the weeping and wailing of the populace, while some of the deceased's relatives threw beads for them to scramble after.

The most important temples lay on out-of-the-way heights in the forest, and only priests and chieftains dared to approach them. Beverley, whose description of Virginia was published in 1705, was early enough to have the opportunity of examining one of them in secret. His description runs:

> "Having removed about fourteen Loggs from the Door, with which it was barricado'd, we went in, and at first found nothing but naked Walls, and a Fire place in the middle. This House was about eighteen foot wide, and thirty foot long, built after the manner of their other Cabbins, but larger, with a Hole in the middle of the Roof, to vent the Smoke, the Door being at one end: Round about the House, at some distance from it, were set up Posts, with Faces carved on them, and painted. We did not observe any Window, or passage for Light, except the Door, and the vent of the Chimney. At last, we observed that at the farther end, about ten foot of the Room, was cut off by a Partition of very close Mats; and it was dismal dark behind that Partition. We were at first scrupulous to enter this obscure place, but at last we ventur'd, and groping about, we felt some Posts in the middle; then reaching our hands up those Posts, we found large Shelves, and up on these Shelves three mats, each of which was roll'd up, and sow'd fast. These we handed down to the light, and to save time in unlacing the Seams, we made use of a Knife, and ripp'd them, without doing any damage to the Mats. In one of these we found some vast Bones, which we judg'd to be the

Bones of Men, particularly we measured one Thigh-bone, and found it two foot nine inches long: In another Mat, we found some *Indian Tomahawks* finely grav'd and painted. . . . In the third Mat there was something, which we took to be their Idol, tho of an underling sort, and wanted putting together. The pieces were these, first a Board three foot and a half long, with one indenture at the upper end, like a Fork, to fasten the Head upon, from thence half way down, were Half hoops nail'd to the Edges of the Board, at about four Inches distance, which was bow'd out, to represent the Breast and Belly; on the lower half was another Board of half the length of the other, fasten'd to it by Joynts or pieces of Wood, which being set on each side, stood out about 14 inches from the Body, and half as high; we suppos'd the use of these to be for the bowing out of the Knees when the Image was set up. There were packt up with these things red and blue pieces of Cotton Cloath and Rolls made up for Arms, Thighs and Legs, bent to at the Knees. . . . But the Head and rich Bracelets, which it is usually adorn'd with, were not there, or at least we did not find them. . . ."

Priests and medicine men were distinguished both from ordinary people and from each other by their own peculiar costume. Their heads were shaven, apart from the usual crest over the crown of the head and a strip along the forehead, where it was smeared with fat and dye so that it jutted out something like an eyeshade. The most distinguished priest also wore a curious headdress of stuffed snake and ermine skins which hung down over his face and neck and was tied together into a tuft at the top surrounded by a crown of feathers. The priest's dress was a short closed cape of hare skin or feathers worn in the customary way over the left shoulder, whereas the medicine men were content with a breech-cloth of otter skin and a stuffed bird fastened above one ear. Their equipment included rattles of hollow gourds filled with small stones, which were used at invocations and dances, *inter alia* to drive out the demons of sickness.

Medicine men had some knowledge of healing herbs and could undertake blood-letting, moxibustion and scratching the skin with snake's teeth. The most widespread form of cleansing, however, both in the literal and in the ritual sense, was the sweat bath, which was taken in a special little hut. Water was dashed on to heated

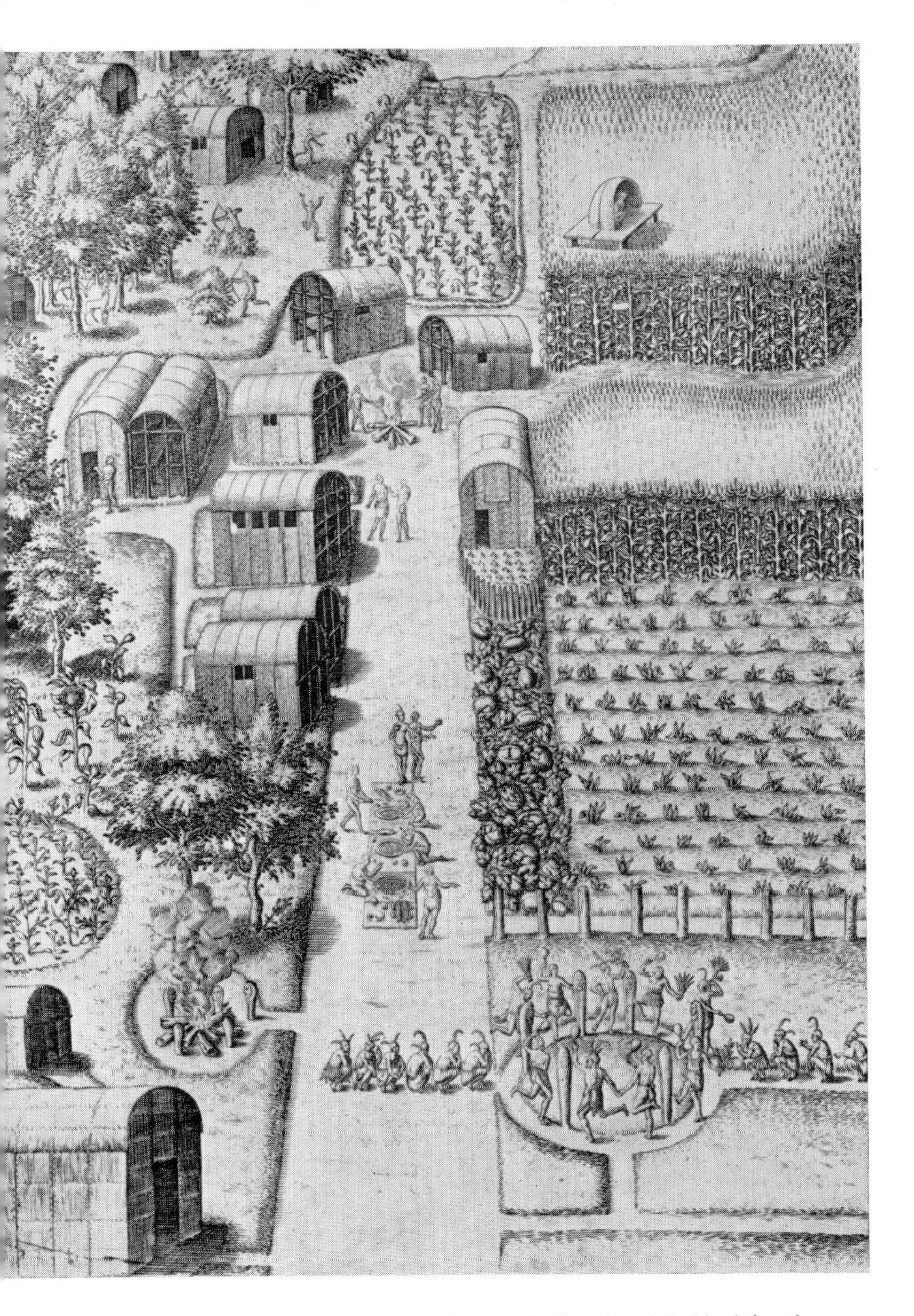

One of the open (undefended) villages in North Carolina inhabited by the Secotan, one of the small Algonkian tribes. Fields of maize, the most important plant the Indians cultivate, grow between the houses.

Men of an Algonkian tribe in North Carolina making a canoe by burning.

Left: Indian methods of fishing employed in Virginia: in the background men are spearing fish and the use of wicker-work weirs to trap them is shown. In the foreground is a dugout canoe: the fire probably served to provide flaming branches to the light from which fish are attracted at night. The Indians speared them.

Above: Algonkian Indians grilling fish. Fishing took place mainly in spring and summer, sturgeon, chad and herring being the principal catch.

Below: Front and rear views of an Algonkian chieftain. The quiver which he carries on his back is made of cane.

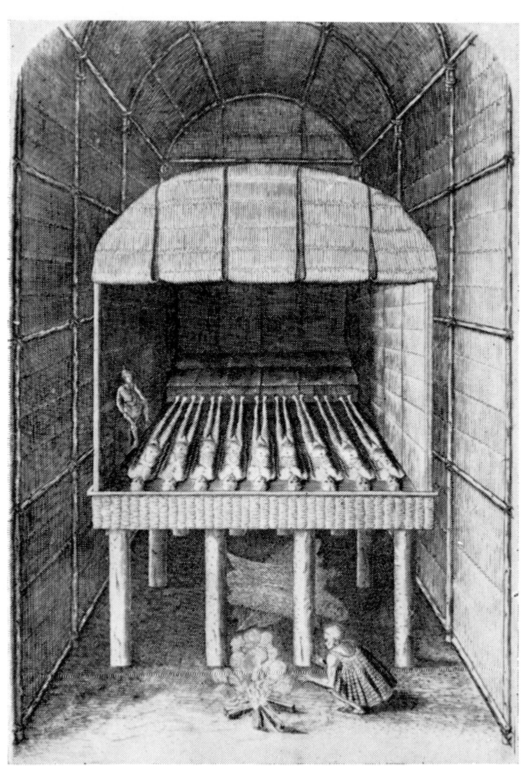

Above: Though this particular Algonkian dance probably was a fertility rite, the round space surrounded by carved stakes was used commonly as a festival place. Compare the picture of Secotan facing page 192.

Left: An Algonkian "temple": it contains the mummies of former chieftains of the tribe.

stones so that the room filled with steam, and the bath concluded with a quick plunge in the cold water of the nearest river.

But how did these priests and medicine men otherwise operate? What form did the relationship between these Indians and the higher powers take on the whole? In this matter, too, we have to bemoan our ignorance, for the old chroniclers saw nothing but devilry in the ceremonies, which they did not understand and from which they turned away in disgust. We are told that outside the temples round the country were stone shrines where blood, fat and tobacco were offered up when men returned from hunting expeditions and campaigns, and that a small piece of food was thrown into the fire before a meal. John Smith relates how the priests peered into the future by sitting for days on end round a fire, round which a circle of maize meal was strewn, and singing for hours at a time. Finally there are references to sun worship (?) and to ceremonies and dances connected with the harvest and to festivals in which the participants were decorated with green twigs—quite obviously a fertility rite—but all these are only references, insufficient for a detailed description, let alone for comprehension of what took place.

* * *

Although our picture of the life and conduct of these Indians is regrettably incomplete, it is none the less enough to form a basis for comparison with the cultures of both their northerly kinsmen and their neighbours. Examining more closely the culture of the southern Algonkian tribes, as Dr. Regina Flannery has done, we are immediately surprised to see how few traces of their northern origin remain. Of the more important features there are really only two connected with hunting, i.e. the division of the country into family territories and the taboo against boys eating what they have killed in their first hunt. The notion of the Great Hare as organizer of the world is also an old northern element. There is far more in common between these tribes and the great south-easterly culture area: first and foremost in everything that pertains to agriculture and, to some extent as a result of that, in many matters connected with religion—not only fertility rites but also idols, temples and the priesthood.

The powerful chieftaincy and its succession through the female line, the rod armour, scalping, the stockading of villages, etc., also suggest the south-east or at any rate the Iroquois, whose culture contains many southerly features. Of course, there are many other elements in the culture whose origin cannot be immediately traced. But in any case it is no exaggeration to say that the southerly elements far out-number those which can be presumed to derive from the north.

How this state of affairs is to be explained is still an open question. As mentioned before, archæology cannot at present help us to decide whether the southern Algonkians have occupied their country for a long period of time or whether on the other hand they immigrated comparatively late. Their language is no more helpful, for the scattered remnants which have been written down are not enough for determining its place within the whole stock. According to their own tradition, the Powhatan had not lived in Virginia more than a few hundred years before the arrival of the English; as to this it must be said firstly, that we have no means of evaluating the accuracy of the tradition, and second, that it may perhaps refer to a move of such limited extent that it is of no cultural-historical significance. In other words it is not necessarily to be taken as meaning that they came direct from their original homeland in the north at so late a period in time.

How these Indians came to adopt the southern culture is a problem, the solution of which depends on the answer to the immigration question. If they have been inhabiting the coastal plain for a long time the answer is simple, for then it is enough to postulate a steady and constant influence from their neighbours. But matters are different if they immigrated comparatively recently. In that case the readiest explanation would appear to be that given by Professor Frank G. Speck, one of the foremost experts in the ethnology of eastern North America. He thought that the immigration had been mainly of military character and comprised only a few warriors who had found wives among the older inhabitants. In this connexion it is significant that the agriculture, which is of course the basis of all the south-easterly culture, is chiefly dependent on the women. Furthermore we know that the abduction of women was one of the chief motives of war in historic times.

There is, however, an objection to this explanation which cannot be ignored. Southern influences in the Algonkian tribes, far from being confined to the tribes in North Carolina and Virginia, continue to a steadily decreasing extent northwards up the coast. Not only was agriculture and the cultivation of maize found as far north as the whole of New England, but of the forty-nine south-easterly elements which Dr. Flannery takes into account, half of them still occurred in southern New England and still more were found in New Jersey and Delaware. This would seem to indicate a steady flow of culture influences from south to north continuing throughout a long period of time. We must hope that new excavations will gradually overcome these difficulties for us. Meanwhile, final conclusions in the matter must wait.

It is, however, not without interest to consider the culture of the southern Algonkian tribes in relation to that of their northern kinsmen, for there is no doubt that at some time or other they separated from them. We must look for their original home in the extensive woodlands of Canada where to this day caribou and moose are hunted on snowshoes in winter, and from canoes in the autumn when the animals are driven into rivers and lakes. A third method is that of scaring them into long lines of converging fences —the same methods that are used throughout the northern forest zone right across to Scandinavian Lapland.

No less profitable than hunting is fishing, and at some time in the past it must have been still more important. Snowshoes, and thus hunting on snowshoes, cannot of course have been known since the dawn of time; on the contrary everything indicates that their use spread to Alaska and Canada across Bering Strait from Siberia. It was, incidentally, this snowshoe complex which later made the reindeer nomadism of the Siberian peoples and the Lapps possible. Before the snowshoe gained acceptance in North America the depth of loose snow in the forests must have made it practically impossible for the northern Indians to hunt in the winter. Their only way of getting food must have been by fishing or catching beaver and musk-rats from the ice of the rivers and lakes.

Though we are for the moment unable to decide when the snowshoe complex reached the northern Algonkians, it would perhaps be possible to determine whether the tribes in Virginia separated from them before or after its arrival. For obvious geographical reasons one would not expect to find either snowshoe hunting or ice fishing as far south as Virginia and North Carolina. Is there anything else then which can help us to find the answer? It so happens that even in the Lake Superior region fishing and beaver hunting on the ice are as important to the Indians' economy as hunting on snowshoes, and as one goes south so more and more of the characteristic components of the snowshoe complex disappear. Farthest south they have not only to all intents and purposes disappeared, but we find that winter hunting merely consists of a continuation of the methods used in the autumn with nothing new added.

Taken together, these facts indicate that the southern Algonkians had already separated from the main group before the snowshoe complex had reached them. This could perhaps be taken as evidence that the separation took place a long way back in time. Such a conclusion would, however, be premature, partly because we do not know how old the snowshoe complex in North America is, and partly because we must bear in mind that the direction taken by the southern tribes in question moved them farther and farther away from it. Whether we shall ever succeed in penetrating any further into their early history the future must decide.

BIBLIOGRAPHY

For the archæology of Virginia, see DAVID I. BUSHNELL, JR.: "Indian Sites below the Falls of the Rappahannock, Virginia" (*Smithson. Miscell. Coll.*, xcvi, 4, Washington, 1937). DAVID I. BUSHNELL, JR.: "Virginia before Jamestown" (*Smithson. Miscell. Coll.*, c, Washington, 1940). CLIFFORD EVANS: "A Ceramic Study of Virginia Archæology" (*Bur. Amer. Ethnol. Bull. 160*, Washington, 1955). ALICE L. L. FERGUSON: "Burial Area in Moyaone" (*Journ. Washington Acad. Sci.*, xxvii, Menasha, 1937). GERARD FOWKE: "Archeological Investigations in James and Potomac Valleys" (*Bur. Ethnol. Bull. 23*, Washington, 1894). KARL SCHMITT: "Archeological Chronology of the Middle Atlantic States" (*Archæology of the Eastern United States*, ed. James B. Griffin, Chicago, 1952).

The cultural position of the Virginian tribes is treated by REGINA FLANNERY: "An Analysis of Coastal Algonquian Culture" (*Cathol. Univ. Amer. Anthrop. Ser.*, 7, Washington, 1939). FRANK G. SPECK: "The Ethnic Position of the South-eastern Algonkian" (*Amer. Anthrop. N. s.*, xxvi, Menasha, 1924). For the Algonkian peoples as a whole, see KAJ BIRKET-SMITH: "A Geographic Study of the Early History of the Algonquian Indians" (*Internat. Arch. f. Ethnogr.*, xxiv, Leiden, 1918). A short survey of the culture of the south-easterly tribes is given by JOHN R. SWANTON: "Aboriginal Culture of the South-east" (*42nd Ann. Rep. Bur. Amer. Ethnol.*, Washington, 1928). More detailed, with numerous quotations from older works, is JOHN R. SWANTON: "The Indians of the South-eastern United States" (*Bur. Amer. Ethnol. Bull. 173*, Washington, 1946).

The most important sources are the following. R. B(EVERLEY): *The History of Virginia*, 2nd ed., London, 1722. THOMAS HARIOT: *Narrative of the First English Plantation of Virginia* (reprint), London, 1893 (of the 1st ed., 1588, only four copies are known!). JOHN SMITH: *The Generall Historie of Virginia, New-England, and the Summer Isles*, London, 1624 (reprinted with other works in *Travels and Works of . . .*, ed. E. Arber and A. G. Bradley, i-ii, Edinburgh, 1910). HENRY SPELMAN: *Relation of Virginia* (*circa* 1613, printed in *Travels and Works of Captain John Smith*, ed. E. Arber and A. G. Bradley, i, Edinburgh, 1910). WILLIAM STRACHEY: *The Historie of Travaile into Virginia Britannia*, 1616 (works ed. *Hakluyt Soc.*, vi, London, 1849).

Among more recent works are DAVID I. BUSHNELL: "Virginia—from Early Records" (*Amer. Anthrop. N. s.*, ix, Lancaster, 1907). JOHN LŒWENTHAL: *Die Religion der Ostalgonkin*, Berlin, 1913 (Inaug. Diss.). CHARLES C. WILLOUGHBY: "The Virginia Indians in the Seventeenth Century" (*Amer. Anthrop. N. s.*, ix, Lancaster, 1907).

For the Virginian Indians in recent times see JAMES MOONEY: "The Powhatan Confederacy" (*Amer. Anthrop. N. s.*, ix, Lancaster, 1907). JNO. GARLAND

Pollard: "The Pamunkey Indians of Virginia" (*Bur. Ethnol. Bull. 17*, Washington, 1894). Frank G. Speck: "The Rappahannock Indians of Virginia" (*Ind. Notes a. Monogr.*, v, 3, New York, 1925). Frank G. Speck: "Chapters on the Ethnology of the Powhatan Tribes of Virginia" (*Ind. Notes a. Monogr.*, i, 5, New York, 1928).

THE MAORI

Tropical Agriculture in a New Environment

Sweet Potato

FOR CENTURIES men dreamt of a great undiscovered southland, *Magna Terra Australis Incognita*, which would provide the southern hemisphere with a counterweight to the northern continents. When one day in December 1642, after nine days' eastward sailing from the island which now bears his name, Abel Tasman, the Dutch seafarer, sighted an unknown coast, he was convinced that he had reached the goal he sought; but an attack on the part of the warlike natives, coupled with stormy weather, made him change his mind about landing, and after following the coast northwards until he came to a promontory which he called Cape Maria van Diemen, he headed once more out to sea and some time later reached Tonga.

Tasman was the discoverer of New Zealand—it fell, however, to the lot of another seafarer, James Cook, more than a hundred years later, to prove that this was no enormous "Southland" but a large twin-island divided almost half-way by a strait. He visited New Zealand on each of his three expeditions to the almost unknown South Seas and on his very first voyage in 1769-70 sailed right round the country and took it into the possession of the British Crown. A new world was thus opened up for exploration and European colonization, though a number of years were to pass before the first settlers arrived, and still more before the British annexation became official. A beautiful country with a pleasant climate, it was a long way off the beaten track. If the globe be divided into two hemispheres, one to include as much as possible of the great land masses and the other the largest possible surface of water, New Zealand will be found to be close to the centre of the latter, surrounded on all sides by enormous stretches of ocean, about as far south of the equator as Italy is north of it and about the same size.

The larger of the two islands which go to make up New Zealand is the South Island. A magnificent chain of mountains, known not without reason as the Southern Alps, stretches along the west coast. The Ice Age shaped its steep, snow-clad peaks—which at Mount Cook reach a height of 12,500 ft.—and furrowed out its deep, U-shaped valleys into which rivers tumble out of high side-valleys in the form of enormous waterfalls. The southern part of the west coast has been broken up by the ice into a maze of narrow, steep-sided fjords just as has occurred in Norway. On the eastern side of the mountains the valleys are shut in to form long lakes which in origin and picturesque beauty are similar to those in the Italian Alps. The mountains gradually disappear in the gravel deposits of the Canterbury Plains, most of which, however, are covered by a thick layer of fertile lœss.

On the slightly smaller North Island the terrain is quite different. Here too are mountains; but they follow the east coast of the island and do not constitute a continuation of the Southern Alps, while large parts of the island are merely undulating. The most characteristic features of the island are the magnificent volcanic cones and volcanic activity in general. True, this activity is very much reduced and mostly confined to occasional eruptions of dust and hot steam; but traces of it are to be seen in the extensive deposits of tuff and lava and its effects still make themselves felt in the form of discharges of poisonous gases, bubbling solfataras and countless geysers which send streams of boiling hot water high up into the air and in many places have deposited the loveliest terraces of geyserite. The volcanic districts are equally well endowed with picturesque lakes, whether they are the result of volcanic explosions filled with water or former valleys dammed up by streams of lava.

In view of its situation a partly subtropical climate might be expected. But only the extreme north approaches this. New Zealand lies chiefly in the zone of westerly winds and variations of temperature are small, with cool summers and mild winters. Regular winter frosts occur only in the south; at the southernmost point the summer might be compared to that of Trondheim and the winter to that of Florence. The westerly winds bring an abundance of rain, and this coupled with the cool summers results in the formation of enormous glaciers along the valleys of the Southern Alps. At the same time the copious rainfall causes the mountains to be covered by an evergreen temperate rain forest of small-leaved beeches, myrtles, laurels and conifers of various kinds as well as innumerable lianas and, in particular, ferns of all sizes from trees to herbs, some growing in the ground, others clinging to the branches of trees—a luxuriant though gloomy forest without the colour of flowers or the song of birds. East of the Southern Alps the country lies in rain shadow; instead of bringing rain the wind fills the air with dust, and the forest gives way to scrub and grass steppes or to large heaths of bracken. In contrast to the South Island the greater part of the North Island was originally covered by forest which in the warmer climate prevailing there was richer in variety and included certain species of palm which do not demand too much heat. Heaths of bracken are also to be found, especially on the pumice stone plains of the volcanic region.

No less characteristic and uniform than the flora is the fauna. Although Australia is the nearest continent, one looks in vain for marsupials. For millions of years New Zealand was cut off from the rest of the world, and apart from seals and whales round the coasts the only original mammals are one or two species of bat which must have found their way in by air. Dogs and rats were introduced, voluntarily or involuntarily, by man. Isolation has also left its mark on the bird life. The absence of beasts of prey and other foes has made possible the development of curious, almost wingless, ratites: the kiwi, similar in size to a chicken, and the extinct moa birds, of which the largest species was three feet taller than any surviving ostrich. Equally remarkable are the parrots, both the owl-parrot, which spends the day in holes beneath the roots of trees, and the kea, which has learnt to tear the wool and skin from the settlers' sheep and has thus done great damage. Nearly half the birds of New Zealand occur nowhere else.

* * *

To this distant country, larger than any other in the South Seas, with its mild, temperate climate and magnificent scenery, there arrived sometime in the distant past the ancestors of the native Maori. Whence did they come? The answer is to be found in the circumstances of their race, their language and their culture. In all respects they belong to the Polynesians of the other South Sea island groups, from the Ellice and Tonga Islands in the west to Easter Island in the east, and Hawaii in the north. But this does not, of course, provide the final answer to the problem and only prompts the further question—where did the Polynesians originate? At this point the help which might be expected from racial research fails us to some extent.

The Polynesians are generally tall, well-built people, with warm brown colouring, smooth or curly black hair and dark flashing eyes. Their facial features are almost European and it is by no means uncommon to meet both men and women who to our eyes are really good looking. Thus, curiously enough, they are very close to the white race. But how this relationship is to be explained is one of many anthropological mysteries; however, it is at least worth mentioning that for example among the Dayak in Borneo, the Naga in Assam, and the Lolo in the mountains of south-western China there are racial elements with similar, quasi-European features.

Even if this be taken as an indication, it does not, of course, provide any proof as to where the Polynesians came from. Many different solutions to the problem have been advanced. One of them which has attracted a certain amount of attention in recent years is that put forward by the Norwegian, Thor Heyerdahl, i.e. that they are a mixture of two peoples who emigrated from the coast of Peru and the north-west coast of North America respectively. Heyerdahl is not the first to ascribe the Polynesians' origin to America. But it is he who has done most to substantiate the theory. A weighty argument at one time against the idea that they emigrated from America, or at any rate from Peru, was the fact that the Indians there had no sea-going vessels, only rafts, and these it was thought could not manage a voyage across the ocean. With his daring journey in the *Kon-Tiki* Heyerdahl has, however, established beyond doubt that it is possible. But it is one thing to prove that it is possible—another to prove that it actually took place at some distant time—and moreover on such a scale that these hypothetical seafarers could have become the ancestors of an entire people.

Heyerdahl has also produced various facts in support of his theory. In particular he has tried to demonstrate a large number of points on which culture of the Indians and the Polynesians tally. But it is here that he appears to run into difficulties. Certain of the likenesses he refers to cannot be accepted; in others the elements in question are as widespread in Asia as in America and thus carry no weight as proof. With one exception, to which we shall later return, there is not a single element in the whole Polynesian culture which can with certainty be said to belong to America. On the other hand there is a great deal more which unquestionably suggests Asia. This applies to the principal cultivated plants and domestic animals such as pigs and hens, it applies to water craft, types of stone adzes and much else, and it applies not least to the Polynesian language which belongs to the Austronesian linguistic stock which is widespread in the Philippines, Indonesia and westwards as far as Madagascar. Thus there is every reason to believe that the Polynesians' home must be sought in Southern Asia—which is the view of all modern ethnologists who have studied the problem.

It appears to be something of a mystery that a Stone Age people—for that is what the Polynesians were, even though they were culturally well advanced in other respects—were able to undertake such enormous journeys with success. No other primitive people are their equal as seafarers, and their craft are the most elegant and seaworthy that have ever been produced by people on a similar cultural level. For use near the coast a dug-out shaped from a single log suffices; but to prevent it from capsizing in a rough sea it is counterbalanced on one side by an outrigger of light wood which is fastened in various ways to the hull by means of cross-booms. This craft was incapable of really long journeys.

For long-distance travel there were proper boats consisting of a canoe with raised gunwales made of boards secured together by ropes of sennit and caulked with coconut husk fibre and congealed breadfruit juice, while, instead of having outriggers, two boats were connected by a platform and made into a single craft. Fore and aft was a half-deck. On the platform a small house served as a cabin, and big craft for chieftains and war canoes had magnificently carved stem pieces. Boats sixty to one hundred feet long were by no means unusual, and some were even longer. They were fitted with either one or two masts and with triangular sails of matting. In western Polynesia they had lateen-sail rigging, in eastern Polynesia a sprit sail pointing downwards. There were no rudders. Instead a special steering oar was used. Food was mainly the boiled and dried meal of pandanus fruit, boiled breadfruit, coconuts, dried fish and the dried meat of giant clams. In addition live pigs and chicken were often taken on board. In the craft was a fireplace where food could be cooked. Water was stored in bamboo containers, gourds or coconuts. In this way the crew could easily have enough provisions on board for three or four weeks, and in any case before a long journey they are known actually to have trained themselves to withstand hunger and thirst.

It was, of course, hazardous to venture out into the trackless ocean. By day they orientated themselves by the sun, at night by the stars. The winds, which blow steadily most of the year, also indicated direction to some extent, and the same was true of sea currents and the flight of sea birds. By observing birds it was possible to set course for the low coral islands a considerable distance off even though they rose scarcely more than a few feet above the surface of the water.

As already stated, there is every reason to believe that the Polynesians' forefathers had spread across the Pacific from Indonesia. One of the most frequent objections to this view is that in such case they would have had the prevailing wind and the currents against them. In reply to this there are two points to be made. It is true that the south-easterly trade wind blows with great regularity three-quarters of the year; but in January and February the wind is slight and its direction variable, and furthermore the Micronesian Islands, which constitute natural stepping stones for their migrations, lie chiefly in the eastward equatorial stream which in the summer is continued in the direction of Fiji. The other point is purely psychological. The Polynesians knew well enough that it was far more sensible to sail against the prevailing wind for then, in the event of drinking water and provisions beginning to run out, it was always possible to get back home again.*

What their reason was for leaving their original home we do not know, nor do we know when it happened. So far as the later journeys are concerned, however, we have some guidance in the 500-year-long Polynesian genealogies; though they have no bearing on the earliest immigration which chiefly concerned the westerly island groups. There can scarcely be any doubt that right from the start the main stream made its way eastwards through Micronesia. Others possibly followed the route farther south along the northern border of Melanesia, but this might be disputed. However that may be, Samoa and Tonga must have been among the island groups they first took into their possession, and significantly they lack the traditional immigration background which is otherwise so characteristic of Polynesia.

Other emigration waves from Micronesia at this period possibly led to the first occupation of such distant places as Hawaii and Raiatea in the Society Islands, whence again New Zealand was discovered. Even lonely Easter Island far away in the direction of South America seems to have been reached; Heyerdahl's excavations, dated by radioactive carbon, have established that it was at

* In his recently published work Andrew Sharp has, with apparent good reason, maintained that the Polynesian migrations were chiefly the results of canoes and their crews being blown off course and not of premeditated voyages. On the other hand it seems difficult to ignore the broadly concordant evidence of the native traditions. As is so often the case, the truth may be mid-way between the two.

any rate inhabited about A.D. 400. Most, if not all of the first settlers brought with them an impoverished culture. The poor, Micronesian atolls must have operated as a filter which kept back various cultural elements: stone is non-existent, so is the paper-mulberry tree the bark of which is used for bark cloth; and most of the useful plants have difficulty in thriving there.

The last decades' excavations have brought to light just such an impoverished culture in New Zealand, in particular at Wairau on the south side of the Cook Strait. It is sometimes stated that the immigrating Polynesians found the country already inhabited by dark-skinned, i.e. Melanesian, tribes, but it must be emphasized that so far not a shred of archæological evidence to that effect has been produced, and moreover what is advanced in support of such a view could equally well be otherwise explained. On the contrary, as far back as culture can be traced in New Zealand, it is not only typically Polynesian but has, moreover, what might be called an old-fashioned universal-Polynesian stamp with no trace of the characteristic development which later appeared.

This stamp is evidenced for example in the quadrangular type of tanged adze, in the fish-hooks with a stone stem corresponding to the bonito hooks with mother-of-pearl spoons of other islands, and in certain peculiar forms of neck ornaments which resemble cachalot teeth.

These first immigrants brought the dog with them but no other domestic animals, and, what is especially important, evidently did not carry any kind of cultivated plant with them. Their dwellings, which are chiefly known from the South Island's east coast, are all in places quite unsuited to agriculture. Their economy has been based entirely on food gathering, primarily bracken roots, which also, together with fishing and hunting, played a big part in supporting them in later times. For the hunters it was of vital importance that the moa birds had not at the time disappeared from the country; the finds have affirmed that they were hunted on a large scale and this, it may even be assumed, played a not inconsiderable part in bringing about the extermination of these remarkable birds. None the less, the population was certainly scattered and few in number, for the dwellings show no trace of the fortifications which are characteristic of the later period with its dense population and eternal tribal warfare.

If it be true that one of the Polynesian immigration waves to Oceania avoided Micronesia, i.e. went alongside or through Melanesia, then that would perhaps be the one which introduced agriculture together with such domestic animals as pigs and hens to the Polynesian islands. Another possibility is that some of the immigrants passed Micronesia so quickly that these elements did not have time to get lost on the way (it must be remembered that even though by far the greater majority of the Micronesian islands are coral formations, this is not true of them all), and a final possibility that must be reckoned with is that the Polynesians, after their immigration, got knowledge of them from Fiji, where there were breadfruit trees, taro, yams and bananas of old, as well as pigs and poultry. But nothing can be said with any certainty about this. Suffice to say, however, that all these cultural elements reached Tonga and Samoa at an early stage, and from Samoa they further spread to the Society Islands which gradually became a secondary focus of development. This is where the legendary Havai'i or Hawaiki is to be found, the point of departure of a large number of expeditions and actually the old name for the little island of Raiatea which, even after the principal island, Tahiti, had arrogated to itself political power over the island group, still retained its privileges in rank and sanctity.

A fresh landnam wave sprang up there in the twelfth to fourteenth centuries with almost explosive force. Over-population gradually threatened the islands, war and unsettlement followed in consequence and, as in Viking days, those dissatisfied had no difficulty in finding new leaders in the ambitious younger sons of the chieftains. Craft headed for Hawaii, the Cook, Austral and Tuamotu Islands, for Marquesas and Mangareva and on to the 1,300-mile-distant Easter Island. And during the same period a new settlement took place in New Zealand. The expedition which was undertaken from Hawaiki under the leadership of a chieftain by the name of Toi presumably in the middle of the twelfth century was thus a forerunner; but the decisive immigration did not occur until 200 years later. Following the old navigational precept "slightly to the left of the sunset" a stately fleet entered the Bay of Plenty on the North Island. At the sight of all the trees with their red blossoms one of the chieftains threw his red feathered headdress into the sea with the words: "Hawaiki's royal colours I hereby discard in favour of the royal colours of this new country which bids us welcome". New Zealand's present day Polynesian population, the Maori, trace their ancestry back to these immigrants with as much pride as the inhabitants of New England trace theirs back to the *Mayflower*, and to this day it is said of the seven canoes in which they came that "their fame resounds unto the heavens".

Now the question is, of course, to what extent the Maori really are descendants of the crew of the "Fleet". We must bear in mind that when they were discovered they numbered about 200,000, perhaps even double that. Even the inhabitants of the North Island can scarcely avoid including moa-hunters among their forefathers—an unpleasant fact which is glossed over in the family trees by simply breaking them off at the arrival of the "Fleet" or by artificially grafting them on to a tree with nobler roots. Moreover, it is likely that a large part of the South Island's inhabitants even in Cook's time were actually fairly pure descendants of the moa-hunters, and particularly among the most southern tribes the blood of the moa-hunters ran almost pure in their veins.

There is, furthermore, confirmation of this in the culture, which is by no means uniform throughout the country. Geographical conditions can, of course, account for the fact that agriculture did not spread to the most southerly districts of the South Island; but it cannot explain the absence of pile buildings, the insignificant development of the art of woodcarving, the partiality for old-fashioned double canoes instead of plank boats, etc., all of which appear to be the result of direct inheritance from the moa-hunters. It was on the North Island, and in its central and northern districts in particular, that New Zealand's culture developed most abundantly. Its inner development has, of course, taken time and was not even interrupted by the start of European colonization. What we now call Maori culture does not go a long way back; and it might be remarked here that the description, *Maori*, which actually means "usual", "normal" or something similar, first came into use as the name of the people in the nineteenth century to distinguish them from the white settlers.

* * *

The special characteristics of Maori culture are due, if not exclusively at any rate largely, to the fact that it has been transplanted from a tropical to a temperate climate. This will be described in detail later. But it was deep-rooted in the general Polynesian culture. This applies to its whole spirit, its outlook on life or, if you prefer, its religion. At the same time it has proved its vitality by bearing fresh fruit even in the European period in the shape of the god Io cult. Io is actually an old deity, not originally very important. Perhaps because of the name, which is related to the word *iho*, "the innermost", "the core", and because of a link in Christian minds between Io and Jehovah, he came to be regarded as late as the nineteenth century by a small circle within the highest ranks of the priesthood as a supreme being and the creator of the world.

The really fundamental and original outlook on life is, however, dualistic. This dualism does not concern the contrast between good and evil, but the contrast between sacred and profane—also expressed in the difference between light and darkness, between heaven and earth, and man and woman. First of all, so tradition runs, there was emptiness or chaos, Kore, which turned into night, Po, and from that heaven and earth, Rangi and Papa, gradually came into being and by their connexion the gods were born. The most important of them in the well-timbered country was Tane, lord of the forest, the trees and wild birds. He separated heaven from earth so that light broke through; but the love of the two did not end and heaven's tears fall on earth as rain, while the earth's sighs rise upwards as the mists of night. Tane is mankind's first ancestor, and in some myths Tiki, the first man, is regarded as a personification of his procreative power. Tane's brothers are Rongo, who looks after agriculture and peaceful pursuits, Tu, the god of war, and Tangaroa, god of sea and fish, protector of seafarers. In addition to the main gods, of which there were many others—Rangi's and Papa's descendants are referred to as the seventy heavenly gods—there were countless minor deities linked to individual tribes and kinship groups, mostly the spirits of ancestors who continually looked after the well-being of their descendants. Maui, whose adventures are the subjects of innumerable tales, must be regarded as a mighty legendary hero. He it was who fished up the North Island from the bottom of the ocean and in memory of its origin it still bears the name of Te Ika-a-Maui, i.e. Maui's fish.

From the principal gods to human beings there is a direct, descending line, which is why so much importance is attached to the family trees which trace the kinship groups back to the circle of the gods. Pride in kin is not arrogance, but religion. Life is unity in which not only gods and humans, but also things which to us are lifeless, have a part. This is expressed in the idea of *mana*, the sacred force that permeates existence. To achieve real understanding of this conception is almost impossible, it being so foreign to all our accustomed ways of thinking. It is connected on the one hand with another fundamental conception among the Maori, *tapu*, the nearest translation of which would be "to bring out one's nature"; it was thus linked to the personality and manifested itself in strength and success in life. On the other hand *mana* could be both given and taken away, could be conducted away like an electric current and so to that extent was something impersonal. The chieftain, who was descended from the gods as the first-born son through all the generations, possessed the greatest *mana*, indeed in a way the *mana* of the entire kinship group. It was inseparable from his prestige and that of the tribe, and if he failed it by, for example, being defeated by his enemies and made a slave, he could never regain his former position, even if he escaped or was liberated. And not only human beings could possess *mana*. In the Cook Straits there are rocks whose power is so great that if anyone looked at them from a passing boat it was held up for a whole day and night.

Life had to be protected from contamination, the holy were not to be infected by the profane, and sacred power of various strengths could not be mixed, for this spelt danger not only to the individual but to the whole of society. From this notion derived the prohibition, *tapu*, which preserved the difference between life and death and between the different spheres of life.* *Tapu* means "regard" or "to have regard to" and was closely linked to the *mana* idea. It applied especially to cooking and eating, since both of them involved dangerous contamination. That was why people who on ritual occasions, or simply because of their particular *mana*, were subject to a strong *tapu*, had to have their food prepared in special ovens and why meals were taken in the open air or in the porch of the house but never inside it.

The chieftain, especially his head, was loaded with *mana* and surrounded by *tapu*. If he had slept in a strange house, he put his hand on the place where his head had rested, raised it up to his face and sniffed his *tapu* back again, and he drank out of his hollowed hand so that his *tapu* should not spread to the drinking vessels and make them unusable for others. A white woman who had once given a chieftain something to drink, is said to have been exceedingly cross when he broke the cup afterwards; she did not realize that he was actually doing her a service.

Priests, too, were *tapu* and—this applied to everyone—the more so the higher their rank. The highest ranks of the priesthood, who quite certainly belonged to the nobility, only concerned themselves with the holiest of rites, while the lower ranks looked after the more everyday rites and among their duties was service as doctors. Lowest in rank amongst them were the fortune tellers and mediums—these on certain occasions became possessed by one of the lesser deities who spoke through their mouths during their trances. The priests possessed a by no means insignificant amount of knowledge, and they underwent long training in astronomy, for example, and of course also in the sacred history of the particular tribe. When an old priest lay on his deathbed he asked his pupil to "bite",

* The Polynesian form of the word is *tapu*, which is therefore used in this chapter instead of the more usual taboo.

i.e. touch with his teeth, some part of his body at the moment of death, so that his *mana* could be transferred to his successor. Like the highest chieftains, who by the force of their divine descent were the only ones able to perform certain rites, the highest priesthood were also trained in schools (*whare wananga*, i.e. houses of learning), which were so sacred that before they went into them the pupils had to take off all their everyday clothes and put on new ones when inside.

The gods were the subjects of offerings and solemn rituals. Usually the offerings consisted of food, and it was one of the gods' privileges to receive the first fruits of the harvest and of hunting; but on special occasions such as before a battle, or at the erection of a house or the building of a canoe, this was not enough. A slave or a member of a weak and subject tribe then had to lay down his life. Invocations were made in settled formulas, *karakia*, which in order to operate successfully had to be recited without the slightest mistake. Only rarely were they directed immediately to the gods. Usually the gods were referred to indirectly or by means of obscure allusions. The words themselves were filled with sacred power. Thus the way lay wide open to conceiving them as pure magic, and in fact many of them were purely magic formulas available to anyone, whereas others were so sacred that only the priests knew them and dared to make use of them.

Each village had its holy precincts or cult place. It could be an enclosed area inside the fortifications; but more usually it was situated some distance from the village at an out-of-the-way spot where its *tapu* would not present any danger to children and others who either without thinking or through ignorance might subject it to contamination. There was nothing to show the extreme sanctity of the place beyond a little pile of earth or unworked stones plus some upright stones or posts and sometimes a little platform on which offerings could be placed. In addition to the cult place proper, there was in the neighbourhood of every village some consecrated water in the form of a pool, stream or well, where ritual cleansing was carried out on such important occasions as birth, war and burial. But the most remarkable of all sacred places was the village latrine. It was situated over a steep drop and consisted of two short posts connected by a cross-bar on which the user squatted while holding on firmly to either one or two posts stuck into the ground in front. Its sanctity was to some extent a practical arrangement in that it prevented evil-minded people from stealing the excrement for the purposes of witchcraft; but in addition, according to Dr. Prytz Johansen, it had a further significance, the horizontal cross-bar separating the world of life from the world of death (excrement). In the event of serious illness and before hazardous undertakings, among them war, the curious rite known as *ngau paepae*, "biting the bar", was performed, the cross-bar being touched with the teeth while a priest recited an invocation befitting the occasion.

One searches the sacred places in vain for any actual idols. Some object or other in which the god occasionally might reside was sometimes hidden in a wooden box or in a small carved house on top of a post at the sacred enclosure. A similar purpose was served by small, crudely formed stone figures representing Rongo, the god of agriculture, who was set up in the sweet-potato fields to promote fertility, and by carved wooden staves which were stuck in the earth to signify that the soil was *tapu*. The gods themselves, however, were invisible, though when they so desired they could, of course, manifest themselves in the form of rainbows, meteors, lightning and different kinds of animals such as lizards and owls.

The entire outlook on life which formed the background to Maori culture indicates the predominant importance of kinship to society. Kinship defined one's relationship to the gods, from whom the chieftains were directly descended, the first-born son's first-born in unbroken succession. Even though a chieftain should prove incapable and lacking in any real authority, he still retained the religious privileges with which his sacred birth endowed him. The chieftain's younger sons constituted the nobility, while the common people consisted of the younger sons of younger relations and the children of freeborn men by slave women, liberated slaves, and so on. In other words the social order was aristocratic in the extreme, even though the dividing lines between the different classes were fluid to the extent that they all belonged to the same kinship group. Only slaves, i.e. prisoners of war, formed an exception. Being outside the kinship group they were also outside society and thus devoid of rights, though their lot was by no means hard, apart from the fact that they ran the risk of losing their lives when a human sacrifice was deemed necessary.

As the kinship group grew, the need arose to divide it into younger groups which separated off from the original clan and took over fresh land for cultivation. None the less ties of blood were not forgotten, and the interrelated kinship groups together formed a tribe whose members could trace their line back to a common ancestor. The kinship group put up an inviolable common front externally, but this did not always prevent internal strife. If by any chance relatives should encounter each other on the battle-field—and with relationship so far reaching this was inevitable—killing was as far as possible avoided, and though cannibalism was a traditional revenge on a fallen foe, a dead kinsman was never eaten, for this violated one's own kinship group and thus oneself. The feeling of solidarity was so strong that even tribes with nothing in common beyond the fact that their forefathers were believed to have come from Hawaiki in the same craft, felt a certain relationship which was simply expressed in the word *waka*, i.e. canoe.

In the life of the kinship group, woman was inferior. She constituted the profane element in the world. Everyday duties were her sphere, and this more or less "impure" nature of hers made it necessary to exclude her from various activities. Her presence was thus prohibited at the building of a new war canoe and she was even forbidden to pass the place where the work was going on; the same applied to the erection of a new house or a fortification, nor was she allowed to be present while a slain enemy was being eaten. On the other hand the very profanity of her nature often bestowed on her the rôle of performing those rites which had to be observed in the lifting of certain *tapu* rules.

But one must not suppose from this that her special position carried any sort of oppression with it. In marriage she was highly respected and only the nobility sometimes allowed themselves to have more than one wife. It could happen though that highly respected guests would be offered a temporary marriage partner. An example of this occurred when one of the first bishops in New Zealand visited a village causing his companion to exclaim in anger: "What? A wife for the bishop!" Whereupon the chieftain in question, evidently at something of a loss, replied, "All right, let him have two then!"

Husband and wife nearly always belong to the same kinship group; but it was a rule that in any event they could not have the same grandparents and preferably not the same great grandparents. Both betrothal and marriage took place with great ceremony and the presentation of gifts, which confirmed the connexion between the families in question. Usually the bridal pair lived with the bridegroom's family; but the rule was not invariable, especially if the bride was the more distinguished, her rank then being taken into account. Even though the father's line predominated, the mother's position was far from being of no significance. A new-born child came into the world in a special hut, which was burned after its birth, and was received and made welcome by the kin. Afterwards the child was carried in solemn procession to the consecrated water of the village, where a priest carried out a kind of baptism and presented it to the gods, while if the child was a boy it was consecrated either to the god of war, Tu, or to the god of peace and agriculture, Rongo. After that the child was carried to the parents' house where the priest again recited sacred formulas and gifts were spread out in the porch. In this way the child's *mana* was secured.

Generally speaking, gifts constituted an important part in Maori life. Gifts established peace, and the chieftain received gifts from the members of the tribe; but like a Nordic Viking king he had to be not only victorious in war but generous in peace. To receive a gift was an honour; but to give one was a still greater honour which increased the donor's *mana*. A certain form of gift was expressed in hospitality. Receiving guests, especially at big festivals, was a solemn and elaborate affair. When the guests made their entry into the village they were received in front of the assembly place by a warrior who, with threatening grimaces and curious writhings of the body, leaped towards them flourishing his spear, which he finally laid on the ground in front of them, during which time the villagers shouted words of welcome and waved green branches. At the guest house everyone came to a halt and started weeping and wailing in honour of those who had died since the two parties last met; this was followed by many long speeches. Only after that, in solemn procession, was the meal brought forth, so that in the meantime not infrequently the food had got cold. At grand receptions the food was displayed in advance on high, festively-decorated staging.

It goes without saying that on such occasions too, distribution of presents took place; but it is important to note that a present always carried the obligation of a present in return. On the other hand there was no question of bartering, for in the eyes of the Maori, trade was degrading. All the same, gifts spread the various regions' products far and wide. Most prized were weapons and ornaments of hard, green nephrite, which occurs only in two sequestered places on the South Island, and of a similar kind of stone (bowenite) which occurs only at one single place. From here it had to be transported by sea along steep cliff-lined coasts or across country through narrow mountain passes and uninhabited forests. Thus old heirlooms were understandably regarded with veneration and love; they themselves possessed *mana* and were gifts which moved to and fro within the kinship group.

Respect and honour were inseparable for the complete development of life. An affront to one's honour was equivalent to a debilitation of life and could lead to suicide, but it also had other violent repercussions. One remarkable form was the traditional plundering, *muru*. If an important man offended his kinship group by holding a wedding without sufficient ceremony, for example, or if he was visited by misfortune—if his son got drowned or his wife ran off with a lover—this was violation of the group's honour, which demanded redress, just as it was also evidence of inevitable misfortune and a bad omen which necessitated a cleansing of the group's life. So the members of the group gathered in full war dress and after a mock fight took away the victim's property lock, stock and barrel. He, however, by no means resented what happened for, apart from the cleansing of life which the plundering brought about, it was, *mirabile dictu*, an honour—though a dearly bought one—which proved his importance in the kinship group.

Outside the kinship group an insult led inevitably to revenge. A man got soaked by rain and when he arrived at a strange village after the rain his damp clothes were steaming. A boy was rash enough to say that he was steaming like an oven. Now cooking is the work of women and slaves, and the unintended insult offended him so deeply that it led to war. No wonder then that war was an almost daily occurrence, even if it was generally confined to reciprocal attacks by minor forces. A total of 140 warriors was the usual; but it could be more if allies were taking part. They were received by a violent war-dance, stamping of the ground, wildly rolling eyes and outstretched tongues. Then followed the traditional welcome with tears for the departed, long speeches and nose rubbing. Before the warriors set out, they performed the ceremony already mentioned of biting the latrine cross-bar (see page 213) and consecrated water from the sacred streams or well was sprinkled over them. They were now subject to war *tapu*, which put them under the protection of "red-eyed Tu", the god of war. Their weapons were spears—some for throwing, others so long that they had to be carried by two men—also long, sharp-edged clubs which ended in a grotesquely carved human head with an outstretched tongue which could be directed towards the enemy as a challenge and in an emergency could serve as a spear head, and finally large, axe-shaped and short spatula-shaped, or asymmetrical, clubs of wood, whalebone or the costly nephrite, the last named more especially intended for thrusting.

What decided the battle was not so much the number of dead as their rank. Greatest honour was connected with slaying the first foe—"the first fish" as he was called. His heart was cut out by the accompanying priest and lifted high in the air as an offering to the particular war god of the tribe. The battle ended with the victors' eating their dead enemies and perhaps using their bones for making fish-hooks. Thus they achieved their revenge and showed the enemy the greatest possible degree of contempt, which stuck to their successors for generations. It was a disgrace which was exceeded only by being captured alive and turned into a slave—and lower than that it was impossible for a Maori to sink.

To one's own dead, however, one displayed extreme respect and care. As soon as the last hour of a dying man was feared to be approaching, he was put in a special hut, and when the spirit had departed to the distant Kingdom of the Dead, which was situated either in the underworld or in the sky, the hut was burned down. Then, dressed in its best clothes, the corpse was laid out for public view while the survivors, with green wreaths on their heads as a sign of mourning, made deep gashes in their breasts and broke into loud shouts of dismay, which alternated with dirges and speeches in praise of the departed. If the dead man was a chieftain, mourners came from near and far and were received with traditional solemnity. Often the dead chieftain's head was severed from the body and subjected to primitive mummification so that the kinship group could mourn over it—or in the case of a fallen foe so that it could be the subject of contempt and all kinds of insult. At the funeral of an important chief a slave was sacrificed also, either so that he could serve his master in the spirit world, or so that his flesh could serve as provisions on the journey to the hereafter.

In addition the corpse was wrapped in a mat and as a rule buried either bent double or outstretched; in woody districts, however, it was sometimes put in hollow trees or on a platform in the crowns of the trees. One tribe at least was accustomed to burn the corpse, a practice which was otherwise only followed in enemy country so that no one could violate it. After the burial there was a big celebration, and food and other gifts were distributed to the sorrowing guests. In some places corpses were dug up after a couple of years, the bones were cleaned, coloured red, and buried in a distant cave.

* * *

Both in religion and in social conditions the common basic Polynesian characteristics are unmistakable; moreover, in many cases they have a peculiarly old-fashioned character—a factor to which we shall revert in a moment. This does not, of course, mean that there has been no separate development in New Zealand since the immigration, for with such vigorous people as the Maori a culture does not remain unchanged for centuries. But the development which undoubtedly has taken place there has its roots only to a slight extent in the new environment which the immigrants found. Things are different, however, when we examine the purely material side of the culture. It stands to reason that on a people whose whole mode of life was originally adapted to tropical South Sea islands the temperate climate of New Zealand and its wealth of forests must have had a far-reaching influence, not only in the matter of clothes but also in dwellings, boat-building and economics.

Clothing material widespread throughout Polynesia was bark-cloth, which was made of the bark of the paper-mulberry tree or of certain wild fig-trees; none of them, however, will grow in the soil of New Zealand. On Cook's first voyage he was shown near the northern tip of the country, as something very rare, six paper-mulberry trees. Otherwise the climate was too cold for them. Now, it stands to reason that any people finding themselves in new conditions will try as far as possible to retain techniques to which they are accustomed, and so it is beyond doubt that the Maoris' ancestors tried to transfer bark-cloth to their new home—this is demonstrated, for example, by the fact that a few bark-beaters carved out of native woods have been found in New Zealand, and in the absence of anything better, efforts have been made to use the bark of the local whauwhi tree (*Hoheria populnea*). But it was unsuitable and gradually bark-cloth disappeared and was replaced by mats. Mats and plaited material for dress are actually well known in tropical Polynesia, where they are frequently made of strips of coconut palm and pandanus leaves; but this material New Zealand was equally unable to provide.

On the other hand there were other plants which could be used—rushes and, in particular, an extremely common liliaceous plant (*Phormium tenax*) which goes under the misleading name of New

Zealand flax or hemp. Even Moa-hunters had known how to exploit its excellent qualities as plaiting material. Its tough sword-like leaves up to as much as six feet in length were split into thin strips, soaked in water and scraped with shells. Especially fine material was obtained by beating the fibres with a round wooden club. Some changes in the technique of plaiting took place, the usual Polynesian method with a twined weft became a sort of "finger-weaving" in which the warp was suspended between two upright sticks. And finally the actual pieces of clothing underwent a transformation, partly in consequence of the new material, partly too on account of the chilly climate.

So far as men are concerned the most widespread Polynesian item of dress is probably a breech cloth of bark cloth. Instead of this a little triangular apron of hempstrips or rushes now appeared in New Zealand. For dancing, and for other occasions as well, instead of the apron the men could wear a knee-length skirt of rushes in scraped and unscraped sections which appeared as dark and light horizontal stripes. Similar skirts were the customary dress for women. But it is obvious that such clothing was too light for New Zealand's climate and so it was supplemented by a cloak, which could be either short or long. The commonest type, which was especially suited to rain and could serve also as a blanket, was covered on the outside by a thick layer of fringes which were either knotted into the lining or consisted of short, free-hanging ends of the warp. Heavy cloaks, which were more or less impenetrable to spears, were worn in war, and for special occasions there were others made of especially fine work with tassels, etc. Chieftains' cloaks could have long strips of dog skin or red, green, white and blue-black feathers arranged in squares and stripes fastened to them. The most expensive cloaks were, however, quite simple but made with choice, silky threads in the warp and coloured edgings in tasteful geometrical designs.

However much pride and vanity the Maori possessed, neither the form nor the number of their adornments achieved such barbaric heights as those of people at a lower stage of cultural development. An exception to this, however, was tattooing on the face, back, and thighs. The features of distinguished men almost disappeared beneath spiral designs and ingenious scrolls which were hammered into the skin with a small adze-shaped bone chisel, whereas the women were content with a few simple lines on the chin and lips. During the lengthy and painful process both the craftsman and his victim were subject to strict *tapu*, and in consequence of his inflamed and swollen lips the latter could take only fluid nourishment which was poured down through an elaborately carved wooden funnel. The idea that the tattoo designs are a kind of tribal mark is based on a misapprehension. The men wore their hair bound up in a knot in which they sometimes stuck a feather or an ornamental comb of wood or whalebone, whereas the women cut their hair short. Actual ornaments were, as already mentioned, quite few. They were preferably of whalebone or, still better, of nephrite and were restricted to various kinds of ear ornaments and small grotesque human figures, *hei-tiki*, which were worn on a string round the neck and originally seem to have been fertility amulets for women.

Like the dress, the dwelling underwent a number of modifications to suit the new surroundings which the ancestors of the Maori found, and here it was an invaluable asset that the country could provide an almost inexhaustible supply of timber. The typical Maori house was a rectangular wooden building with a slightly sunken floor and a saddle-shaped straw roof. Simple houses would have no walls at all, the roof resting immediately on to the earth.

The best-built houses were to be found on the North Island where the culture generally speaking was highest. The wall of the front gable end was slightly retracted under the roof so that an open porch was formed in front of it, and in addition to a low door there was also a window opening in the wall which allowed the smoke from the fire to escape. Both doors and windows had shutters which could be closed at night. Rich carvings decorated not only the door- and window-frames of important houses but also the corner posts and gable boards, and at the gable angle where these met a fantastic mask or human figure with its tongue defiantly outstretched could be set up. Assembly houses, in particular, which could reach the impressive length of eighty feet, and a corresponding width, were richly embellished with wood carvings and were quite simply called *whare whakairo*, i.e. carved houses. The posts supporting the ridge posts were carved with figures representing ancestral heroes and mythical beasts, while similar carvings decorated the wall posts.

There always had to be an uneven number of these on each side and between them were finely made cane panels. Along the walls on either side of the fire were grass sleeping places covered with mats. In front to the right were the places allotted to guests while those for the inhabitants were on the left.

The building of an assembly house was a tremendous task which involved a complicated system of exchanging gifts and doing reciprocal services on the part of everyone concerned. It was the pride of the village and stood in the open square where visiting guests were received and public affairs transacted. Cooking was absolutely forbidden in the houses, being relegated to special cooking huts where it was carried out with the aid of hot stones in earth ovens. In addition, there were stores for supplies—some of them raised on several poles, others on a single pole—and earth pits where sweet potatoes were kept until they were to be used.

The Maori possessed a highly developed sense of beauty and tried to locate their villages in beautiful places; but the factor which was of prime importance was that they could be effectively defended. Some villages were surrounded by strong palisades, others were open; but in this latter case in troublous times the inhabitants frequently would seek refuge in the fortifications which were such as to arouse the admiration of the old seafarers. They formed a characteristic feature of the culture of the North Island, whereas they were rarer on the South Island with its sparser and more scattered population. Sometimes in open fields, but more frequently on a ridge of rock and other inaccessible places, it is still possible to find remains of many of these refuges. In days gone by they were enormous installations, consisting of earth works, deep trenches and strong palisade walls, sometimes in several rows one behind the other and surmounted by terrifying, carved human figures. One has to go as far west as distant Tonga and Fiji before finding anything at all like these fortifications; but whether there is any connexion between them and those of the Maori is undecided and may even be doubtful: perhaps they came into being in New Zealand spontaneously in consequence of the warlike tendencies of the people.

The same skill in craftsmanship apparent in housebuilding is displayed in the building of boats. Right from the start the Polynesians have been on intimate terms with the sea, which carried them regularly to distant island groups. Their simplest craft consisted merely of dug-outs, and these are still in use on the lakes and rivers of New Zealand.

For long voyages across the open sea the Polynesians used double boats and outrigger canoes. Such craft were also brought to New Zealand by the immigrants and were found still in use by the first European seafarers, Tasman and Cook, mainly on the South Island, where older types survived longer than was the case farther north. The wealth of timber gradually led, however, to the development of a new kind of craft, the enormous tree-trunks available making possible craft of such width that outriggers and double canoes became unnecessary. Such boats could be up to a good 100 ft. long and over 6 ft. wide. The gunwales were raised by boards securely lashed, and the projecting stem was carved and jutted out in the form of a stylized bird and a complete human figure or a mask with outstretched tongue, while a stern post of carved fretwork rose 6 ft. above the surface of the water. Up to ninety paddlers drove the boat rapidly forwards by means of narrow paddles to the rhythm of songs and movements by a song leader, and if the wind was favourable a triangular sprit sail of mats was hoisted.

During such exacting work as the erection of the large houses and the building of the equally big craft, the workers were subject to strict *tapu*; and it is astonishing to realize what they managed to achieve with the few stone tools at their disposal: first and foremost polished quadrangular or three-sided adzes of basalt, nephrite or other suitable stone, simple stone chisels, knives of sharp obsidian blades and a kind of drill driven by a thong. Still more impressive, however, is their skill in the matter of woodcarving, which has developed on the foundation of their timber work. Masks and human figures, which have already been mentioned several times, were a favourite motif. Their attitudes are stiff and static. The great head, with its wildly staring eyes and its broad, curiously shaped mouth, almost like a figure 8, with outstretched tongue and often large tusks, rests on a long body with short bandy legs and hands which, for some reason or other, are given only three fingers, resting on the stomach. Painted in red ochre mixed with shark's oil and often provided with eyes of opalescent mother-of-pearl, they make a fantastic and barbaric impression. Sometimes the figure was wry-necked with the face in profile and the mouth drawn out into a long bird-like beak, and sometimes one leg was shrunken and the other extended into a sort of long, winding tail, in which case the figure was supposed to be a man-eating sea monster.

Other favourite motifs are the spiral and double spiral, which together with winding S-bends form the basis of tattooing patterns and of the ornamentation not only on houses and boats but also on wooden boxes in which feather decorations were kept, weapons and ceremonial adze hafts, whistles . . . in short all kinds of implements beyond the crudest tools. This decorative art was most richly developed on the North Island, and poorest in the extreme south, where simpler, straight-lined designs predominated. It seems, however, as if spiral ornamentation in a more or less highly developed form is of great antiquity throughout Polynesia. There are also traces of it on the Marquesas Islands, and perhaps via certain parts of Melanesia it goes as far back as the East Asian Bronze Age.

In the light of the Maoris' skilled craftsmanship and love of art it is in general reasonable to state that they saw nothing degrading in manual work, of which even chieftains did their share. Though one cannot refer to the rise of an actual craftsman class, there were certain experts or *tohunga*, whose help was sought when difficult and elaborate tasks made it so desirable and who

Above: A Maori house. In a land rich in trees it was natural for wood to be the principal building material. The typical house was rectangular, with a slightly sunken floor and a saddle shaped straw roof. The best-built houses were to be found on the North Island. The door and window frames, corner posts and gable boards of important houses were very richly carved.

Right: An old Maori before his house. In his hand is a patula-shaped club. The protruding tongue of the carved figure is a symbol of defiance.

Maori women. *Left:* females are tattooed on lips and chin only.

Below: two women rub noses in greeting.

Above: One of the big, richly carved Maori canoes such as Captain James Cook saw on his first coming to New Zealand. Though early Maori craft were simple dugouts, the enormous size of some of the trees led to the development of craft which could be up to 100 ft. in length and over 6 ft. wide. Such boats could carry some 90 paddlers and could safely undertake long voyages on the open sea. The paddlers worked to the rhythm of the songs and movements of a song leader.

Right: An old Maori man with characteristic spiral tattoo marks.

Below: The *Haka*, a ceremonial dance, is also a popular diversion.

Above: Maori war clubs of greenstone and wood and a charm made of greenstone. Like the other objects on this page they are in the National Museum at Copenhagen.

Left: The craftsman who carved this wooden figure with a stone knife worked so skilfully that he has been able to represent in elaborate detail the traditional tattooing of the face.

Below: This elaborately carved wooden box was used by the Maori for keeping feathers in. Despite the elaborate tattooing of the face and body and the rich carving of utensils, homes and boats, the Maoris did not in their dress achieve the barbaric heights attained by some peoples of a more primitive standard of culture.

were paid by gifts and reciprocal work. It is significant that also the priests were reckoned amongst these *tohunga*; they were, of course, the experts in religious matters.

* * *

No other aspect of life was so fundamentally affected by the new environment which the ancestors of the Maori encountered as their economics, and in some respects this had to be completely changed. It has already been mentioned that the earliest migrants to Polynesia had probably had to give up agriculture during their journey through the atolls of Micronesia. However that may be, New Zealand's first settlers brought no cultivated plant with them, but had to rely entirely on gathering wild plants, fishing and hunting moa-birds and other game. In later times, too, when new immigration waves had brought cultivated plants to the country, the importance of the earlier methods of providing food remained unaffected, particularly on the South Island, where agriculture only became established in the northern districts and was completely absent farther south.

The roots of bracken (*Pteris aquilina*) which covered large tracts of heath, were everywhere a source of food of prime importance, and were known as *te tutanga te unuhia*, "the food that never fails". The roots could be gathered all the year round; after being dried, they were baked—not in the traditional earth oven but over charcoal—after which they were hammered with a wooden club, the hard fibres removed and what was left baked once more. In addition to bracken, many other wild plants figured on the menu: the underground stem and part of the leaves of what is known as the cabbage tree (*Cordyline australis*) which would, however, grow only in the extreme north, the pith of a kind of fern tree, roots and pollen of reed-mace, young fern shoots which were boiled as vegetables, various kinds of berries, and so on.

In addition to this there was hunting. Forest game was as indispensable as forest timber, and, like human beings, the trees and birds were considered to be the descendants of the god Tane. It was *te wao tapu nui a Tane*, "Tane's great and sacred forest". Thus it had to be shown veneration and respect. While the birds were broody and their young could not fly it was *tapu*, and breaking the *tapu* was punished by general plundering of the malefactor's property. The manufacture and repair of hunting implements had to be carried out in a special house, and while the work went on the workers were also *tapu*. The forest itself was a living being, subject to the same life principle as man, on which depended the growth and procreation of trees and animals. For this reason the forest was not to be violated, and before a hunting party went in to it, the priest had to be convinced that the forest's "life" was assured; often the latter was concealed in a stone buried under a tree. The first bird to fall a victim to the hunt was brought as an offering to Tane, and, after a ritual meal, the forest's *tapu* was lifted.

By far the most important game were the birds. The moa had already disappeared from the North Island before the arrival of "the Fleet", and possibly it never lived alongside human beings there. On the South Island, however, it was exterminated at the latest 200 years afterwards. After that the kiwi, certain kinds of parrot and pigeons together with sea fowl, such as the albatross, stormy petrels, etc., were the object of the Maoris' efforts. The wingless kiwi was hunted by dogs and sea birds by the aid of outstretched nets or, so far as the albatross was concerned, simply by hooks.

Other birds were caught in snares, some of which were fitted on a long stick with a side branch; the huntsman concealed himself on a platform high up in the crown of a tree where the birds nested, and when one of them alighted on the side branch of the stick he pulled a string and thus captured his prey. Such snare trees were personal property. To decoy parrots a tame decoy bird was used. This was tethered by a string fastened to a ring of bone or nephrite round the bird's foot. In addition, there were special bird spears with barbed bone points. The only mammal which served as food and which was thus much coveted was the native South Sea rat (*Rattus exulans*) which is considerably less unappetizing in its habits than its European relatives. It was caught partly in pitfalls and partly in snares fastened to a flexible branch which sprang up into the air when touched. During the first day of the hunting season the rat hunters were subject to *tapu*, and when they returned after having set their snares they were not allowed to speak until the next morning. Both birds and rats were pickled in their own fat and stored in bark containers or big bottle gourds.

It cannot be denied that the paucity of animal life put a strict limitation on hunting, and though they were kept in many parts of Polynesia, neither pigs nor poultry were to be found. Dog meat was considered a delicacy; none the less hunger for meat rose to such heights that cannibalism, which undoubtedly originally was a ritual ceremony, just as it was elsewhere, to some extent lost this character and lone wanderers outside their own tribal area ran the risk of being killed and eaten.

Generally speaking the Maori were not quite so at home on the sea as most of their kinsmen on the small Polynesian islands, though this did not prevent fishing in many places from providing an indispensable supplement to the diet. Like hunting, it was subject to a number of *tapu* regulations. This applied especially to sea fishing, during which, for instance, it was forbidden to carry food in the craft. The first fish caught had to be put in the sacred enclosure or hung up on a tree as an offering. Shark fishing, under pain of general plundering, could take place on only two days of the year, and was carried out collectively by a large number of boat teams. At a given sign, all the craft pushed off from the shore and raced to the fishing ground, which was the joint property of the tribe, and great prestige attached to the one fortunate enough to get the first catch. Hooks suitably shaped according to the catch were used both for shark and for other fish. Some hooks were almost circular, others oval; some were of wood with bone points, others entirely of bone, and a pointed insult to a fallen enemy was to make them out of his bones. For trolling, a piece of mother-of-pearl which functioned as a spoon was set into the stem of the hook.

Nets were used in all shapes and sizes, from three-quarter-mile long drag-nets, the opening of which could be drawn together by a line so that it shut in the catch, to dip-nets fastened to the end of a long stick. The last named were used for various kinds of fish and also for shell fish. Knotting the big nets for dragging meant that the work place had to be *tapu*, so that neither fire was lighted nor food cooked in the place, and before a festive occasion at which strange guests were expected, new nets had to be made, since the old nets had been used to catch fish which had been eaten by people subject to *tapu*. The first time a new net was set out, the operation had to be accompanied by the recital of a long spell, and the first fish to be caught in it was put back into the water.

In the rivers, stone weirs or fences made of branches were erected to act as fish traps. As was the case elsewhere in the South Seas, the catching of the big Pacific Ocean eel was of considerable importance. At night they were speared by torch-light, or enormous eel-weirs were built, work which, like boat building, was strictly *tapu* for women.

With the introduction of agriculture, the Maori were faced with fresh tasks, for it was either impossible to transfer the tropical cultivated plants to the cooler climate, or possible to do so only with great difficulty. The coconut palm would not grow, and the memory of the breadfruit tree only survived in tales and in a single place name. One or two species of cabbage tree (*Cordyline*) were presumably imported, but one of them at any rate did not flourish outside the most northerly districts. The common yam plant could not survive anywhere else either, and even there its cultivation was so unprofitable that it ceased completely during the course of the nineteenth century. The bottle-gourd (*Lagenaria*) which was grown as food and more particularly so that its hard shells could be used as containers, succeeded on the South Island only in the most favourable places. The taro and, especially, the sweet potato, which was the most hardy and therefore the most widespread cultivated plant in New Zealand, were more successful; but even the sweet potato did not reach farther south than the Canterbury Plains on the South Island, where it was the object of the world's most southerly agriculture.

All ground belonged to the tribe, and the chieftain could not dispose of it. "People die, get killed, move away and disappear, but not so the earth; that remains for ever," say the Maori. The tribal ground was divided between different kinship groups and the groups' ground again into family lots.

Though agriculture was restricted to the more favourably situated areas, this did not mean that it stood at a low level. True, artificial irrigation was not employed as it was at so many places in Polynesia; but the Maori had excellent knowledge of the varying characteristics of the soil. They well knew that taro prefers humid places and light sandy soil and that the sweet potato likewise avoids heavy soils, so that if necessary they mixed gravel into the soil. The fields lay for preference on slopes facing the sun, and on the South Island fences were put up as windbreaks. Both sexes worked in the fields, though there were differences in work distribution. Generally the men cleared away the forest, worked the soil and undertook both planting and harvesting; the planting of sweet potatoes was as a rule barred to women, though they undertook weeding. Tools were few and simple. Apart from the adze which was used for clearing, there were only a spade of hard wood, a digging stick with a support for the foot, and a short-hafted wooden hoe which was used in a sitting position for loosening the earth's crust and breaking the soil up fine.

The sweet potato, of which several varieties were known, certainly formed the basis of Maori agriculture. Its history is remarkable. Even before Europeans came to the South Seas, it seems to have been cultivated over large parts of Polynesia. The Maori say that they got to know it even before the great immigration which arrived with "the Fleet" in the middle of the fourteenth century, for a canoe from Hawaiki with sweet potatoes on board had been blown off her course by a storm. Craft were then fitted out to fetch this useful plant from the island, and at about the same time as they returned, "the Fleet" also arrived, bringing to the coast not only sweet potatoes, but also taro, yam and other useful plants. Now, all botanists are unanimous in their belief that the original homeland of the sweet potato is to be found in South America, where the Indians have cultivated it from very early times, and its Polynesian name, *kumara*, is the same as that used by the Quechua of Peru in the form of *cumar*. It was formerly believed to have been first introduced to the Pacific by the Spaniards after the discovery of America, when they set up regular navigation between the New World and the Philippines; but this, of course, conflicts with Polynesian tradition. If the truth of this is accepted it means that Polynesian seafarers must once have reached the coast of Peru and from there carried the sweet potato back to their own islands. In view of their brilliant seamanship there is nothing intrinsically unreasonable in such a theory. But there cannot have been extensive intercourse for if there had been one would expect there to be far more similarities in the cultures of Polynesia and Peru than do in fact exist.

A field of sweet potatoes could usually be harvested three years in succession before it had to lie fallow. When fresh soil had to be brought under cultivation, the forest was cleared late in the autumn or during the winter so that the trees could dry out before they were set on fire in the spring. Everything connected with the cultivation of the sweet potato was surrounded by *tapu*, but whether this was because the sweet potato was considered from the first to be something foreign which demanded special attention, or whether it was because it was of such fundamental importance to the whole of existence is a question which remains unanswered. Both planting and harvesting were accompanied by extensive ritual which, incidentally, varied to some extent from place to place.

In the course of the spring, preferably in September or October, planting took place at a time when the position of the stars promised a good crop. The soil was first heaped into suitable mounds, and each family brought two seed potatoes which were put into a consecrated basket. This, with its contents, was then carried out to the *mara tapu*, the sacred field, where a priest, reciting formulas concerned with the legend of how the sweet potato was acquired, planted the sweet potatoes from the baskets in the mounds already prepared, and when this was done, the basket was destroyed and the remains buried. Afterwards came the turn of the profane field; but so long as the work went on, no food could be cooked or eaten. Various efforts were made to ensure a plentiful crop. At daybreak on the east side of the field a green branch was set up and crude stone figurines which were symbols of the gods—their "resting places" as they were called—were buried in its soil. Before the harvest they were taken up and carried to the sacred precincts. In addition, the prepared heads of the deceased might be stuck up on stakes and put out in the fields to promote fertility, while on the actual cult place god sticks with grotesque carved faces were set up. The field, moreover, was carefully weeded, and while it was growing the crop was strictly *tapu*.

Before harvesting, this *tapu* was lifted and digging up the sweet potatoes took place to a ritual as involved as that at planting. Harvesting was started by one of the priests digging up a sweet potato from the first mound on the sacred field with the aid of a branch, which was used just as it had been broken off from the tree, while he recited a prayer befitting the occasion; as soon as this was done, however, the potato and the branch were buried again, only to be dug up anew when the remaining mounds had been emptied—thus this potato was harvested both first and last. The sweet potatoes from the first mound, which were believed to contain the "vital force" of the harvest, were baked in a special oven, and the first to be taken out of the oven was carried to the cult place as an offering to Rongo, the god of agriculture, while the rest were eaten by the priests and chieftains. Only after all the harvest was done and a new ritual meal had perhaps taken place, were the sweet potatoes freed for general use and then could be stored in the partially underground storage rooms or pits which, however, continued to be *tapu* to women.

Methods of storing provisions are as characteristic as they are necessary in New Zealand where both taro and sweet potatoes give only one crop a year. As mentioned already, both wild birds and roots were pickled in fat and stored for winter use. Generally speaking, the changing seasons led to a regularly recurring cycle of employment. The fact that this was not identical throughout the country is a natural consequence of the different conditions north and south, on the coast and in the forests inland.

Broadly speaking, life on the North Island proceeded as follows.

The year was reckoned as starting at midwinter in June, at the first new moon after the appearance of the Pleiades or Rigel. This was the season for hunting birds and rats, while inland there was fishing and the gathering of mussels. If new fields had to be laid out, then clearing the forest took place at this time. September to November were busy spring months, when trees which had been felled were burned, the soil worked and planting carried out; at this season sea fishing also started, to continue throughout the summer, when comparatively calm weather and seas could be counted on.

In the course of the summer the fields were weeded, and towards its end, i.e. in February, the *tapu*, which till then had lain over the crop as a protection against its premature use, was lifted. It was at this time of the year, incidentally, when work did not require too many hands, that most of the war raids took place. When Vega came into view above the eastern horizon, i.e. in March, autumn was introduced by the harvesting of root crops, and then, too, was the season for the important task of eel catching. Then, with the store-houses full and food plentiful, it was customary to entertain relations and friends, until gradually the year's cycle was completed and it restarted anew.

* * *

In the foregoing description there have been various opportunities of mentioning the culture changes caused by New Zealand's characteristic geography—changes which understandably enough are most apparent within certain areas of the culture's material side. It would therefore be superfluous to go more deeply into these conditions. But it would be relevant to glance at the features which remain after the special adaptations have been disposed of.

The Polynesian culture area falls broadly speaking into two sub-areas, one western, in which Samoa and Tonga constitute the chief island groups, and one eastern, the centre of which is the Society Islands including Tahiti and Raiatea—Hawaiki of the old traditions. New Zealand belongs rather to the eastern area; but if its culture is compared with that of the Society Islands, many differences will none the less soon be discovered, and these cannot immediately be ascribed to geographical conditions but are evidently due to the fact that they either came to the Society Islands or were actually developed there after the ancestors of the Maori had left. On these islands we find, for example, religious structures with enormous stone-built terraces instead of the modest assembly places and sacred enclosures we know from New Zealand, and we also find the idea of Ta'aroa as the highest of all gods, whereas Tangaroa of the Maori was a comparatively minor sea-deity. On the Society Islands there was almost an autocratic kingdom with deified rulers wielding far greater power than the Maori tribal chieftains did, even though they too claimed descent from the gods.

In some cases, the similarity between New Zealand and the remoter east-Polynesian islands is especially marked, as for example in mythology as far as Hawaii is concerned, and in the spiral ornamentation and cannibalism of the Marquesas Islands. The fact that it is on the marginal islands that these elements have survived is easily explained. The powerful urge to expand which was the basis of the voyages from Hawaiki, soon weakened, and the connexion with the distant island groups became broken. There is thus no evidence that new immigration waves reached New Zealand after the arrival of "the Fleet". From then on its culture has developed along its own lines independent of anything that happened elsewhere, increasingly adapting itself to local conditions on the basis of the old foundations it had once been given.

BIBLIOGRAPHY

The Polynesian background of Maori culture is brilliantly presented in TE RANGI HIROA (=SIR PETER BUCK): *Vikings of the Sunrise*, Christchurch, etc., 1954. See also EDWIN G. BURROWS: "Culture-Areas in Polynesia" (*Journ. Polyn. Soc.*, xlix, New Plymouth, 1940). Heyerdahl presents his theory on immigration in THOR HEYERDAHL: *American Indians in the Pacific*, Oslo, 1952. It is keenly contested by, for example, ROBERT HEINE-GELDERN: "Some Problems of Migration in the Pacific" (*Wiener Beitr. z. Kulturgesch. u. Linguist.*, ix, Wien, 1952) and by C. H. M. HEEREN-PALM: *Zwerftochten door de Zuidzee*, Meppel, 1956. A short account of other immigration theories is given by KAJ BIRKET-SMITH: "An Ethnological Sketch of Rennell Island" (*Kgl. Danske Vidensk. Selsk. Hist.-Filol. Meddel.*, xxxv, 3, Copenhagen, 1956). Cf. also ANDREW SHARP: *Ancient Voyagers in the Pacific*, Pelican Books, Harmondsworth, 1957.

Among older works particular reference is made to the following: JAMES COOK: *An Account of a Voyage round the World* (=JOHN HAWKESWORTH: *An Account of the Voyages . . . in the Southern Hemisphere*, ii-iii, London, 1773). JAMES COOK: *A Voyage towards the South Pole and round the World*, 2nd ed., i-ii, London, 1777. JAMES COOK AND JAMES KING: *A Voyage to the Pacific Ocean*, 2nd ed., i-iii, London, 1785. JOSEPH BANKS: *Journal of the Right Honourable Sir . . . during Captain Cook's First Voyage*, London, 1896. F. E. MANING (=A PAKEHA MAORI): *Old New Zealand*, Christchurch, etc., 1906. J. S. POLACK: *Manners and Customs of the New Zealanders*, i-ii, London, 1840.

Excellent surveys of Maori culture are given by ELSDON BEST: "The Maori, I-II" (*Mem. Polyn. Soc.*, v, New Plymouth, 1924) and TE RANGI HIROA: *The Coming of the Maori*, 2nd ed., Wellington, 1950. See also JAMES COWAN: *The Maoris of New Zealand*, Christchurch, 1910. MAKERETI: *The Old-Time Maori*, London, 1938. For archæological conditions see ROGER DUFF: *The Moa-Hunter Period of Maori Culture*, 2nd ed., Wellington, 1956.

Among the extremely comprehensive literature are ELSDON BEST: "The Art of the Whare Pora" (*Transact. a. Proceed. N. Zeal. Inst.*, Wellington, 1898). ELSDON BEST: "Maori Marriage Customs" (*Transact. a. Proceed. N. Zeal. Inst.*, xxxvi, Wellington, 1904). ELSDON BEST: "Maori Forest Lore" (*Trans. a. Proceed. N. Zeal. Inst.*, xl-xlii, Wellington, 1907-9). ELSDON BEST: "The Maori Canoe" (*Domin. Mus. Bull. 7*, Wellington, 1925). ELSDON BEST: "Maori Agriculture" (*Domin. Mus. Bull. 9*, Wellington, 1925). ELSDON BEST: "The Pa Maori" (*Domin. Mus. Bull. 6*, Wellington, 1927). ELSDON BEST: "Fishing Methods and Devices of the Maori" (*Domin. Mus. Bull. 12*, Wellington, 1929). ROGER S. DUFF: "The Evolution of Native Culture in New

Zealand" (*Mankind*, iii, Sydney, 1947). RAYMOND FIRTH: *Primitive Economics of the New Zealand Maori*, London, 1929. J. PRYTZ JOHANSEN: *The Maori and His Religion*, Copenhagen, 1954. H. D. SKINNER: "Culture Areas in New Zealand" (*Journ. Polyn. Soc.*, xxx, New Plymouth, 1921). H. D. SKINNER: "The Origin and Relationship of Maori Material Culture" (*Journ. Polyn. Soc.*, xxxiii, New Plymouth, 1924). TE RANGI HIROA: "Maori Plaited Basketry and Plaitwork" (*Transact. a. Proceed. N. Zeal. Inst.*, liv-lv, Wellington 1923-24). TE RANGI HIROA: "The Maori Craft of Netting" (*Proceed. a. Transact. N. Zeal. Inst.*, Wellington, 1926). TE RANGI HIROA: "The Evolution of Maori Clothing" (*Journ. Polyn. Soc.*, xxxiii-xxxv, New Plymouth, 1924-6). WALSH: "The Cultivation and Treatment of the Kumara" (*Transact. a. Proceed. N. Zeal. Inst.*, xxxvi, Wellington, 1903). JOHN WHITE: *The Ancient History of the Maori*, i-vi, Wellington, 1887-90 (generally considered somewhat unreliable).

ELSDON BEST: "Some Aspects of Maori Myth and Religion" (*Dom. Mus. Monogr.*, i, Wellington, 1922). J. PRYTZ JOHANSEN: "Studies in Maori Rites and Myths" (*Kgl. Danske Vidensk. Selsk. Hist.—Filos Medd.*, xxxvii, 4, Copenhagen, 1958).

Numerous treatises apart from those mentioned are to be found in the *Journal of the Polynesian Society*, New Plymouth, N.Z.

ADAPTATION AND CULTURAL DEVELOPMENT

The Urban Revolution

OUR JOURNEY across the world is done. We have come to know the life of man at widely differing economic stages. We have seen the significance to be ascribed to geographical situation and thus to the accessibility of new influences, and we have seen how, both positively and negatively, adaptation of cultures takes not only creative but also selective forms. It clearly appears, furthermore, that a single historical event can set the process of adaptation off in a new direction. This happened with the horse among the plains Indians, and perhaps, too, with the horse, and certainly with the camel, among the Tuareg. And finally it is clear that increasing adaptation is necessarily rooted in specialization which ties the culture more and more to the locality and to that extent makes it unsuited to existence elsewhere, except under the conditions under which it was bred. Adaptation in fact involves one-sidedness in development.

But another thing emerges from our investigation: culture does not climb upwards in a straight line. Its ways are devious, going up, going down and sometimes ending in a blind alley. The culture of the plains Indians is the result of an intensification of hunting life as it existed not only amongst original hunting tribes but also among a number of agricultural peoples. The Lapps' reindeer breeding has its root in a hunting culture, but has adopted many features from cattle breeding peasants, and only attained its full development when hunting failed. On the other hand the ancestors of the Tuareg seem once to have lived as agriculturists who also kept sheep and goats, and presumably horned cattle, and it is not improbable that the nomadic life of the steppes of West and Central Asia had a similar origin, even if this cannot at present be stated with certainty. The oldest remains of domestic animals so far found do in fact derive from agricultural cultures; but such enormous areas of the actual steppe zone have still to be archæologically explored that no one would dare to say that future excavations could not alter the picture.

The Virginia Indians developed in what would generally be considered a normal way from hunters to semi-agriculturists, whatever the details of the development might have been. The situation is entirely different with the Maori, and possibly with the earliest immigrants to Polynesia as a whole, since their cultivated plants were either completely or partially lost, so that from being wholly agricultural they were forced down to the level of hunters, from which the southern Maori tribes never succeeded in rising again. Thus they form an instructive contrast to the South American Chiriguano Indians, who were originally hunters and semi-agriculturists, becoming, as a result of their migration to the foothills of the Andes with their paucity of game, entirely agricultural.

* * *

Settled dwellings are usually interpreted as a sign of a higher level of culture; but even a mode of life which is based on fishing and sealing can in itself lead to a fairly high incidence of settled dwellings. The coasts on both sides of the northern Pacific provide evidence of this, and the same was probably true of the circumpolar woodlands as a whole before the arrival of the snowshoe and skis which, by contrast, led from settled winter camps to nomadism with reindeer herds. The hunting tribes of the High Plains of North America similarly gave up their permanent houses in favour of tents, and to a large extent the same thing happened with the Tuareg.

Settled dwellings are scarcely even an essential requirement for the emergence of a high culture. In Central America the Maya created their culture on the basis of slash-and-burn agriculture, which must have led to constant shifting of the villages; their so-called towns were grandiose temple buildings and places of pilgrimage rather than actual centres of habitation. One of the principal reasons for the decline of the Maya culture, on the other hand, is to be found in the inadequate agricultural methods, which in the long run could not carry the imposing superstructure. Settled dwelling is thus neither indissolubly linked with a high culture nor a requirement for its development, only for its lasting existence. Of decisive importance, on the other hand, is surplus production, which can free a sufficient number of hands from the daily struggle for food. In the long run only advanced agriculture can achieve this.

Within the framework of the oldest agriculture in Asia, which was the cradle of our civilization, there was a remarkable difference between east and west, a difference which can be traced even today without difficulty. Among the primitive tribes in India, South China and Indonesia, cultivation seems to have been primarily concerned with tubers such as taro, yam, etc., while horned cattle were chiefly sacrificial animals and a sign of wealth and prestige; in any case milking, and thus the use of milk, was unknown. In West Asia, on the other hand, it was the cultivation of cereals, wheat and barley, which laid the foundations of further development, while from early days oxen were to a marked extent milking animals. Broadly speaking the two types of agriculture correspond to the monsoon and winter rain regions. Whether this means that agriculture generally is double rooted is for the present a question no less obscure than that concerning the interplay between the origins of the western agriculture and the breeding of cattle.

Suffice to say that it was in the west that the big revolution took place—a revolution which gradually transformed the simple village communities into the awakening city states of antiquity. In southern Mesopotamia, Sumer of old, this development had already run its course in prehistoric times, at the end of the Uruk period and the subsequent Jemdet Nasr period, sometimes combined under the heading of the "proto-literary time", i.e. the second half of the fourth millennium B.C. Trade and religion both contributed to the rise of the towns. The fertile delta plains were deficient in stone, metal and building timber, all of which had to be imported and paid for in corn, dates and wool from the large herds of sheep, and this trade was widespread, not only as far as the mountains of Elam and Syria, but right across to Oman and Hadhramaut in southern Arabia and even as far as the distant Indus. The temples were the religious, economic and administrative centres of the new cities.

In Lagash, which in the third millennium was a town of some 19,000 inhabitants, many of the craftsmen belonged to the temple of the goddess Bau: bakers, brewers, wool preparers, weavers, etc., with attendant slaves and slave women. In the wake of the extensive administration came the full development of cuneiform writing which had already begun in the previous period, thereby opening up unimagined possibilities for the future. At the same time the increasing extent of town life led to a breaking of the ties which had formerly united mankind and nature. Nature now became something remote, whose regular course lay in the hands of the gods and was no longer dependent on humans in the guise of a cult drama. Gradually this brought the individual's personal salvation rather than the well-being of society to the forefront of religion. The development of writing and the observations by the priesthood of the movement of the stars across the nocturnal sky sowed the seeds of future science. And with the interplay between the townspeople and the nomads, the Sumerian city states became the territorial states of Babylon and Assyria.

Both materially and spiritually urban culture meant the breakthrough of that civilization in the continuation of which we are still living. The creation of towns separated man and nature. The influence of environment thereby became not less, but in many respects less immediate.

BIBLIOGRAPHY

For differing views concerning the decline of the Maya civilization, cf. S. G. Morley: *The Ancient Maya*, Stanford, 1946. J. Eric Thompson: *The Rise and Fall of Maya Civilization*, London, 1956. The urban revolution is described in V. Gordon Childe: *New Light on the Most Ancient East*, 5th ed., London, 1954.

INDEX